Pra

"Kim is utterly REVOLUTIONARY in reshaping trauma recovery where many therapists and psychiatrists are at a silent loss as to how to truly help their clients fully heal. I've personally witnessed thousands of students in our global community make profound shifts back into their Hearts to find sustainable peace, joy, and long-lasting stability as a result of her trauma work. As an educator and counselor myself, I believe there is no model of healing that's as complete as the process presented in this book."

—Daniela Hess Grant, MSEd, CTACC, Co-founder of Yoga Farm Ithaca

"The author is expanding boundaries in the field of trauma recovery... past the limits that confine some mental health practitioners. This book takes the reader on an enlightening deep dive into healing the traumatic root cause of anxiety and depression through a multi-layered approach."

—Jennifer Kuebler, Licensed Marriage and Family Therapist

"Kim is an extraordinary visionary and healer who has integrated various interventions into a well-defined treatment program to address childhood trauma and the whole person."

—Jessica Desrosiers, PsyD, Clinical Psychologist

"In this book, Kim Beekman delineates a comprehensive method for uprooting deeply held trauma patterns through a multi-pronged approach that bridges healing systems and spans dimensions of consciousness. By sharing her wisdom in this very digestible framework, Kim creates a blueprint for burgeoning and seasoned practitioners alike to confidently release trauma from a client's field *for good*. This approach has dramatically shifted my own life, and the lives of my clients, many of whom are healing practitioners still in need of healing childhood trauma."

—Trish DeRocher, PhD, Professor and Author

Inner Alignment
Soul Retrieval
for Healing
Childhood Trauma

a systematic approach to healing the root cause of anxiety and depression

Kimberly Beekman

First edition

Acknowledgements

My growth in consciousness, and therefore this book, would not have been possible without the many people who have contributed to my life's path. Gratitude to my husband and three daughters, who have loved me and supported my growth and expansion. To my teachers who have come before me with such incredible wisdom. To the Divine for the never-ending flow of Divine Wisdom, Love, and Strength. To my colleagues and coworkers, especially Laura Killian, for co-creating such magnificence in the world from a deep commitment to inner healing for others.

It is an incredible honor to have experienced such an intense path of healing on my own journey. I cherish every dark corner of my cave and every shadowed master teacher who has presented me with the opportunity to heal my past. These experiences, and the experience of helping so many others heal, have informed every single word in this book.

I have deep gratitude and reverence for the clients who have been with me along this learning journey, as I weaved the tools and techniques of the system together. As with every rich experience, there were many failures along the way, and I appreciate the grace given to me. *I'm sorry, please forgive me, thank you, I love you,* all of you.

This work is dedicated to every healer and mental health practitioner that has helped me on my path (too many to list!), and to those who have dedicated their lives to the healing of humanity and the relief of suffering on this planet.

If you are on the frontlines of the mental health crisis that is facing our world today... I assure you that the root causes of disease—anxiety, depression, suicidal ideation, addiction, physical pain, and illness—reside in the trauma packets that we carry around from childhood. When we heal the root cause, the ripple effect on life is tremendous, shifting us back to the space of deep inner connection.

Blessings to you on your journey!

Table of Contents

Foreword

By Jessica Desrosiers, PsyD, Clinical Psychologist

It is with great honor and gratitude that I offer this foreword. Having completed Kim's Inner Alignment Soul Retrieval (IASR) Program myself, as well as being a Clinical Psychologist with a specialty in the treatment of trauma, I am able to understand the whole-body transformation presented in this book.

Kim is an extraordinary visionary and healer who has integrated various interventions into a well-defined treatment program to address childhood trauma and the whole person. Through her program, individuals suffering from childhood trauma, unmet developmental needs, mental health symptoms, relational problems, and overall dis-ease can now experience bliss and embody life to their fullest sacred potential. Healers and lightworkers from all disciplines can benefit from the concepts and fundamental protocol provided in this book, as it can shift the mental health paradigm.

I have been trained in several evidence-based treatment (EBT) modalities for trauma, such as Eye-Movement Desensitization Reprocessing (EMDR), Attachment Focused EMDR (AF-EMDR), Cognitive Processing Therapy (CPT), Cognitive Behavioral Therapy (CBT), Prolonged Exposure (PE), Dialectical Behavioral Therapy (DBT), Emotional Freedom Techniques (EFT), and Seeking Safety. I have treated hundreds of individuals who have experienced both complex and single-incident trauma. While my patients with symptoms of Post-Traumatic Stress Disorder (PTSD), depression, and anxiety will often show improvement using these modalities, they do not fully remit and the effects are usually temporary. For the majority, the coping skills learned from the various treatments are not sustained in life outside of therapy. Clients continue to struggle with an overall dissatisfaction in life. Ongoing self-judgment and shame sustain their lack of self-care and thoughts of worthlessness. Emotional reactivity leads to unstable relationships. Difficulty tolerating painful emotions results in persistent avoidance behaviors. The past continues to live in the present moment. Being mindful of their cyclical maladaptive patterns, thought distortions, and emotional reactivity interrupts the trauma re-enactment, yet does not heal the root trauma. Processing the trauma via EMDR or EFT addresses the root issues, yet does not transfer to life outside of therapy. Only when individuals engage in a supportive, compassionate container of group therapy in addition to or after completing individual therapy do they remain accountable to themselves and practice their skills. Yet, there is still something missing. An emptiness, a separation from parts of themselves, and a disconnect from their Divine worth prevails. I find that the aforementioned modalities do not address the individual as a whole, and how the trauma is stored in the mental, physical, energetic, emotional, and spiritual bodies (all six layers). Although the person's thoughts and emotions may shift, their energetic and spiritual bodies are often left untouched, and the individual remains in suffering, disconnected from their Divine Truth.

In the treatment of my own trauma, therapists used treatments such as CBT to challenge my thought distortions, inner child work to reparent the wounded parts of myself, and EMDR to process specific traumas. CBT did not address the root cause of my anxiety and depression, and only fostered a deeper level of defense, given my tendency to intellectualize. EMDR processed the trauma, effectively decreased my physical and emotional reactivity, and shifted some of my beliefs specific to the traumas. However, my underlying sense of worthlessness and lack of self-compassion, so deeply ingrained by childhood trauma, persisted.

With the loss of my son, my spiritual awakening, and festering negative thoughts about myself, I was guided to the Inner Alignment Soul Retrieval program with Kim Beekman. It was not until I started the program that the layers of perceived worthlessness were addressed. For the first time in my life, I connected to my internal goodness through this intensive two-month program comprised of rewiring my brain and healing childhood trauma via soul retrieval and active empowerment in the dimensional space the trauma occurred. The program created space for me to discover my energetic makeup and how to create balance within my body, address ancestral energetic barriers, fully forgive myself and the perpetrators of the trauma, manifest my desires in life, and connect to my spirituality at a deeper level. I needed the supportive, compassionate, and loving environment created by the healing team and group participants to surrender my armor, open my heart, and finally heal. The Inner Alignment Soul Retrieval system is a holistic and comprehensive approach that treated my entire person, within my six-layered body, unlike other mental health treatment modalities I have been trained and participated in.

Not only was the IASR program monumental for my own personal growth, it also restructured the way I conceptualize and offer healing to others who have experienced trauma. With awareness now that the whole person and all the layers of the body are necessary in the healing of trauma, I integrate skills learned from IASR with trauma treatment modalities.

Here is a poem I wrote to reflect my experience of IASR:

Aligned

The pain and suffering bleeding from her heart,
Covered in stained illusions and falsehood.
Squelching the painful memories to move forward,
Masked, untreated, unwanted.
All to "live," all to "do,"
Never to "be."
Bubbling out of her pores,
She no longer can "live" in the depths of pain in her heart and soul.
Struggling, searching, finding,
Uncovering, embracing, empowering, releasing.
She has always been good and enough,
Has always had worth.
She now envisions and has returned home to her Truth.
Aligned now with...
Her inner Light.
Her inner Goodness.
Her inner Divine Being.

About the Author

Having been on her own healing journey for over 30 years, Kim Beekman has overcome the effects of her childhood trauma and developed a system of healing to help others do the same.

Her journey started as many others have, with well-meaning parents who had substance abuse and personality disorders. Through childhood, she experienced physical and emotional abuse, attempted sexual abuse, and neglect. By the age of 13, she developed bulimia and depression. At 15 years old, she admitted herself into an inpatient psychiatric hospital to break the pattern of abuse and start her healing. At 16, she moved out on her own and put herself through high school and college.

In college, Kim continued talk therapy, studied psychology, interned at psychiatric hospitals, and ran peer eating disorder support groups. She began working for the Catholic Church as a Eucharistic Minister and Director of Programs, gathering spiritual community, creating interfaith groups, and working on distilling religion into spirituality.

She entered graduate school—Master of Public Administration at the Maxwell School at Syracuse University— with an intention of eventually revamping the mental health system, which started to break down in the 1990s when insurance companies started dictating mental healthcare.

During her time in graduate school, she discovered the law of attraction, and attracted her husband (and later, her children), and a deeper expression of her healing process. This led to her becoming a yoga and meditation teacher and a trainer of teachers (500hr E-RYT). She deepened her study of spirituality through Yogananda's system of meditation (Kriya Yoga), Transcendental Meditation (TM®), the connection to the Divine Light and Sacred Fire, and the deeper understanding of layers of the body and chakras. Additional study of Ayurveda at the Sivananda Ashram opened her to developing expertise in Ayurvedic psychology as she became an Ayurvedic Wellness Counselor. Study of Shamanism and other healing systems followed.

Even with all the education and training, the most profound teachings came when she started sitting with people to do law of attraction sessions. Upon seeing people repeat the same pattern over and over (e.g., manifest something wonderful and then lose it through self-sabotage), she started begging the Divine to reveal the deeper healing process. Through continued attempts, she was shown how to access trauma packets, heal them, and bridge spiritual consciousness to the old wounded spaces. After about 250 sessions, the process for healing became clear.

Through trial and error, she realized that the trauma packet work must be sustained over two months, revealing the necessity of incorporating the neuroscience of healing into the system. She learned how to hold the healing space for people without triggering old patterns by holding a sacred container built through a loving team and structured system.

After an additional 500 sessions, the process became standardized and repeatable. She started to train others in this reproducible modality so they could create a healing experience for clients too. To her delight, with the Divine's help, she was able to develop a comprehensive Inner Alignment System: Level 1 Inner Alignment Soul Retrieval for Healing Childhood Trauma, Level 2 Inner Alignment Coach Certification, and Level 3 Soul Retrieval Healer Certification.

Her three teenage daughters keep her humbled and motivated to continue her own inner work and awakening, while staying grounded in practical application. Her marriage has been a stabilizing diving board for her ongoing healing system development. Her co-creative healing team serves as the foundation for her organization's impact in the world.

Kim's ultimate vision is to implement this system worldwide. By training every awakened healer on the front lines of the mental health crisis, she hopes to shift the face of mental healthcare in our communities.

Section 1:

Understanding Trauma Packets and the Six-Layered Body

Chapter 1:
Overview

The Mental Health Crisis

Our society is currently experiencing a mental health crisis, and lacks the resources and wisdom to heal the root cause of anxiety and depression. The root cause is childhood trauma trapped deep within the body. The solution? Well, society doesn't have an effective solution. The mental health system is just beginning to recognize that the problem goes much deeper than the mind and emotions. Talk therapy doesn't touch the space where trauma is stored and is therefore ineffective at healing stored trauma and its resulting life patterns.

Many approaches to healing attempt to resolve emotional issues through just one layer of the body. We see doctors prescribing medications to address the physical brain chemistry. Clinical therapists address thoughts and behavior, and expression of emotions. Spiritual counselors help to create a spiritual connection. Acupuncturists and Reiki practitioners work on the energetics. Do these single-layer approaches ultimately work for long-term relief of embedded childhood emotional patterns? No, because it is like a game of whack-amole, where one layer may feel better but the issue shows up in another layer of the body, or a different area of life. In the process of these temporary fixes, people feel more broken, more depressed and more lost. So often we see someone who has been doing talk therapy consistently for five, ten, or even twenty years. Much of that time has been spent on a cocktail of psychiatric medications, with a few Reiki sessions in between, and they still can't find happiness. They are doing what is generally recommended and can't seem to get unstuck.

When we have childhood trauma, society teaches us to learn how to cope. Put a band-aid on the trauma, learn to live around the issues, and limp through life merely surviving. That's the way, right? We believe there's no way for us to *really* recover. We just talk about it in therapy and do a lot of yoga or meditation to calm the negative thoughts and emotions reverberating through us. We do this hoping to feel a temporary moment or two of relief from the consistent fight-or-flight reaction that sends us into what seems to be a permanent state of anxiety or depression. Having a happy, joyful, abundant, blissful life is not an option. We are doomed to a life of swimming upstream, because we are damaged. We are broken. There is no hope.

You adjust to survival and band-aids, because there have never been modalities available for overcoming childhood trauma and sustaining your healing long term. No matter what type of trauma you experienced—molestation, abuse, beatings, shaming, parental instability, moving ten times, rape, neglect, a narcissistic parent who was always right—it still lives within you. The trauma stored in your body reverberates through your being and dictates how you feel in every moment. It determines how you react at work, with your partner, and to your family. Life feels like one big emotional reaction to other people and issues. Or worse, that trauma has caused you to disconnect from yourself altogether.

Over time, you think you are stuck with these negative feelings and the same trauma patterns in every relationship (e.g., fighting, avoiding communication, awaiting punishment). As soon as that trauma gets trapped in the body, it stays as our base vibratory experience of life. Those well-worn pathways in our body, emotions, and thinking, determine almost everything we attract from that point forward. We begin to feel *stuck* because we haven't been able to get out of the trauma cycle and into a new way of being.

However, the reality is that we are not stuck. There's just old trauma, trapped in the six layers of the body, that has become deeply embedded and patterned into our lives.

The question is, how do we stop the trauma patterns?

Inner Alignment Healing

There are three aspects of healing childhood trauma, all of which are executed concurrently. First, we need to heal the trauma in the body by accessing the past, which is still living in the body in the present moment. By using the Inner Alignment Soul Retrieval process, we get to the core of the past trauma to release the base vibrations that cause anxiety or depression. Once the trauma is healed at the root, we need to rewire the six layers of the body to sustain the newly healed vibrations, so that the old pathways of fear, anxiety, and depression transition into a new way of being. Lastly, we must address the core of the trauma and rewire the brain through and within a container of love, because love is that which does all the healing.

Soul Retrieval to Heal the Origin of Trauma

The Inner Alignment Soul Retrieval process gets to the root of the trauma embedded in the body. Upon accessing the original trauma experience, we can shift vibrations back to a space of peace and wholeness.

When you're a child, most trauma experiences come straight into your body. Your body has a vibrational and physical experience of each situation. It immediately absorbs the trauma experience before emotions or thoughts are processed. Think about how children experience life. They explore with big eyes, an open heart, and full receptivity. They put the stick in their mouth, run for a hug without reservation, or throw the ball through the window with amazement. There's not a lot of rational thought before they do things and experience life. They just take it all in. When they do, they build neural pathways in the brain at rapid speed—millions of new neural pathways from their new experiences. They are building their construct of how the world works: thought pathways, emotional body chemistry, belief systems, emotional tendencies, nervous system and breathing habits, movement patterns, and filters through which they see the world.

Children aren't guarded and shut down like adults, who think about an experience before actually experiencing it. Children's brains and bodies go *all in* to every experience in life. Therefore, when children face a traumatic event, the same thing happens. They experience it through the body. Fully. They take it all in. The impact of the trauma will embed into the six layers of the body—into their physical body's nervous system, energy field, Heart and emotions, thoughts, and spirit.

Like gum in fabric, once the trauma is in there, it's not possible to just pluck it out. The trauma is frozen in time and space at the age when it occurred. The emotions, thoughts, and body sensations experienced at that moment are stored within the body. The fear is trapped within the frozen trauma and continues to replay that scenario, with corresponding feelings, well into a person's adult life. The adult eventually begins to feel imprisoned or even haunted by these old vibrations, which are replaying automatically and unconsciously like a broken record in day-to-day life. With these repetitive vibrations, the soul, in a sense, becomes fractured. Pieces of the soul get left in each of these frozen experiences. The soul no longer feels whole.

These trapped trauma vibrations affect the six layers of the body—physically, mentally, emotionally, energetically, and through the awareness and bliss bodies.

The trauma seeps into the *physical body* and eventually creates pain. Often, it shows up as intermittent pain or fatigue, such as fibromyalgia, chronic fatigue syndrome, or some other autoimmune disease that has no apparent root-cause treatment and gets worse with stress. It can manifest more physically, as well, as low back pain or recurring headaches.

The trauma plagues the *mental body* with thoughts of unworthiness, helplessness, mistrust, or a sense of abandonment. This penetrates deeply into the belief systems and eventually shapes how the person sets up their whole life. For example, a person can create a life paradigm of avoiding men or staying small, to reinforce the corresponding beliefs set up in trauma.

The trauma appears in the *emotional body* throughout life. A person can experience panic attacks that seemingly come out of nowhere; anxiety that feels gripping and has no quick fix; or depression that feels like a heavy blanket weighing on the heart. Explosions of anger or rage can feel uncontrollable.

The trauma permeates the *energetic body* with elusive energetic imbalances. Ungrounded energy can feel like manic nervousness, or heavy energy can feel like extreme fatigue. Energetic imbalances can block a person's ability to feel safe, connected, motivated, loved, heard, or to see beyond the current situation.

These manifestations of trauma result in a barrier in the *awareness body*, which keeps us from being able to see what's blocking us from our inner connection. The barriers also keep us from feeling the deep love, peace, freedom, and joy of the *bliss body*. The trauma creates a deep sense of disconnection from self. It prevents us from seeing the whole picture of our life versus a micro situation that feels difficult in the moment.

Even though this trauma lives in the past, it plays out in the body in the present moment, so it's possible to access the past vibrations, thoughts, memories, and emotions where the trauma originated. Once we access it, we can work to bring this part of the self back to peace... to pick up the pieces of the fragmented soul and restore wholeness.

When healing through the Inner Alignment Soul Retrieval process, we access the frozen trauma and facilitate healing for that childhood experience, so the person can begin to feel safe and have a deeper understanding of the past situation. They can reconnect with the Divine and remember wholeness, because they've restored the part that they had lost. They feel more positive emotion and become empowered to handle these situations in the future. They stay connected to the present-moment adult self in a way that feels protected from that point forward.

Note that this is a very different approach from the traditional mental health model. Since these trauma vibrations live in every layer of the body, they cannot be healed through just the layer of the mind, which is where talk therapy focuses. This trauma needs to be healed where it started, where it is stored, in all six layers. Any attempt to work at it from the mental layer of the body—by analyzing it, role-playing it, hypothesizing the effect of it—is limiting in terms of what healing is possible. Even if it provides momentary relief, the mental body healing doesn't hold. The healing has to happen where the trauma lives, deep within the body.

Rewire the Six-layered Body to Sustain Healing

Trauma is a complex web of thoughts, emotions, energetics, neurosynaptic wiring and chemistry, and spiritual disconnects that reverberate through the physical body. The root of the trauma is in the past, where all these layers intersect.

Trauma gets wired into the brain, usually based in some form of unworthiness such as *not good enough, unlovable,* or *not worthy of being heard.* The brain builds the neural synaptic patterns created by the frozen trauma experience. These brain synapses give off corresponding hormones and chemistry to support this wiring, and signal the unworthy feeling to the cells. The neurotransmitter receptors in the cells get organized to support the synapses in the brain, permeating this feeling through all systems of the body. In this way, the brain, body chemistry, and cells all become wired to the trauma experience.

Most people have some form of trauma generating some flavor of unworthiness deep within. Many of us with childhood trauma have body wiring that is conditioned to feel depression or anxiety, which are generic labels for negative vibrations stored in the body. Whether and how you feel depression or anxiety depends on how your six layers wove the trauma into your body. Trauma can be expressed through the six layers of the body as: physical symptoms and sensations (pain, illness); emotions (anger, sadness, anxiety, shame); negative thoughts (*I am bad, I'm not good enough, I am unlovable*); imbalanced energetics (unhooked, unsafe, heavy, inertia, fiery); awareness blockages (*There's nothing beyond this dismal moment; I am hopeless for a greater future*); and spiritual disconnection (*Nothing and nobody has my back. There's no support from the Universe. God isn't here for me*).

These trauma patterns, established early in life, become reinforced and continuously give off those same vibrations every single day. For example:

> It was unsafe in my childhood home, so my brain wired in a deep feeling of *unsafe*. Each day, I think thoughts about how nobody is here to support me. I believe there is no God or Universe to provide for me. I feel a constant state of anxiety. I spend my life trying to create safety externally, through my job or my marriage. Yet, I continuously feel like my life will fall apart at any moment, just like I felt when I was younger. Because I feel this way, through the law of attraction, I continue to attract situations where I feel unsafe.

> OR

> I didn't feel loved growing up. As a result, I wired in thoughts about how nobody has or will ever love me. God doesn't love me. I can't see myself beyond

this unlovable-ness. So I spend my entire life scanning the world for those who love me and who don't love me. I externally seek the love I need to cover my fear of dying alone. But the very act of doing so keeps love at bay (because through the law of attraction, I can't sustain love and keep it in my life). So I end up feeling perpetually alone with deep grief and depression.

Once you start healing those trauma packets through the Inner Alignment Soul Retrieval process, the part of you that feels unsafe or unloved begins to get its needs met. This creates a sense of empowerment to handle life, which reverberates through your being. **However, if you don't practice these new vibrations of safety or love consistently over two months (which is the time it takes to wire them into the body), you won't be able to sustain this feeling of love or safety, even if the trauma has healed at the root.** Despite the deep healing, you will likely re-habituate back to feeling unsafe and unloved. Why? Because the change wasn't wired into the brain, body chemistry, neurotransmitter receptors, emotions, and thoughts for the duration required to change the neural networks of your brain and body.

You can learn something new, building new neural pathways in the brain, and feel really good after an *aha!* moment or healing experience. However, after a few days, if these new neural networks are not fortified and practiced consistently, the new pathways will truncate and you will feel the same way you felt prior to healing. Therefore, you need to rewire all six layers of the body consistently over two months if you want to *feel* healed. Each layer needs to be rebuilt in a way that supports the work done in the Inner Alignment Soul Retrieval process, so that the healing can be sustained.

In summary, once a few old traumas are healed through Inner Alignment Soul Retrieval, a few layers of the onion are peeled away. The person must consistently hold this new vibration for at least two months so it can get wired in. This leads us to the next important aspect of healing, which is a supportive community that can hold the vibrations of love, safety, and accountability throughout the rewiring process.

Hold a Consistent Container of LOVE

We've all heard that *love heals* and *God is Love*, but what does that *love in action* look like when it comes to a practical approach to healing? How can we, as flawed, conditionally loving humans, bring that depth of love into someone's life so they can heal the fractured self?

That is the Divine art of healing childhood trauma. It has to be done in the frequency of love—unwavering Divine Love. That's where the vibrations of worth and safety come from: from earth, from Divine, from the Heart[1]. Without orchestration from the spiritual layers of the body, the bliss body, it's not possible to weave a new fabric of the inner being.

Many healing practitioners haven't worked their spiritual layer of the body enough to guide true healing. So many are still carrying around their own religious trauma—from religious dogma and rules; distortions that make people good or bad; concepts of God being punishing and only giving love under conditions of behaving in certain ways; God-fearing thoughts— so it's difficult for them to help their clients understand the immense unconditional love of the Divine without the duality of good or bad, or right or wrong. The Divine's immense love was distorted by religion and human ego beliefs for many centuries. An effective healer must be deeply connected to a universal flow of the Divine love to help another person tap back into the Divine love that they are. Peeling the Divine away from religion is critical work to be done prior to holding someone else through the development of their spiritual body. Allowing the Divine to be represented by the client's view—whether that be sun and earth, God, Love, Buddha, Jesus, Divine Light, Shiva, Krishna (or nobody)—is critical to the person being able to integrate their spiritual body.

Most practitioners are still carrying their own inner pain, getting retraumatized through their work with clients. Many are getting depleted from their service instead of giving from their overflow. Most haven't done the depth of work required to heal

---

[1] Note that "heart" is capitalized to signify the spiritual Heart.

the childhood trauma within themselves so they can hold the container for others. True healing requires practitioners who have done their own Inner Alignment work. This healing within their own Hearts is what provides the overflow of Divine love, into which their clients can connect.

In the Chapters That Follow...

This book walks you through a very thorough review of childhood trauma: where it lives and how it is stored in the body; how it behaves in the brain and nervous system; how it permeates our energetics, thoughts, and emotions; and how the spiritual layers of the body are affected. Once a deep understanding is established in Part 1, you will learn the pathway to healing in Part 2.

Chapter Contents

In **Section 1, Understanding Trauma Packets and the Six-Layered Body**, we explore the major concepts of how trauma is stored and operates in the body.

In Chapter 1 Overview, we introduce the three aspects for healing.

In Chapter 2 Trauma Packets, you will get a clear sense for how we define trauma and the frozen trauma experiences that live in the body.

In Chapter 3 Trauma in the Six-Layered Body, you receive an overview of the six-layer lens through which we explore trauma.

In Chapter 4 Physical Body Layer, we will examine the effects of trauma on the nervous system from the perspective of the autonomic, sympathetic, and parasympathetic nervous systems. You will learn how the neural pathways, neural chemistry, and cell structure are impacted by trauma.

In Chapter 5 Energetic Body Layer, we introduce the Ayurvedic perspective on diagnosing and balancing imbalances in the elemental dosha constitutions and chakra energy centers.

In Chapter 6 Mental Body Layer, we take a close look at belief systems, consciousness, and brain structure as they relate to thinking and the impact of trauma on the mind.

In Chapter 7 Emotional Body Layer, we examine the purpose of negative emotion, and how death fear vibrations, pain bodies, and fear reactivity result from trauma.

In Chapter 8 Awareness Body Layer, we explore the effect of trauma on inner awareness, and move beyond the mind, through the nine dimensions of consciousness.

In Chapter 9 Bliss Body Layer, you will discover how trauma affects the soul through soul fragmentation, and how to move through interference energy to gain soul residence.

In **Section 2 Pathway to Healing,** we explore the steps for healing trauma.

In Chapter 10 Healing Trauma Packets, we review the three aspects of healing childhood trauma.

In Chapter 11 Inner Alignment Soul Retrieval, we go into depth on the process for transforming childhood trauma within the trauma packets in the body.

In Chapter 12 Rewiring the Six-Layered Body, we share the Inner Alignment steps for rewiring the body over two months for lasting relief of trauma.

In Chapter 13 Love as the Basis, we reveal the most important aspect of healing and why it works.

In Chapter 14 Inner Alignment Healing System, we share the levels of work that can be completed to heal yourself, why other modalities are ineffective, and how to help others heal through this comprehensive system.

If you're like me, you may want the author to get to the point, and if that's the case, you might want to read Chapters 1, 2, and 3; skim body layer Chapters 4 through 9; and then skip to Chapters 10 through 14 to devour the healing system. Then, you may want the details about *why* the system is designed as such, and you may have wished you continued through the layers of the body.

Blessings and thank you for the opportunity to share this incredible approach to healing.

Chapter 2:
Childhood Trauma

Defining Childhood Trauma

Childhood trauma is the emotional, mental, physical, energetic, and spiritual response to an event or series of events in childhood which created fear that completely overwhelmed an individual's ability to cope, make sense of, or integrate the ideas and emotions involved in that experience. Most often, traumatic childhood events are most difficult to process when there is no loving caregiver present to help bring understanding, comfort, care, and support throughout the experience and aftermath of the trauma situation.

Childhood trauma occurs between birth and age 25, in the time before the brain is fully developed, and prior to having a rational mind. Up to age 25, we're trying to make sense of the world from an incomplete, not-yet-rational perspective.

In our Inner Alignment definition of trauma, we go a step further to say that just about everyone has *some* level of trauma—being in a human body, going through our archaic education system, being raised by confused parents, and interacting with kids who were raised by traumatized parents. Relationships and life situations can be overwhelming and make it difficult to cope, make sense of, or integrate the thoughts and emotions that we experience. In short, we're all starting with some sort of frozen trauma in our bodies.

Big T & Little t Trauma

Trauma occurs when something happens either in our internal world, meaning a thought occurs to us, or in our external world, meaning someone said something, did something, or didn't do something. When a trauma event happens, there is typically some flavor of deep fear attached to that situation.

There are two types of trauma: trauma with a *big T* and trauma with a *little t*. This is an important distinction, because as a society we typically just identify big T experiences as trauma. There are millions of people walking around believing that they don't have trauma, but most everybody has trauma with a little t. The human condition alone creates a certain level of separation that keeps us from feeling truly integrated with ourselves.

Little t traumas are normal life events, such as moving during the teenage years, being picked on by a sibling, or having two overworked or stressed-out parents. This type of trauma can seem like a normal experience, but to a child who lacks understanding, it feels like a huge event that can leave a mark for an entire life. For example, a bruised arm after you fell from the monkey bars; a negative experience with the kids excluding you on the playground; the mean teacher who laughed when you got the answer wrong; your grandmother who shamed you for speaking up; or your parent who repeatedly told you not to cry. Any of these seemingly benign experiences can register in children's bodies as a little t trauma, and influence how children think and feel about themselves.

Big T trauma life issues can be:

Physical abuse such as being hit (or threatened with spanking); physically handled in a violent manner; physically separated from love or care; or not getting physical needs met (food, shelter, hygiene, quiet, personal care).

Childhood sexual abuse can be any look, glance, or touch that feels inappropriate, dirty, or sexual—whether consensual or not when underage—and of course, rape or molestation (single event or sustained over time).

Caregiver emotional neglect or over-control can be traumatic. Being told that it's not OK to have feelings or that feelings are inappropriate. Punishment or shame when emotions are felt or expressed. Manipulation with emotions, through control or fear. Being ignored or *cut off* when feelings are present. Having an absence of emotion modeled, where stuffing or numbing emotions is the norm. Parents and family members who numb emotions through addictions—abuse of food, alcohol, drugs, sex, gambling, gaming. Emotional neglect due to parental anxiety, depression, anger, or yelling. Or simply an emotionally checked-out caregiver, not living in the Heart with love.

Mental abuse can cause trauma through excess criticism, negativity, favoritism, insults, gaslighting, or teaching that there are only certain ways to behave to be accepted in the family. Religious abuse through the building of bad/wrong/sinner concepts; being rejected by community or God. Over-responsibility for other family members. Bullying or exclusion from the social community, at school, in extended family, or even in the neighborhood.

There are also external traumas that don't stem from abuse, such as accidents, illness or death of a close relative, loss of income, divorce, moving away from home or friends, personal illness, etc.

Just about any experience can register as a trauma if there's fear, overwhelm, and an inability to process the experience. Imagine how prevalent childhood trauma is from this broader definition.

Trauma Packets

Whether you experience trauma with a big T or little t, these trauma experiences affect us very deeply, and often seem to be permanent. The overwhelm occurs at every layer of the body:

Physical Body: The nervous system gets activated into fight or flight; hormone and cortisol levels increase; cardiovascular abnormalities occur and heart rate increases; the immune system over-activates; and digestion and elimination halt.

Energetic Body: Breathing is held or stopped; tightness in chest, fire in belly, or a lump in the throat occurs; fear rattles through the energy field; and a feeling of impending doom or death permeates through the body.

Mental Body: Immediate and often spontaneous thoughts such as *I'm not loved, not safe, not worthy, don't belong,* or *can't exist or express* show up; and beliefs around scarcity, powerlessness, or abandonment arise.

Emotional Body: Fear arises, accompanied by sadness, anger, or incessant worry or anxiety.

Awareness Body: Awareness shuts down, with an inability to see beyond the current fear to access a different way of being.

Spiritual/Bliss Body: Spiritual disconnection occurs with a deep sense of being alone. Dissociation, soul loss, and soul fragmentation create separation from self.

During trauma, every layer of the body is affected at the same time, which makes the system feel completely dysregulated. Unlike animals, children can't shake it off and move on. The overwhelming trauma vibration gets stored at every layer of the body until it is processed out of the system. For many, it is *never* processed out of the body and the person limps through life with these burdens firing off trauma vibrations daily. Once the trauma occurs, it is deeply embedded and will continue to re-fire the trauma vibrations throughout life.

Children don't have the emotional skills, self-awareness, or maturity to process the trauma out of each layer of the body during or after an experience. Because children don't have the cognitive ability (fully formed prefrontal cortex) to process the trauma until their mid-20s, the trauma stays deep within, frozen inside the body for decades, wreaking havoc on all six layers, until the adult starts their trauma-healing journey. It's like shattered glass has been smashed into their system. It's impossible to extract the shards of glass until they find the right tools to do so. Most often, children have to live in the trauma scenarios (school, parents, community) for many years after the trauma, so there is a lack of outside perspective to move through the experience.

When the trauma freezes, it gets stored in a physical and energetic space within the body, specific to how the person experienced the trauma. For example, if it is a safety issue, the fear is stored in the base of the torso or the legs. If the trauma was related to belonging, shame, or guilt, or was sexual in nature, it is typically stored in the low belly or back region. If it was related to feeling powerless and not valued, or has anger, it can be stored in the upper belly. If it has to do with being loved or cared for, and has sadness related, it might be stored in the chest. If the trauma is related to never being able to speak or be their truth, it's stored in the neck. If the trauma is about not knowing, or feeling lost or unclear, it could be stored in the head.

In Inner Alignment, we call these frozen trauma experiences *trauma packets*. The trauma packets are frozen at the age of the trauma. If the trauma occurred when the child was seven years old, then the trauma packet is filled with seven-year-old thoughts, seven-year-old emotions, and seven-year-old confusion and overwhelm. In that trauma packet lives a little seven-year-old girl who separated from the wholeness of herself, her soul. Since her father hit her, she has been curled up in the corner of her childhood bedroom, feeling unsafe and scared from the time when the trauma occurred. Fears of her father doing it again, fears of death, and thoughts of unworthiness roll through her seven-year-old mind. She lives in this constant fear and emotion, with a deep feeling of unloved.

This is not a metaphor. The entire trauma situation lives, unresolved, in the chest and hips of her adult body and continues to give the six layers signals that the trauma is still happening (fluttering in the chest, sadness and grief, thoughts of being unlovable). Since the traumatized seven-year-old girl is frozen in this trauma, encased within the adult body, she remains scared, playing the scenario over and over like a broken record, because her seven-year-old consciousness can't resolve the trauma. She can't make sense of why this would happen or what she can do to feel safe and loved. The reality is that the trauma is still happening to the seven-year-old in the adult body, and is filling the adult's thoughts with seven-year-old thoughts, emotions, vibrations, and experiences. There is a full-on fight-

or-flight experience being kicked up to the adult's nervous system. Her adult self feels like she is under attack and is going to die. She spends her entire adult life with her nervous system in high gear, desperately searching for safety and love in every single relationship and continuing to be disappointed.

For 30 years, she spends most of her time trying to understand *why* she feels broken. She is told she has anxiety and depression and that she should practice mindfulness or go on medication. Neither solution fully works, and she feels even more broken as a result. All along, there is a trauma packet re-activating inside her, which keeps her in the unsafe, unloved, powerless vibrations that she experienced decades prior.

To illustrate this further, we can explore some of Julia's little t trauma packets. Julia had a generally good childhood, with a few issues here or there. She wouldn't have classified herself as having childhood trauma, but a lot lurks under the surface.

The top of the next picture is a trauma packet that lives in her chest. This is how Julia's parents modeled love to Julia. Home life looked like there was love, but it felt empty. Her parents always had the façade of getting along, and her mom always did what her dad asked. Everything seemed happy but it felt bad, lonely, and disconnected. This left a hole in Julia's Heart. Love felt empty and unattainable. She wasn't able to make close friends in school. As an adult, Julia wound up recreating her parents' marriage with her husband, in a partnership that looked good but felt empty.

The middle trauma packet lives in Julia's upper belly. Julia's grandfather lived with her growing up. He was a kind man during the day, and at night a somewhat unpredictable alcoholic. She loved to spend time with him because they would do special things together, but she feared who he would turn into by evening. Sometimes, after a few drinks, he would yell at her for the most insignificant mistakes. She began to feel like she couldn't do anything right. She was frozen with fear when she was around him. Later in life, she found herself scared around any authoritative male figures. At work, she would feel constantly unworthy of promotion or acknowledgement because she felt like she could never do anything right.

Julia's Trauma Packets

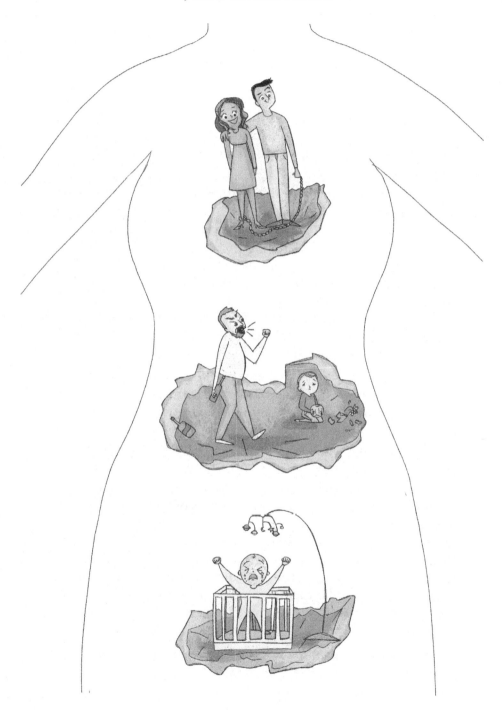

The bottom trauma packet lives in Julia's low belly. As an infant and toddler, she felt scared and alone in her crib. In the middle of the night, she would weep for her parents, but nobody would come. This felt like a deep abandonment, and made her feel scared and alone. As a middle schooler, when she was alone at home, she would have a deep sadness and go straight into the abandonment feeling, so eventually she turned to food for comfort. As an adult, she felt this when her husband traveled, was distracted with work, or simply wasn't paying attention to her. Through adulthood, she continued her habit of using food for comfort.

These trauma packets live within Julia and reverberate through her body as feelings of being unlovable, unworthy, and abandoned. She feels unsafe and lonely, sad and confused. Although Julia can understand these trauma packets and where they originated through years of self-help, the understanding doesn't change the way they reverberate through her body and affect the way she feels in present-day situations. Those trauma packets become triggered in seemingly benign circumstances, where she knows she's safe and loved, but can't seem to work herself into *feeling* that way.

She finds herself repeatedly needing validation in her relationships, and without it, she feels even more abandoned. In her abandonment, she seeks comfort and numbing, which has distorted her relationship with food and her body. Now, food equals love, and she feels like she can't break these numbing patterns, even though she can clearly see what is happening.

These trauma packets live within her, deep below the surface, and replay without her awareness of where or why they are replaying in her body. Sometimes she can analyze sources of negative thoughts from childhood experiences, but analyzing them hasn't stopped them from reactivating and overlaying her current life experiences. The past distorts the present moment and makes it feel like the old situations. She's never free from the past, even though she has created a new and different life for herself.

Here are other examples of common trauma packets:

Loss of a Loved One (big T trauma packet)

Natalie was six years old when she witnessed her four-year-old brother drown. She was in the sailboat offshore when she saw him wander from the beach into the water, and she sat there in shock when he didn't come back up above water. Her body was frozen and she felt outside of herself as she watched him drown. Afterward, when back at the house, she actually didn't feel sad like she thought she should. She couldn't feel anything at all, just complete shock. (This experience became a significant trauma packet that lived within.)

In the days that followed, nobody said anything in front of her. There was no emotion, no expression of thoughts or grief. Everyone spoke of logistics and it seemed like life went on, stoic as usual. At the funeral, she went to hold her mom's hand and her mom let go of her. Immediately, she felt a heaviness in her heart. So sad. Unloved. (This moment became an even more significant trauma packet that got stored and replayed within.) After the post-funeral reception, she sat in the corner feeling abandoned. That was exacerbated when her mom fell into a deep depression in the months that followed. She lost her brother, and then soon lost her connection to her mom.

She would say that she lost a part of herself that day, and she spent the next 52 years watching life without connection to her body or her Heart. She felt a sustained sense of disconnection and sadness. This felt like a heavy bowling ball that lived in her low belly and a heavy weight on her chest. Decades in therapy never seemed to change the way she felt. She went through the motions of life—college, husband, and kids—until one day, a clash with her son got so bad, the disconnection pushed her into her healing journey.

The week her brother died, she lost connection to her Heart and spent most of her life in complete disconnection from her soul and her emotional body as she replayed these trauma packets. Diagnosed with depression, and unable to connect to any joy, she felt like an empty vessel. Interactions with her extended family always seemed to exacerbate this depression, because they triggered the same family of origin trauma packets. Later in life, she developed physical manifestations of this heaviness in her low belly, as fibroids in her uterus.

Narcissistic Mother (big T trauma packet)

Barbara grew up as a child of a single parent. Her mom worked a lot and wasn't around very often. When her mom was around, she would spend her time criticizing and controlling most of what Barbara did and said. Nothing was ever good enough for her mom, but Barbara always tried harder so she could get her mom's positive attention. Good grades would usually get her a hug. Cleaning the kitchen would please her mom. Doing and achieving were her access points to more positivity in the house, so she did that as much as she could to get a snippet of positive attention and love from her mom. Repetition of these patterns created well-worn pathways of *results equal love*. (This *not good enough* trauma packet lived in her upper belly as burning pain and nausea.)

As an adult, Barbara became an overachieving workaholic. She defined herself by her job and what people at work thought of her. Her work life was consumed by stress, not because the position was especially difficult but because the trauma packet created immense fear of failing. Failing to get successful results was not an option because results were her only source of joy, so she spent most of her life obsessing about her work projects, team member responsibilities, deadlines, and many other things that were seemingly out of her control. A promotion or validation from her boss was what she lived for. Criticism from coworkers felt like death.

At night, she used alcohol to numb the pain of the activated trauma packet so she could feel less failure and loneliness. In fact, alcohol became her companion. She stayed single because relationships were too painful, and just confirmed how unlovable she was. She was diagnosed with anxiety and depression. As the years went on, she developed acid reflux and heart palpitations from the reactivated trauma packet.

Sustained Sexual Abuse (big T trauma packet)

Vera was a shy girl who lived with her mom and her mom's boyfriend, Dan. Dan moved in when Vera was three years old, and spent time with her while her mom worked nights. When she was young, Vera and Dan would cuddle and watch TV before bed. When Vera was around five years old, Dan started bathing her and tickling her private parts. At first, this felt good and fun, but as time went on, she didn't want to be touched and tickled. She was too shy to say no, and didn't want to lose their connection, so she continued going along with what he wanted. By the age of 10, she found herself disconnecting from her body and going to another place to sustain the activity. Other times, she pretended to be sleeping when he touched her. This carried on until she was 15 years old, keeping it their *little secret*. (The sustained abuse accumulated as a series of trauma packets across different stages of her development.) After telling her mom in her teens, she was devastated because her mom did absolutely nothing. (This became the loudest trauma packet in her body.)

Through her teen years, she isolated herself from men completely. It always felt like they would make her do something she didn't want to do. It never felt safe around them. She created closeness with women and decided it only felt safe for women to touch her or get close. She spent her life avoiding male bosses and friendships, and felt justified *writing off all men*.

As an adult, this feeling welled up in the lower part of her body. She experienced extreme low back pain that traveled down her legs. She put on extra weight so she would not be noticed by men, but this caused other problems, such as diabetes.

She felt shame for having let the touching go on for so long. She had confusion about enjoying it some of the time. This trauma packet would be triggered when she felt any pleasure, like enjoying food or time with friends, and the associated shame would surface as well.

She was resentful that Dan did that to her for so long. She hated her body and wouldn't even look at herself in the mirror. A glimpse of herself would trigger the self-hatred.

Even with women, connection and sexual pleasure was missing. She just got through sex and went out of body to sustain the connection, which led to dissociation as an adult, and a lack of connection with others. This lack of connection led to a deep state of depression.

Not Good at Math (little t trauma packet)

When Jen was 11 years old and in fifth grade, she had a strict math teacher who got easily annoyed with her. Mrs. Drake would call on her when she was daydreaming and Jen wouldn't know the answer. One day, Mrs. Drake sent Jen to the chalkboard at the front of the room to do a math problem, and ultimately made a fool of her. Her classmates laughed and made fun of her on the playground, saying she was stupid. By the end of the school year, Jen had anxiety whenever she started her math homework.

This 11-year-old experience got frozen into Jen's body in that moment at the front of the classroom. The feelings of overwhelm and embarrassment, the thoughts of not being smart enough, the physical sensations of her heart beating very hard, with sweaty hands and a quiver in her voice. She almost felt outside of herself while she stood in front of the class being humiliated. The 11-year-old experience got stored in her upper belly as *I'm stupid* thoughts that felt like a hot, burning, moving sensation. It got stored in her chest, thoughts of *Nobody likes me*, as a jumpy, jittery sensation. From that point on, any time she did math, any time she had to answer a question in front of others, and most times she was in a classroom setting, she had these same vibrations.

As an adult, whenever she had to do a presentation or answer something in a meeting, she felt the same jittery chest and burning in her belly. She called this anxiety. It didn't matter how much she talked about these past situations in therapy, as it never seemed to shift these recurring experiences. She could only find band-aids for the situations, like memorizing her speeches and calming her nervous system beforehand. No matter how many self-help books, hypnosis, or energy sessions she did, the pattern would replay because she had a trauma packet that could at any point be reactivated and replayed through a present-moment trigger. No matter how much her mind understood the cause and source of the issue, she couldn't bridge that understanding to a resolution in her body.

Busy Parents (little t trauma packet)

Rachel was the middle daughter. Her parents were incredibly busy with work and three small children. She felt like they never listened to her, never met her needs, and never hugged her because they were too distracted. As a result, she became super clingy and insecure. When they left her with a babysitter, she cried the whole time they were gone. When she played soccer, she was devastated if they didn't watch. She always hung on her mother and never felt safe when they left. They called her *velcro kid* and were always peeling her off their legs. She never felt safe in childhood, and this unsafe trauma packet persisted and replayed throughout her life.

As an adult, Rachel suffered from anxiety and panic attacks. She felt like she just couldn't handle *adulting*—paying bills, keeping a job, organizing her apartment, or holding onto a boyfriend for more than a few months. She felt like she was failing in life and just couldn't get it together.

Every person she partnered with, from roommates to boyfriends, characterized her as too clingy. The more needy she got, the more they pushed her away. She cycled through relationship after relationship, never able to create consistency or reliability anywhere in her life.

The doctors prescribed different medications to calm her anxiety and the overwhelming sadness from being alone. Even on medication, she still felt alone with or without others around. The trauma packet of being pushed away recreated that feeling, whether it was happening or not.

Trauma Fire in the Basement

In Inner Alignment, we think about the trauma packets as if they are a fire in the basement of a house. The small fires in the basement are blazing and kicking up smoke to the upper floors of the house.

There's so much smoke in the kitchen and bedrooms that it's hard to breathe. It feels impossible to merely exist most days. We do our best to blow the smoke out of the house, but the smoke exists at all six layers of the body, so it's pretty pervasive. We do yoga, meditation, EMDR, acupuncture, etc. We've tried it all, but nothing ever gets rid of the smoke. Most of the relief is temporary and only touches the surface.

In this metaphor, talk therapy is like sitting in the attic window reporting on the smoke and fire. *Well, let's see… I can see some flames coming out of the basement. There's definitely some smoke on the first and second floors of the house. I can see some debris floating out into the front yard.* The prefrontal cortex, where the analysis happens, is so far from the source of the fire in the body. If anything, it practices the neural pathways of the trauma by re-engaging the thoughts, stories, and emotional patterns.

Most people are managing the *effects* of their trauma packets through smoke management. They may exercise to release some endorphins. They do somatic work to feel the smoke and more effectively blow it out the window, or they receive energy work to move the smoke through a new pathway. They rewire the brain and memory through EDMR, leaving remnants of the phantom experience vibrating through their body. They may meditate and transcend the body so they don't have to feel it as much. Or they build mindfulness practices to interrupt the smoke.

There is no gateway from the attic of the thinking brain to the basement, where the fire is roaring in the body. What you think about, what you figure out, has very little effect on the actual fire, on the sensations of the trauma packet stored within. Some understanding is good, so you can transform belief systems later, but overall, the 20 years of talk therapy can make people feel more broken. All that effort, understanding, band-aids, and money can lead to a feeling of hopelessness because the layers of the body still hold the trauma. The fire is still burning no matter how much you look at it.

Of course, blowing out the smoke is helpful to maintain survival. If you can't breathe, you can't live. However, it must be viewed as smoke management (effects management), not putting out the fire or addressing the root cause. Moving energy around doesn't put the fire out. Thinking new thoughts in the mind doesn't change the thoughts from the seven-year-old trauma packets.

The *cause* of trauma vibrations lives in the trauma packet in the body. Healing only happens when you start putting the fire out, when you access the vibrations in the trauma packet and rework the thoughts, emotions, vibrations, energy, awareness, and spiritual connection in the original space of the trauma. The experience may have happened in the past, but it lives and replays in every present moment, so it is accessible and changeable. The fire can be put out with the right tools.

Trauma Packets and the Law of Attraction

The law of attraction gives explanation to the cause and effect of the Universe. Like attracts like. Current thoughts, feelings, and vibrations that live in your body will attract more of the same. Whether you believe in the spiritual laws, or simply focus on the neuroscience that your brain filters for what matches the thought objects of your past experiences, you'll arrive at the same place: Your past patterns and their vibrations predict the future.

If you feel like you're worthy, and you think you're worthy, then you'll filter your world as if you *are* worthy, and then through the law of attraction, you will likely attract situations that correlate with that worthiness (e.g., new jobs, great partners).

If you think the world is out to get you and feel like nothing ever works out for you, and you vibrate these sensations in your body, chances are you'll run into situations that affirm that the world doesn't support you.

If Natalie sets up her brain, nervous system, and other body layers around fear, sadness, and loss, what do you think she will get more of in life? More situations where she can never keep the love or joy, affirming that happiness will always get taken away.

If Jen's trauma packets set up her wiring to think she's stupid and that people don't like her because of it, she will set up her whole life around that paradigm. She will work hard at school and feel like she never measures up. She will assume her coworkers don't believe in her and come up with many reasons why that's true. She will avoid applying for promotions because she believes she's not smart enough to do the job. She will hyperventilate when she has to balance her project budget because she's not good at math. She won't be able to attract others' confidence in her because she doesn't have confidence in herself. She will burn herself out trying to prove her value to the world, and always feel like she falls short. Through the law of attraction, this trauma packet wiring will be reflected through all her interactions, through everything she attracts in life. She will consistently run on the hamster wheel until she simply can't do it anymore.

If Vera's trauma packets contain thoughts and emotions that make her feel like men aren't safe, it will be difficult for her to attract a sense of safety in her male relationships. She may continue to attract male friends who seem great, but in the end, betray her in one way or another. Is this coincidence? No. Her trauma packets will continue to draw, through the law of attraction, similar vibrations and scenarios. Why? Because our trauma packets are the loudest vibration in our bodies, and fear attracts fear.

Whatever resistance, fear, or difficulty lives enmeshed in your body's trauma packets will continue to attract similar experiences. Feeling unlovable will likely attract a partner incapable of a deep, connected love. Feeling unworthy will likely attract a boss who simply can't acknowledge quality work. Feeling abandoned will likely attract an inability for people to really show up when needed. Like attracts like. So, when trauma packets are vibrating loudly through us, we will likely attract new situations that mirror old situations from our past.

Interestingly, those who follow New Age spirituality's interpretation of the law of attraction believe they should bypass those old vibrations and use positive thoughts to override the negativity so they don't attract something negative. They stay super focused on *keeping a high vibration* so they don't attract the negative, but here's the thing: Whether you ignore them or not, those trauma packet vibrations are living in there. They are loud and kicking up dirt and negative vibes, either way. You can ignore them and pretend they don't exist, but the Universe responds to the loudest vibration in your body. You can't be miserable and walk around with a smile just to get something better. You can't practice positive thoughts and make a gratitude list, and then spend the rest of the day in fear and anxiety, hoping to get more positive manifestations in life. Even if you attract the better scenarios, it would be difficult to maintain the situation because of your inability to hold that positive vibration. Through a lack of resonance, your life will revert back to the trauma vibrations in that trauma packet.

You actually have to *feel* better, happier, in the present moment to draw something better from the world. You have to fully live life in this experience to receive abundance in the future. You have to *feel* worthy and deserving of what you desire. You must *feel* like the Universe supports you and that what you want is possible, actually inevitable.

You must *feel* this way to attract it, but if you have some heavy trauma packets creating misery, unworthiness, and impossibility, then it's pretty tough to feel this way consistently enough to attract and sustain this new experience, right? That's why this deep soul retrieval and rewiring is critical for creating new patterns, behaviors, thoughts, emotions, and pathways for future potential. It's like cutting off the anchor that keeps pulling you underwater so you can finally swim to the next destination.

Chapter 3:
Trauma in the Six-Layered Body

We often confuse ourselves as being our mind or our physical bodies, but we are so much more complex than that. We have physical bodies composed of organs and systems (physical layer). We have an energy field with energy centers and channels (energetic layer). We have thoughts, beliefs, and habits of behavior (mental layer). We have emotional responses to situations, such as love, fear, sadness, or anger (emotional layer). We have the ability to become aware of ourselves in a way that brings higher intelligence (awareness layer). We have euphoric love built into ourselves (bliss layer).

Because trauma is like glass that gets shattered and spread throughout the layers of the body, we must understand these layers and their complexities in order to root out the remnants of trauma that have settled deeply into each layer. Fear is stored within each layer in corresponding trauma packets depending on what happened at the time of the trauma. The trauma packets penetrate the layers and intertwine deeply into every crevice of our being.

In Inner Alignment, we refer to sensations that can be felt in any layer of the body as *vibrations*. For example, a vibration can be felt as pain in the physical body, sadness on the emotional body, heaviness on the energetic body, a negative thought in the mental body, or a blockage in the awareness body or bliss body.

Six Layers of the Body

To thoroughly understand how and where trauma is stored, we must examine how trauma manifests and behaves within each layer.

Physical Layer

The trauma penetrates our physical body in such complexity, penetrating our nervous system, body chemistry, hormones, digestion, respiration, and cardiovascular system. From the Inner Alignment perspective, the following aspects of the physical body are relevant for healing:

- Activation of the nervous system, specifically how the sympathetic and parasympathetic nervous system's response (fight, flight, freeze, fawn) impacts the autonomic nervous system's processes;

- Neuroscience of trauma packets as it relates to the neural pathways, neurotransmitters and hormones, and neurotransmitter receptors;

- Re-traumatization through triggered trauma packets; and

- Body awareness and the ability to feel sensation, pain, resistance, and restriction.

Energetic Layer

The energetic body is less understood in our society, and has previously fallen in the category of being spiritual, but in our work, we distinguish between the energy body and the spiritual body. Luckily, Eastern philosophies such as Chinese Medicine and Ayurveda provide ample description on the energetic body to guide us on the energetic effects of trauma. In Inner Alignment, we lean on the ancient system of Ayurveda to understand the energetic body, mainly the body layers (koshas), energy centers (chakras), and the elemental balance or imbalance (doshas).

- The koshas are the layers of the body that we are examining in *this* chapter: physical, energetic, emotional, mental, awareness, and bliss bodies. Classic kosha study categorizes the emotional and mental bodies as one layer, but our system requires a different approach to each of these layers. Seeing a body from this layered perspective helps us pinpoint imbalances more effectively.

- The chakra system is a subtle but complex energy system that consists of energetic centers located within specific areas of the body that intersect every other layer. Any combination of imbalance within these seven chakras can create chaos and difficulty within any layer of the body.

- The dosha system correlates to the elements—earth, water, fire, air, and ether—that govern the layers of the body and can create the perfect storm with the short- and long-term effects of trauma. We must understand the makeup of the individual's elemental constitution to determine how to restore their unique energetic balance.

With the lens of the koshas (body layers), doshas (governing elements), and chakras (energy centers), we can see how trauma has created energetic imbalance, and use this data to restore balance in conjunction with the other body layers.

Mental Layer

The mental layer of the body governs our thoughts and belief patterns in terms of how we think about our world. In our system, we separate the mental body from the emotional body because they operate very differently, though they both may create fear vibrations. We break down the mental layer as follows:

- The relationship of thoughts, choices, and behaviors that lead to specific emotional patterns;

- Delineating expansive Heart-based belief systems from limiting fear-based belief systems;

- The repetitive trauma response of the Animal Brain, and the thoughts that form as a result in the Thinking Brain;

- The nature of the death fears that live within trauma packets, which create noise throughout the layers of the body;

- The layers of consciousness—subconscious ego-mind, conscious mind, and superconscious mind—to delineate higher versus lower consciousness;

- The subconscious ego-mind's fear-based belief systems such as scarcity, powerlessness, entitlement, control, and knowing, and the mind's habits of negative thought momentum, judgment, and projection; and

- Thought and belief development as it relates to trauma packets and how to bridge the conscious mind into the trauma packets.

Emotional Layer

The emotional layer of the body governs how we feel, specifically related to fear-based emotions: sadness or depression, frustration or anger, and worry or anxiety. Each of these emotions originate from an underlying fear that often sources down to trauma packets. We examine this layer through contemplation of the following:

- Fear- versus love- based emotions;

- The wisdom of negative emotions and the emotional inner guidance system;

- The pain body, its accumulation, and how it relates to trauma packets;

- The difference between trauma packet emotions and present-moment emotions;

- Fear reactivity response patterns (fight, flight, freeze, fawn) that are activated in trauma and wired in at a young age;

- Neuroscience of emotional wiring;

- Anxiety and depression as they relate to doshas, pain bodies, and trauma packets; and

- Emotions as they relate to the energetic body chakras and doshas.

Awareness Layer

The awareness body gives us the ability to observe ourselves from a more expansive perspective. Our awareness body can witness self from a place of deeper wisdom. This layer of the body is undeveloped for many people, as they stay merged in the minutia of life. However, when it awakens, life starts to change dramatically and people find themselves on a spiritual path or personal growth journey, searching for answers and learning about themselves more deeply. To look at this layer of ourselves, we will examine the following:

- Stepping out of automatic thought and emotions;

- Developing innocent perception and a questioning nature;

- Creating awareness of automatic fear responses;

- Law of attraction as it relates to developing awareness; and

- Navigating and integrating the spiritual dimensions of consciousness as they relate to trauma packets and chakras.

Bliss or Soul Layer

The bliss layer of the body is most closely related to what many would call the experience of the soul, or the Heart of who we are. The spiritual Heart vibrates in the consciousness of love, peace, freedom, and joy. Inner Alignment is the process of aligning back to the bliss layer of the body, back to alignment with the Heart. Bliss is always there—it's our most natural state—but it tends to get covered up or distorted by fear. Trauma packets play a big role in distorting our natural state of soul vibration. We examine the bliss body through the lens of:

- Soul fragmentation;

- Accessing bliss body through the Sacred Heart and defining our unique connection with Divine Source;

- Interference energy and its effect on accessing bliss body; and

- Bliss body resonance for soul residence, and barriers such as dissociation or watching life from outside of self.

Healing the Layers

As we examine each of the body layers in the chapters that follow, we hope to convey the complexity and depth of the embedded trauma at each layer. In understanding how trauma becomes enmeshed into each layer, we can better comprehend how to heal through soul retrieval and rewiring processes.

At the end of each body layer chapter, we present the Notes for Healing section, which summarizes the main aspects that must be healed at each layer. Specific tools for healing are described in detail in Section 2: Pathway to Healing.

Chapter 4:
Physical Body Layer

Our Inner Alignment process was built with a focus on spiritual, mental, and emotional inner work, so the understanding of the physical body was revealed as the system unfolded. As my team and I realized how effective the six-layered approach was, we were able to better understand the way the cranial brain, heart brain, nervous system, and feeling senses were being affected through the Inner Alignment Soul Retrieval and rewiring processes.

The impact of trauma on the brain and nervous system is offered here as a general overview, given that our team is not composed of doctors, scientists, or neuroscience scholars. We lay this groundwork to provide understanding of the nervous system and neural circuitry for assimilating key concepts around healing in Section 2: Pathway to Healing.

Nervous System

The long-term effects of childhood trauma on the nervous system are well-documented, so we highlight how we view this from our Inner Alignment System.

Autonomic and Sympathetic Nervous Systems

The autonomic nervous system controls our internal organs and glands and generally operates outside of voluntary control. It can be further subdivided into the sympathetic and parasympathetic systems. The sympathetic nervous system is involved in preparing the body for stress-related activities (our fight-or-flight response), while the parasympathetic nervous system is associated with returning the body to routine, day-to-day operations (our rest-and-digest response). The two systems have complementary functions, operating in tandem to maintain the body's homeostasis.

When the sympathetic nervous system (fight or flight) is active and in persistent survival mode, it affects every aspect of the autonomic nervous system, with all body systems in high gear. This sympathetic response, sustained over time through persistent trauma packet activation, can create long-term damage on organs and physical systems of the body. The effects of chronic stress or replayed trauma on the autonomic system body processes can have a major impact on health and well-being. In the cardiovascular system, it can manifest as increased or erratic heartbeat, increased blood pressure, and reduced heart rate variability. Hormonally, excess stress hormones are released, and hormonal imbalance occurs. The digestive system can halt and become inefficient in digesting nutrients and eliminating waste. In the respiratory system, breath becomes irregular resulting in less oxygen to the brain and body, and less detoxification. Immune function gets unnecessarily triggered, which can create inflammation and autoimmune dysfunction.

When trauma packets are created and frozen into the body, the fight-or-flight response from the original situation can become a part of the automatic firing. A thought like, *I don't matter* can bring up an increased heartbeat, cortisol stress hormone release, burning in the stomach and diarrhea, breath-holding, and immune response. If this gets retriggered frequently enough, it becomes a person's base physiological state. The sympathetic nervous system continuously fires, and the nervous system becomes chronically dysregulated. Spending too much time with the sympathetic system activated in this way can create dis-ease in *every* layer of the body over time.

The Vagus Nerve

When looking at nervous system responses in Inner Alignment, we identify the primary fear response that is being triggered: fight, flight, freeze, or fawn. These responses seem like behavioral patterns stemming from the mental or emotional body; however, they can be pre-wired nervous system responses that originated in early childhood trauma packets and continue to activate through adulthood.

According to Dr. Stephen Porge's Polyvagal Theory, the autonomic nervous system is comprised of a three-part structure: the dorsal vagal system, the sympathetic nervous system, and the ventral vagal system.

- The dorsal vagal system, which is the oldest of the systems, is part of the parasympathetic nervous system. It immobilizes the body in response to life-threatening situations by facilitating a shutdown, *freeze* or faint response to traumatic stimuli.

- The sympathetic nervous system, which is more evolved, mobilizes the body in response to threat by activating the fight-or-flight response, so the response in the body is to *fight* the stimulus or take *flight* from the situation.

- The ventral vagal system, which is the most evolved of the structures, is the branch of the parasympathetic nervous system that helps you relax and connect to others when you feel safe. This is often called the social nervous system, and it can lead to a *fawn* response when activated with fear.

The dorsal vagal response is to freeze or shut down (freeze response), which subdues the autonomic functions of the body. An animal would freeze when a predator comes, or even faint to make the predator think it's dead. The same is true for recurring childhood trauma. A child might freeze until their mother's mood changes. A recurring freeze response can create a dissociation from the physical, mental, and emotional bodies over time (often regarded as dissociation). When this is wired in, or associated with stressful situations, it can become a default response, creating significant stress and ongoing damage to every layer of the body. In time, through trauma packet reactivation, someone can become programmed to a place of being stuck or frozen in everyday situations because of the habitual triggering of the dorsal vagal response.

The sympathetic nervous system response is to fight or flight. In this case, the body's autonomic functions go into overdrive and the body is revved up. Often, depending on a person's energetic body tendencies, personality, and childhood experiences, a fight response could look like gearing up for an actual physical fight, a right/wrong debate, blaming, or simply a perpetual state of doing (such as cleaning the house or performing tasks to stay busy and burn off the cortisol). The flight response is to flee from the situation, or to continue moving away from or around the person creating the trigger. Over time, this can become a perpetual habit of fleeing when we can't find emotional safety in a situation or relationship (e.g., avoiding communication, leaving the party, or changing partners).

The ventral vagal response is a more evolved response that allows us to create a sense of relaxation and connection to others. Instead of going into overdrive (sympathetic fight or flight) or shutdown (dorsal vagal freeze) response, we have the option to stay calm and maintain the social connection when triggered. This brings the nervous system back into a state of homeostasis. This ventral vagal response is ideal for a mindful response to a stimulus or triggering situation.

However, an over-reliance upon the ventral vagal circuit (or social nervous system) for the purpose of appeasing and pleasing others could result in a fawn response, which involves reading the social and emotional cues of others and working to care for their needs in order to create an external experience of safety and love (usually before caring for one's own needs or providing love for self). The fawn response is often confused as the more caring or compassionate response, but if the response is coming from reactivated trauma packet fear, and is used to create external safety (versus inner safety), then it's just another fear response prompted by the trauma packet's impact on the nervous system.

Let's simplify these polyvagal concepts in a way that you would find in many mindfulness resources. The sympathetic nervous system increases autonomic functions and creates the stress response (fight or flight). With this, the vagus nerve is the key to activating the parasympathetic functions (rest and digest) to bring the body back to a relaxed state. Stimulating the vagus nerve can slow down your heart rate, lower your blood pressure, and settle your respiratory response. This is an important factor in healing the long-term effects of childhood trauma on the physical body, such as heart disease and high blood pressure, endocrine disorders, digestion issues (irritable bowel, blood sugar management), inflammation (rheumatoid arthritis, rashes or hives), etc.

The vagus nerve plays a critical role in letting your body know that you are safe and that things are going to be okay. Heart Rate Variability (HRV), controlled by the vagus nerve, is a good measure of this inner resilience. The more variation or complexity in your heart rate, the more resilient and adaptable you are. To activate the vagus nerve, one must breathe into the diaphragm. Since a deep inhale increases the heart rate, creating an upward spike in heart rate, and an equally long exhale decreases the heart rate, creating a downward spike, this creates a highly variable heart rate and a more resilient heart.

The vagus nerve transmits information from the heart to the cranial brain, facilitating homeostasis throughout the body. Through the science of neurocardiology, which studies the brain cells within the heart, Dr. Armour discovered in 1991 that the heart has a little brain, or intrinsic cardiac nervous system. This *heart brain* is composed of approximately 40,000 neurons that are like the neurons in the brain. The heart brain communicates with the cranial brain via the vagus nerve, which carries information from the heart and other internal organs to the brain. The heart actually sends more information to the brain than the brain sends to the heart. The HeartMath Institute's research on the wisdom of the heart demonstrates that the heart can receive and process incoming data and experiences *before* the brain receives them; the heart essentially has a mind of its own. This means that the vagus nerve influences brain function and most of the body's major organs and plays an important role in our mental and emotional experiences and the quality of our lives.

If we take this information and apply the negative effects of childhood trauma to the wiring of the heart brain, and the heart brain's communication to the cranial brain through the vagus nerve, then we can consider the role of the heart brain in rewiring these effects in the healing process.

Brain and Neural Pathway Development

One of the simplest and most profound descriptions of the neuroscience of emotion was the following by Debbie Hampton:

"A thought is an electrochemical event taking place in your nerve cells producing a cascade of physiological changes. There are thousands upon thousands of receptors on each cell in our body. Each receptor is specific to one peptide, or protein. When we have feelings of anger, sadness, guilt, excitement, happiness or nervousness, each separate emotion releases its own flurry of neuropeptides. Those peptides surge through the body and connect with those receptors which change the structure of each cell as a whole.

Where this gets interesting is when the cells actually divide. If a cell has been exposed to a certain peptide more than others, the new cell that is produced through its division will have more of the receptor that matches with that specific peptide. Likewise, the cell will also have less receptors for peptides that its mother/sister cell was not exposed to as often.

So, if you have been bombarding your cells with peptides from negative thoughts, you are literally programming your cells to receive more of the same negative peptides in the future.

What's even worse is that you're lessening the number of receptors of positive peptides on the cells, making yourself more inclined toward negativity.

Every cell in your body is replaced about every two months. So, the good news is, you can reprogram your pessimistic cells to be more optimistic by adopting positive thinking practices, like mindfulness and gratitude, for permanent results."

Most cranial brain development happens by the time a person is seven years old and then slowly continues on through young adulthood. Because the majority of brain development happens before a child enters first grade, it's important to examine how these neurons are developed and the effect of trauma on the development of the cranial brain's neural pathways.

At birth, the brain contains about 100 billion interconnected cells. Each cell forms thousands of connections, called synapses, with other brain cells. An infant's brain has about 2,500 synapses per neuron. New synapses are created every time a child experiences a new sensation or processes a new stimulus. Over the first three years of a child's life, those original synapses multiply to nearly 15,000 per neuron. At this point, the brain begins to eliminate lesser-used or dormant synapses and strengthen the ones that are used frequently. The strongest synapses persist into adulthood after the brain stabilizes around the age of 25. While the brain is always changeable and adaptable, it becomes more difficult to significantly alter brain pathways after this stabilization occurs.

Whatever emotions, reactions, or experiences a child has on a regular basis will become the foundation of their brain function for the rest of their life. When early childhood traumatic experiences remain unaddressed through the rest of brain development, they become cemented into the brain's pathways and can lead to anxiety and depression later in life.

Auto-Associated Neural Networks

"Neurons that fire together, wire together." Neuropsychologist Donald Hebb first used this phrase in 1949 to describe how the neural pathways in the brain are formed and reinforced through repetition. The more the brain does a certain task, practices a certain thought, or exercises a certain emotion, the stronger the neural network becomes, making the process more efficient within the structure of the brain each time it is repeated. Any two cells or systems of cells that are repeatedly active at the same time will tend to become associated, so that activity in one facilitates activity in the other. Gordon Allport, a

Harvard psychologist, reinforced this by suggesting that if the pattern of activity were to occur repeatedly, the set of active elements constituting that pattern will become increasingly inter-associated. That is, each element will tend to turn on every other element and turn off the elements that do not form part of the pattern.

Psychologist Deann Ware, Ph.D., explains that when brain cells communicate frequently, the connection between them strengthens, and messages that travel along the same pathway in the brain over and over begin to transmit faster and faster. With enough repetition, these behaviors become automatic. There are many complicated behaviors that we do automatically because neural pathways have formed and the patterns become *auto-associated*.

The application of these neuroscience-based concepts to the understanding of childhood trauma is profound in describing the neural synaptic causes of anxiety and depression. Let's say that as a child, when your father was angry and punishing, you felt unsafe, unloved, and lonely. In reaction to this, you did nice things for him (e.g., did the dishes, brought out the trash, got him his beer), which caused him to be nice to you, and then you felt loved again. Those experiences, when repeated, can become auto-associated and create a habit of becoming a caregiver to feel safe and loved.

I'm unloved thoughts + *lonely* and *unsafe* feelings + *doing nice things for someone who is angry with me* behaviors + *feeling loved again* emotions + *holding my breath* respiratory patterns + *fawn* fear response during nervous system activation... can create auto-associated wiring where punishment becomes an indicator that it's time to fawn over others so you can win back their love and feel safe again. Any of these thoughts or feelings can trigger each other by just one being activated. Feeling unloved gets associated with feeling unsafe, and vice versa, feeling unsafe imports an automatic feeling of being unloved. When someone is angry, an automatic pattern of fawning and caregiving is activated to regain safety. Feeling unsafe becomes associated with getting love. And love gets connected to feeling unsafe. The nervous system activates into fear when in loving relationships, so fear becomes auto-associated with love. Fawning over others becomes associated with getting love. Ultimately, these auto-associations lead to love never feeling good because you have to jump through hoops to get it, and it's only temporary. The resulting feeling is hopelessness and depression due to the auto-associated dysfunctional wiring of love, safety, and fawning.

This understanding of how the brain gets wired—with emotions, thoughts, breathing patterns, nervous system, fear—gives us a basis of understanding why adults walk around with such mixed emotion and confusion around relationships. If a child gets consistent messages and experiences that are trauma-based, rooted in fear and negativity (a lack of love), that child will be completely wired into that paradigm. Imagine how the brain of a young child gets wired up during a repetitive trauma situation during childhood: a narcissistic parent that always needed to be right, an older sister that always teased, a loving grandfather who repeatedly touched inappropriately. The paradigm will persist until they develop their prefrontal cortex and awareness body to reevaluate and rewire auto-associated patterns, thereby transitioning into a more loving and joyful existence.

Neurotransmitters and Hormones

Communication across synapses or between the brain and body happens due to two types of chemicals: neurotransmitters and hormones. The body produces these two substances—neurotransmitters in the brain and hormones in the glands—to regulate everything from mood to heart rate. Neurotransmitters include dopamine, norepinephrine, and serotonin, while hormones include oxytocin, cortisol, and insulin, among others in each category. Serotonin, for example, is connected to mood and sleep patterns, and having low levels is linked to depression and insomnia. Oxytocin creates the warm-and-fuzzy feelings of closeness that encourage socialization and regulate stress.

Traumatic experiences in childhood can alter the production of neurotransmitters and hormones. Studies have shown, for example, that people who experience childhood abuse or neglect can suffer from thwarted neurotransmitter development. Underdeveloped oxytocin pathways greatly affect the ability to feel loved, positivity, happiness, and closeness to others. Low levels of serotonin lead to depression. Unformed dopamine receptors dramatically reduce a person's ability to experience pleasure and happiness. All of these inhibitive changes to neurotransmitter production can lead to mood issues, inability to regulate stress, and an overactive sympathetic nervous system.

Neurotransmitters and Neurotransmitter Receptors

Neurotransmitters and their receptors act like a lock-and-key system. Just as it takes the right key to open a specific lock, a neurotransmitter (the key) will only bind to a specific receptor (the lock). If the neurotransmitter is able to connect to the receptor site, it triggers changes in the receiving cell.

If a neural pathway or circuit is set up to transmit neurotransmitters associated with depression, it will also have neurotransmitter receptors that receive the corresponding neurotransmitters. In other words, if someone experiences trauma and has fear and depression pathways, their body sends out fear and depression neurotransmitters, and has cells set up with mainly fear and depression receptors. Because of this, we say that their brain is wired for fear and depression.

It takes about two months for the neurotransmitter receptors to change and accommodate new types of neurotransmitters. For example, for a depressed adult, it would require the brain to consistently release neurotransmitters associated with happiness for two months for the depressed neurotransmitter receptors to change into happy receptors, so the chemical feeling of happiness can be sustained. An interesting thought: If you feel depressed and want to get happy, you have to feel happy consistently for two months in order to change the receptors to hold those new happy neurotransmitters. This is quite the conundrum for those who have been chronically depressed since childhood. They have to create and maintain a body chemistry they're not wired for, and sustain it for two months. This highlights the need for a systematic approach to trauma recovery and rewiring that supports the neuroscience of healing over the two months it takes to rewire the circuitry and chemistry of the brain and body.

Re-Traumatization Through Triggered Trauma Packets

In Inner Alignment, we hypothesize that when we initially store a frozen trauma packet in the body, the six layers of the body experience different sensations that fire together, replay, and therefore wire together. Since trauma packets can continue to activate once they have been stored in the body, the replay of these auto-associated components—thoughts, emotions, energetics, nervous system firing, and behavioral patterns— become well-worn circuitry.

For example, a teacher scolds a child for the first time... physical sensations (fight-or-flight response, chest fluttering), energetic sensations (heat moving from belly to chest), thoughts (*I'm stupid*) and emotions (embarrassed and disliked), a feeling of death, and soul dissociation from the body... are fired together at the same time, for the first time. Because the overwhelming trauma experience is not processed out of the body, it continues to replay itself over and over again and creates auto-association through repetition. The thoughts and feelings begin to transmit as a group faster and faster. It becomes a well-practiced set of body system experiences that fire together on their own, sometimes as a result of a present-moment trigger, and often seemingly out of nowhere.

It takes the firing of just one component of that packaged set of thoughts, emotions, or energetics to activate the whole set. Further, the auto-associated packet can fire on any layer of the body. From the above example, either a thought of *I'm stupid* in the mental body, or emotions of embarrassment from the emotional body, can bring all the other components into action. As a result, the re-triggered trauma packet will replay in every layer of the body. This is why people spend much of their lives replaying the trauma packets stored within.

Many healing modalities tend to stir up the trauma packets by accessing the thoughts or emotions, and the corresponding auto-associated vibrations from the body. Essentially, this requires the person to re-live the experience through the six-layered body, bringing it all up to the surface, which can reinforce the pathways of the trauma, firming up the beliefs, emotions, and nervous system response. Often, people will leave treatment feeling worse than before. This is because the trauma packet was re-activated, without any healing for the root cause of the sensations that live in the trauma packet.

Natalie, who lost her brother to the drowning accident, and then her mother to depression, wired up a thought paradigm around loss and being alone. She believed that any time she was happy, she would just be waiting for the other shoe to drop. She believed it was just better if she didn't feel anything. She kept up a life of disconnection by pursuing computer science so she didn't have to navigate social-emotional dynamics. She married her husband because it made sense, not because she felt love, since she couldn't feel any emotion. She did what she could physically for her kids, but wasn't capable of feeling love, giving love emotionally, or teaching them how to love. Her brain and body only knew survival, getting through life, and she was stuck in a perpetual freeze response emotionally. Natalie set up every aspect of her life with these thoughts, beliefs, emotions, and body sensations. She continued to re-trigger these feelings of numbness through the life she built for herself. Any time she felt that constant disconnection, she felt the familiar feeling of loss associated with being alone.

Feeling Sensation in the Physical Body

When the body gets wired to trauma, when the fight/flight/freeze/fawn response becomes so habitually auto-associated with old trauma thoughts and emotions in this way, the person begins to feel like they are living in an inner hell. Primal fear automatically activates through the nervous system (and corresponding body chemistry) and becomes unbearable. Because of this uncomfortable sensation in the nervous system, which seems to have an auto-associated life of its own, the person may begin to dissociate from their body. They will often go numb, disconnecting from all physical sensation and body signals, which in the moment feels better than experiencing all the confusing sensations that make the body feel like it's under constant threat, even though the rational mind knows there's no imminent threat.

This disconnection from the physical body's messages causes a new set of issues: a habit of ignoring signals (hunger, elimination, etc.) or habits of numbing the sensation through addictive behaviors. This can result in overeating, use of alcohol or marijuana, self-harm, relationship connection issues, and disconnection from the emotional body and its inner guidance system.

We must feel the sensations of the body to discern what's going on within each layer. A rumbling in the belly can suggest hunger. Droopiness in the eyes may suggest energetic fatigue. Pressure on the chest could indicate sadness. Dizziness could indicate ungroundedness.

Interestingly, most people aren't connected to their bodies, and if they are, they often don't know how to decode the messages that the body is sending through the vagus nerve. For many, the sensations are scary and confusing, and they just want them to go away. Befriending sensations, learning the unique messages from the physical body and the corresponding systems, can be a critical map back to well-being. Our body's sensations can lead the way back home.

Notes for Healing the Physical Layer

The three main areas that must be healed in the physical layer are: the autonomic nervous system's dysregulation, the neural circuitry's tendency toward negative thoughts and emotion, and the inability to navigate feeling sensations in the body. To heal this layer, the following must be addressed in the healing process:

1. Regulate Heart Rate Variability (HRV) and create resilience in the cardiovascular response.

2. Regularly modify the respiratory rate to balance the sympathetic/parasympathetic response (e.g., activate the parasympathetic nervous system through vagus nerve stimulation in the case of sympathetic response).

3. Rewire the neural pathways in the brain to sustain more positive thoughts and emotions that can build new neural circuitry over two months.

4. More consistently release neurotransmitters and hormones that sustain greater amounts of happy hormones (such as oxytocin, dopamine, and serotonin) so the neurotransmitter receptors can

be built and the chemistry can be supported in the cells.

5. Shift out of re-traumatization through the replay of trauma packets, into a more sustained positive repetition of positive neural circuitry, through the ability to pause the negative feedback loop.

6. Learn the unique feelings and sensations of the body's signals to lessen the fear and feel more equipped to listen and respond to body sensations without fear.

7. Through Inner Alignment Soul Retrieval, root out the negative physical sensations and nervous system patterns that were frozen in the trauma packet of the childhood trauma experience to stop them from replaying automatically. Replace them with physical sensations of safety and peace for a more grounded state of nervous system regulation.

Chapter 5:
Energetic Body Layer

In order to comprehend the effects of trauma on daily living and heal the root cause within the trauma packets, the energetic body must be understood. While Westerners haven't developed a clear system to work with the energetic layer, we can lean on ancient Eastern Medicine to guide us in the understanding of the energetic body, and help us gauge whether someone's energetics have been affected by the trauma packets stored in the body. Through the 5,000-year-old system of Ayurveda, we can examine trauma packet energetics through the lens of chakras and doshas.

Chakra Energy Center System

Referred to as the *chakras* in Eastern modalities, the energy centers serve as a major puzzle piece in understanding the specific effects of trauma stored in trauma packets. Because the energy centers intersect the physical, emotional, mental, and awareness bodies, imbalances are indicators of where trauma is stored and how it has manifested in the various systems. For example, an energetic imbalance in the Will Chakra can appear in the mind (mental body) as perfectionism, in the emotions (emotional body) as anger, or in an organ (physical body) as stomach ulcers.

Trauma packets and their associated vibrations will first be apparent on the subtle layers before densifying more tangibly on the physical layer. Attuning to the blocked energetic spaces is a good start to identify the actual location and layers affected by trauma packet vibrations. When we see the effects of imbalances span across the body layers within a chakra, it indicates an underlying trauma packet wreaking havoc in this area of the body.

Chakra Energy Centers

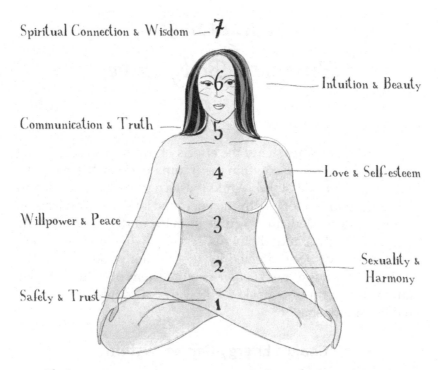

Chakra energy centers are spiraling hubs of energetic frequencies within a location in the body. They correlate to every body layer—specific organs and glands, types of emotions, thought themes, aspects of behavior, life issues—and serve as precise indicators of balance or imbalance. Depending on the type of situation and emotional reaction, we can immediately know where the trauma packet resides and how it is manifesting based on the chakra-related topic:

1- Root Chakra: Safety and trust

2- Sacral Chakra: Relationship connection and harmony

3- Will Chakra: Worth and strength

4- Hearth Chakra: Love and compassion

5- Throat Chakra: Truth and expression

6- Third Eye Chakra: Intuition and wisdom

7- Crown Chakra: Divine connection

The Inner Alignment System leans heavily on the intersection of the emotional body feelings and physical body sensations in the space of the specific chakras to point to the precise issue that needs work. For example, if the person says they feel pressure in the chest and feel unloved by their spouse in daily life, we can deduce that the old trauma packet lives within the Heart Chakra, and inner work needs to heal specific Heart-related issues. By focusing on the situation in present life, the issue that's bothering the person right now, we can follow the sensations related to the chakra and work the trauma very precisely, based on what we know needs to exist within that chakra. In this example, that would be a base vibration of inner love within the Heart, unburdened by past relationships.

This approach is very different than having someone come in for trauma work and say that they were neglected by their parents, and talking about their parental issues from the mind. As a result of that neglect, depending on how the child stored that parenting experience, the child could feel unsafe (Root Chakra), abandoned (Sacral Chakra), unworthy (Will Chakra), unloved (Heart Chakra), like they don't matter (Throat Chakra), or like they shouldn't exist (Third Eye or Crown Chakras). The body's sensations provide data on the most damaging aspect of the neglect for that specific person. The sensations give a roadmap for where the trauma got trapped across the layers of the body, how the person internalized the experiences from childhood, and the pathway for healing it.

Let's take a look at how trauma packets reveal imbalance on the energetic layer of the body. Note that chakras can be imbalanced in either direction—too little energy in the chakra (weak-imbalanced) or too much energy in the chakra (excess-imbalanced). We trace these from the bottom to the top of the body.

#1 Root Chakra: Safety (relates to earth element)

At the physical level, the Root Chakra (#1) is located from the tailbone down to below the feet. This chakra governs the connection to the earth, and our connection to our physical body. When balanced, we feel grounded, safe, and financially secure, and have a sense of trust in our existence in the world. When weak-imbalanced, we can feel unsafe, ungrounded, fearful, and generally overwhelmed and unhooked. When excess-imbalanced, we feel stuck, stagnant, and resistant to change.

Trauma often weakens the Root Chakra because it inherently threatens our sense of safety on any layer of the body, i.e., emotional safety, physical safety, safety in our sanity of mind, and safety in how we feel energetically (e.g., overly sensitive to others' energies) and spiritually (e.g., feeling spooked by spirits).

Without a solid Root Chakra, that deep sense of unsafety can form our outlook in life, the way we perceive and experience the world. Thoughts and emotions connected to being unsafe can be built into our brain's neural pathways and belief systems, resulting in paranoia, anxiety, and panic attacks. A weak Root Chakra can interfere with our ability to feel capable of adulting, getting and keeping a job, interacting with others, etc. Thoughts such as *I'm unsafe* and *I can't trust people* may surface, generating significant fear and overwhelming the person's ability to move beyond the survival response. One might experience paranoid emotions relating to a deep fear of death and looping thoughts of unsafety, such as fear of illness, fear of energies, and not trusting self or others.

A trauma packet that lives in the Root Chakra could have sensations (or absence of feeling) in the legs, or excess movement in the head (dizziness).

#2 Sacral Chakra: Connection (relates to the water element)

The Sacral Chakra (#2) is located in the low belly and low back, and governs our connection to our family, our tribe or community, and our ability to have a sense of emotional harmony and intimate connection to others. When balanced, we have a sense of secure connection to those around us and a value for relationships.

When weak-imbalanced, we can feel disconnected from others and emotionally aloof, producing a deep sense of disharmony in our relationships. On the thought layer, relationships may seem disposable. If a partnership doesn't work, you might just move on to the next person without much regard or compassion for the original partner. On the emotional layer, you may not move past the surface connection to create deeper emotional intimacy. Sometimes a weak Sacral may appear on the physical layer as a lack of sex drive or an inability to have children.

When excess-imbalanced, the excess water can make us over-emotional and too sentimental (e.g., big emotions over a small event). Individuals with this imbalance may become too attached to those around them, relying on them for comfort and feeling abandonment when their emotional or sexual needs are not met. Emotionally, this person may appear dramatic in seemingly small situations, as they are swept away in the tidal waves of emotions. Or perhaps they grow overly attached within a relationship, focusing only on their partner's needs at the exclusion of their own. This can result in not setting personal boundaries, because the need for relationship harmony supersedes one's own truth or desires.

Trauma within our birth family can create a significant imbalance in our ability to feel connected in future relationships. For example, we might avoid relationships due to an inability to create harmony, or conversely, make it our job to be the caregiver to avoid losing relationships. Either way, this creates an inner imbalance that keeps us from unencumbered, balanced relationships with friends and family members. A balanced Sacral keeps us from bailing on relationships or losing ourselves in them.

Mentally, thoughts of *I'm not worthy of connection* and *They will leave me* can form our belief system. Thoughts related to perceived abandonment may be accompanied by emotions of grief, betrayal, sadness, guilt, or shame. In the end, one can end up feeling lonely, empty, or even selfish.

A Sacral Chakra trauma packet could be felt in the physical body as a heavy bowling ball (or emptiness) sensation in the low belly.

#3 Will Chakra: Worth (relates to the fire element)

The Will Chakra (#3) is located in the upper belly and mid-back, and governs our willpower, motivation, confidence, and ability to see ourselves as worthy. When balanced, we have a sense of knowing who we are, our value in the world, and motivation toward the results or outcome we desire.

When weak-imbalanced, we can lack a sense of self-worth, courage, passion, or desire. We can have difficulty making decisions or getting clarity on what we desire. This can result in overwhelm, flightiness, and confusion. Often, a weak Will Chakra can lead to depending on others to decide for us, to be our strength and define our truth, which leads to giving our power away to others. This voluntary powerlessness doesn't feel like a decision due to a lack of fire and will, which can lead to feeling victimized in relationships and unable to maintain boundaries and self-worth through self-advocacy.

When excess-imbalanced, it can show up as controlling, jealous, perfectionistic, rageful, and even narcissistic. With too much Will Chakra fire, we get attached to successful results and plow over others who are in the way of that end result, damaging relationships in the process. This excess fire, like a wildfire, can burn up other people, intentionally or unintentionally, due to the pure force that comes from a strong will. Because the ego is seated within the Will Chakra, too much energy in this space can be very concentrated on the individual's needs, without consideration for others' needs or desires.

Depending on the nature of the trauma, our own perceived self-worth can get distorted. Thoughts of *I'm not valuable* or *I'm not deserving* may be present. Someone might feel low self-esteem or self-worth, unmotivated, powerless, or unable to do anything *right*. In contrast, the person may have a sense of angry entitlement (*They should have done it my way!*) with frustration, anger, or arrogance.

In order to feel our power in life, we have to activate the Will Chakra, the fire within ourselves. When our Will is activated, we believe we can change or transform our relationships and situations (jobs or exchanges), and impact in the world.

When raised by angry parents, someone may consider *all* anger bad or wrong and shut down their Will Chakra. Their experience of anger can get associated with violence because the parent lacked love when abusive, and therefore felt unsafe. Without a strong Will Chakra, they find themselves unable to truly make their life what they want it to be. They lack direction because they can't connect with their desire. They struggle with the expression of their truths because they haven't activated their will. When the will is shut down, their truths are often shut down as well.

(Note that anger without love is scary. Anger while connected to the Heart is manageable and important for expression in relationships. Very few people know how to access their anger and express it while staying grounded in the Heart).

Physically, this can manifest in the stomach, small intestine, liver, gallbladder, spleen, or pancreas. The sensations of imbalanced Will Chakra on the physical and energetic body can feel like burning or stabbing in the upper belly.

#4 Heart Chakra: Love (relates to the air element)

The Heart Chakra (#4) is located in the chest and upper back, and dictates the way we process love—give love, receive love, love others, love ourselves, and have compassion—all matters of love and attracting (or pushing away) love from our lives. When balanced, we can give love to others freely and receive love back. We develop loving relationships that honor the exchange of love and care, without guarding our Hearts for fear of getting hurt. We are able to love ourselves fully through acts of self-care, self-forgiveness, self-acceptance, and self-compassion.

If imbalanced, we get hyper-focused on getting love from outside of us, from others, which we ideally would be giving to ourselves and receiving from the Divine. We might lose the Heart connection to life and to people, and feel deeply unloved by those around us, as if nobody cares. This dependency on others usually leaves us feeling unlove-able.

When weak-imbalanced, we have trouble giving or receiving love. We look to others to care for us, to love us, to be there and give us compassion, and are not able to sustain that for ourselves. A weak Heart Chakra could also mean that we are good at receiving it from others but never build the capacity to give care, love, or compassion to others.

When excess-imbalanced, we become *bleeding hearts* that care too much and give so much love that we become depleted and lost in others' lives and situations. This usually sets up relationships where we are the giver but never receive. Part of the reason the giver never receives is because their relationship patterns were set up from the start as *I'm the giver and you're the receiver.*

To understand this confusion, we must examine love as a frequency versus an emotion that we generate for each other as a currency to feel safe or loved. The frequency of love that gets generated and emanates from our Hearts is not necessarily personal or romantic love. Our Heart connects us to above and below—the Divine love from above, and the sacred earth presence from below. Our Heart connection is about accessing the abundance of love that already exists within our Hearts from these Divine and sacred earth frequencies.

Since love is a fundamental feeling that governs us as humans, and it is usually distorted or absent in trauma situations, there is a lot of confusion about love. How do we get love from others? What's the *right* way to give love? Must we be *selfless* in our sharing of love, and does that mean that our own needs are left out? Are we entitled to love in our adult relationships or must we earn the relationship, and therefore love, in our intimate connections? If we love, are we then vulnerable, i.e., can someone break our heart? This confusion can get wired up as distortions of truth within our trauma packets. Many people with trauma feel that they weren't able to get the love they needed from family members with blocked Heart Chakras. Due to a lack of pure love existing in childhood, people will shut down their Heart, feel unloved, or simply not know how to give or receive love.

Thoughts can lead to *I'm unloved* or *Nobody cares for me*, which can send someone searching for that love from every future relationship. This can come with a great sense of emotional grief, loss, sadness, depression, or neglect. Physically and energetically, this often feels like pressure on or in the chest, squeezing of the heart, or like a heavy weight inside the chest.

Typically, we see the Heart and Sacral Chakras linked in imbalance—unloved and abandoned. Someone will be searching for that love and connection through their relationships, versus generating love within themselves to share with others. The dependency creates unhealthy attachment and fear, because secure love can never come from others. It must first originate from within ourselves.

#5 Throat Chakra: Truth (relates to the ether element as sound)

The Throat Chakra (#5) is located in the neck, and governs the expression of our inner truths and receiving of others' truths. When balanced, we can communicate our desires, express our needs or boundaries, listen to others, and live out our truth through our life purpose. We feel like we have a voice in life, like we matter. We like to be witnessed and feel seen by others.

When weak-imbalanced, we can feel muted or shut down, like our truth doesn't matter. We feel unable to know how to respond to people, or how to share what we feel or think in relationships or situations. Those with weak Throat Chakras feel unseen and invisible, which compounds with feeling unheard, and results in feeling like they don't matter. They can feel stuck in their inability to find their purpose or live in alignment with what they desire. Due to the inability to express truth, they might resort to lying or deviant ways of sneaking to get their needs met (e.g., telling white lies, cheating in a relationship).

When excess-imbalanced, we might take up too much space through excess talking or sharing. This could look like gossiping or getting into other people's business, sharing too much about self and others, or not filtering confidential information. Too much talking could lead to not being able to listen to others' truths, an inability to be silent to allow space for others, and not being able to receive what they have to say.

Trauma has a huge effect on someone's ability to express their truth, especially if their truth was thwarted, or made wrong or bad. If someone was told that *A child should be seen but not heard* or *It doesn't matter what you feel/say/think,* this can color their expression for the rest of their lives. If you are told not to cry, yell, or have outbursts, then those words can literally get stuck in your throat as trauma vibrations.

Thoughts show up such as *I don't matter* or *What I think doesn't matter* or *I'm not important* or *Nobody considers me*. This can lead to feeling invisible in life. Emotions include feeling shy, embarrassed, withdrawn with a fear of speaking up, and feeling *less than* others; or with too much, feeling aloof, having *more important* truths than others, or being loose-lipped with information.

Often the Throat and Will Chakras can be linked in blockage. The desire or will is cultivated in the upper belly and moves upward, to be expressed through the throat. When the Will Chakra is weak, we can't find our truth, boundaries, or confidence in expression. When the Will Chakra is in excess, we spew our opinions and judgments everywhere. When the Will Chakra is charged but the Throat Chakra is weak, we may feel our truths stored there but unable to come out. This can often feel like a lump in the throat, quite literally, or like someone is choking or squeezing the neck.

#6 Third Eye Chakra: Intuition and Wisdom (relates to the ether element as light)

The Third Eye Chakra (#6) is located in the middle of the forehead, through the center of the head (pineal gland), and at the base of the skull. It governs the ability to access inner wisdom, intuition, clarity, and creativity, as well as the ability to see life beyond this moment from the bigger picture. When this chakra is balanced, we are able to see the high-level view of life beyond the current situation to envision our future. We are able to access our own inner wisdom, soul clarity, and the way forward. Through this chakra, we see beauty, create new ideas, and pursue creative endeavors.

When weak-imbalanced, this chakra shows up as an inability to be spontaneous or creative, or access intuition. It feels like a lack of awareness, flow, and creative thoughts, which leaves the mind dull. We might feel confused, with no sense of direction or way out of the current situation.

When excess-imbalanced, we can get overwhelmed and distracted, internally or externally. We can't organize all the thoughts or ideas, or material belongings around us, which creates messiness and disarray. We find ourselves starting many projects, but likely never finishing due to lack of focus on one thing. By picking up on others' energies or emotions, one might feel like an empath or energetically sensitive person who can't protect their energy field enough to discern their own truths.

Thoughts are usually related to feeling stuck or feeling overwhelmed, like *I can't see my way out of this* or *I don't have direction* or *I can't choose one of the many options or directions.* Emotions may feel hopeless or stuck, scattered or overwhelmed.

When the Third Eye is in excess, and the three lower chakras are weak (Will, Sacral, and Root), there is often an inability to translate all the ideas into action. When the Third Eye is in excess and the Root Chakra is weak, there are ungrounded thoughts looping around lack of safety (emotionally, physically, or spiritually).

Because this chakra is physically related to the brain, pineal gland, and nervous system, trauma has significant effects on the Third Eye Chakra, as mentioned in the chapter on the physical layer of the body.

#7 Crown Chakra: Divine Connection (relates to the ether element as space)

The Crown Chakra (#7) relates to the top of the head, and governs our spiritual connection to Divine Source energy. In our society, spiritual connection is as elusive as the energetic body. It gets confused with religious rules and practices, versus the relationship with Source energy.

When balanced, there is a palpable connection between individual soul to Source—to Divine Light, God, Angels, Ascended Masters (e.g., Saints, Buddha, Jesus), or simply the Divine Presence in the form of the sun or earth. When balanced, communication and relationship with Source becomes as important as relationship with family members and partners. Guidance, love, and companionship with the Divine governs life. Life feels like there is a higher purpose.

When weak-imbalanced, the physical realm is all there is, which can feel limited and bleak. It can feel like there's no point to life, no real purpose. Dependency on others or physical belongings (house, shopping, food) becomes dominant, and inner connection to the soul feels unreachable. Someone can feel an existential abandonment or a feeling like they should have never been born.

When excess-imbalanced, someone can get disconnected from their body and health due to overfocus on spiritual connection. They might struggle with keeping a job or relationships in the physical realm, because of impatience with the human condition (e.g., *the low consciousness, non-awake, unevolved egos around us*). General adulting can become difficult due to a disconnection in one or all of the lower chakras. One might be inundated with spiritual energy, messages, and sensitivities, which can create a feeling of being overly spiritually sensitive and unable to digest or take action due to spiritual overwhelm.

Often, in trauma packets, there is a lack of Divine assistance, a deep sense of *I'm alone in this* that feels existential. Thoughts of *What's the use in living?* can be accompanied by emotions of feeling uninspired, or energetically and spiritually disconnected.

Religious trauma can also create trauma packets and imbalance in the Crown Chakra. Unfortunately, religion and Divine connection can feel linked together, so when religious distortions are discovered, someone can also throw out the concept of Divine connection and spirituality, shutting down the powerhouse of love and vibrational light that is available to them. Witnessing flawed and distorted egos acting as enlightened religious leaders can lead some to write off the Divine altogether, or create a stance against God. Mental, physical, or sexual abuse—or abuse of power or authority—within or around a spiritual community can also turn people off to Divine Source.

Because people are often disconnected from Divine Source during a trauma, they don't feel the presence of Divine assistance. They might resent God because they don't feel guidance or protection. Or they don't understand *how God could let that happen*. These thoughts and beliefs live as distortions in the trauma packets. This stems from a lack of understanding of free will—Divine Source cannot intervene unless invited into a life or situation in every instance.

Elements Through Ayurvedic Doshas

It may feel like a stretch to those who identify the body as just flesh and bones, but as we examine the energetic aspects of the body, we can see the elements that make up our planet—earth, water, fire, air and ether—as the foundational elements within our bodies. From the Ayurvedic perspective, these elements make up the layers of the body, and their balance dictates how we feel emotionally, energetically, physically, mentally, and spiritually. We are born with our own unique mix of these elements, and through the stress of life (i.e., big or little T trauma), these elements can get imbalanced. Let's discuss the basics and then explore the effect of trauma on these elemental energetics.

The Ayurvedic Doshas and their elements show up on each layer of the body in different ways, based on the person's Ayurvedic Constitution. Doshas, which translates to *that which can cause problems*, are a combination of elements that can create imbalance within the body systems. There are three different doshas: vata (air and ether) which we call *air constitution*; pitta (fire and water) which we refer to as *fire constitution*; and kapha (earth and water) which we call *earth constitution*. There are seven different combinations of these elemental combinations: air, air/fire, fire, fire/earth, earth, air/earth, and tri-doshic (air/fire/earth). Each element has its unique qualities, and as you can imagine, each combination has its own expression on all layers of the body. Since there are three different elements that can manifest in different combinations on each layer of the body, can you see the complexity this brings?

While we are each born with our own specific combination (called *prakriti*), stress and trauma can create imbalances (referred to as *vikruti*) that present in different ways. This means that throughout childhood, trauma scenarios that induce specific issues will create doshic imbalances based on the nature of the issue stored in the trauma packets. Ayurveda is very complex, but we will simplify it to paint the understanding that imbalanced energetics can result from trauma, and trauma packets can create a perfect storm of air, fire, and earth elements—like a hurricane (wind), wildfire (fire), or mudslide (earth)!

Energetic Constitutions

	Air (Vata)	Fire (Pitta)	Earth (Kapha)
Body	Thin, tall, small features, long-limbs, dry hair/skin, low stamina	Medium build, muscular, freckled	Large build, padded joints, high endurance
Mind/ Emotion	Creative, expressive, inspired, playful	Sharp, strategic, intellectual, clarity	Easy-going, kind, loyal, forgiving, consistent
Digestion	Gas, bloating, constipation	Heartburn, colored stool, diarrhea	Heavy after eating, undigested stool
Imbalanced emotion	Worry, anxiety, fearful, overwhelmed, spacey, forgetful, inconsistent	Angry, resentful, jealous, critical, controlling, demanding	Sad, depressed, lethargic, greedy, resistant to change
Other symptoms of imbalance	Insomnia Dizzy Pain (neck, back, hip) Nervous system issues Large intestine issues	Infection/Inflammation Skin rash/acne Migraines Eyes/Liver/gallbladder Mid-back pain	Head/chest congestion Excess mucous Fluid retention Swelling

Let's look at the tendencies of each Ayurvedic Dosha.

Air Constitution (The Bird)

Air constitution consists of air and ether. Note that air and ether govern Chakras #4–7 (Heart, Throat, Third Eye, and Crown). You can think of this constitution like a bird or a butterfly, flitting around from flower to flower, with beautiful sounds emanating from them. Delicate and light, always moving.

On the mental body, when balanced, air will show up as creative, expressive, inspired, spontaneous, and adventurous. When imbalanced mentally, air shows up as worry, panic, paranoia, overwhelm, confusion, inconsistency, and messy. Thoughts of being unsafe and insecure loop in the mind focused on fearful worst-case scenarios.

On the emotional body, when balanced, air can feel lighthearted, playful, and sociable...pure emotional lightness. When imbalanced, air can experience anxiety and panic attacks. Air constitution can get emotionally overwhelmed and check out of their body so they don't have to feel the intense emotions. This is how air constitution experiences depression.

On the energetic body, when balanced, there is a sense of lightness, movement, and flow. When imbalanced energetically, there is an ungrounded or unhooked feeling.

Physically, air imbalance shows up in the nervous system causing mental health issues, and in the colon as gas or constipation.

For those with imbalanced air constitution, *adulting* and taking care of normal everyday physical realm living (cleaning their home, working a 9am–5pm job, and creating consistent relationships) can be tremendously difficult. When they compare themselves to other constitutions, they tend to feel broken or like there's something wrong with them because they don't have the energy that someone with fire or earth has. If they are severely imbalanced, they wake with very little energy (e.g., their gas tank at 5%), but over-spend and dip into reserves, which leaves them depleted. They typically don't understand that the air constitution body needs significantly more self-care, or their system begins to break down more quickly. They need stability in their routine, although they are often terrible at keeping rhythm. They crave spontaneity and adventure, which throws them further out of balance. They require more than eight hours of sleep and a clean diet because their gut is prone to imbalance.

Air imbalance usually indicates trauma packets that contain unsafe circumstances that led the person to feeling helpless, unsafe, ungrounded, disconnected, or disempowered. They spend the rest of their life feeling generally unsafe and disconnected. Often with a lack of fire, they don't know how to transform their life situations, so they just change up the scene with a new job or relationship when they feel stuck.

When those who have air imbalance begin to observe how they become further imbalanced through lifestyle habits (e.g., lack of sleep, unhealthy foods, inconsistent daily rhythms), they start to learn the roadmap for creating more balance. Note: Their awareness of their lifestyle choices creating imbalance is often met with resistance because they compare themselves with other constitutions, who may not have to be impeccable with self-care like those with air imbalance. Accepting and implementing lifestyle changes for better grounding and self-care usually starts the path of healing on an energetic level.

Fire Constitution (The Lion)

Fire constitution is primarily made of fire and water. Note that fire governs the Will Chakra (#3), and water governs the Sacral Chakra (#2). You can think of fire constitution as a lion, hungry and planning its next meal; using strategy, strength, and force to catch its prey; and becoming the leader of the pack.

On the mental body, when balanced, fire manifests as being smart, strategic, clear, motivated, and results-oriented. They can also be passionate, spirited, and charismatic. They are good at staying focused and getting things done. When imbalanced mentally, they can be manipulative, controlling, demanding, jealous, or perfectionistic—potentially showing up as egotistical or narcissistic at times.

On the emotional body, when balanced, their emotional drive and passion can make them feel alive and full of life. When imbalanced, fire can be angry, resentful, or full of rage. Fire constitution anxiety is focused on pressure and control around a result. Their depression occurs when they don't feel like they have control, so they disconnect altogether.

On the energetic body, when balanced, fire can feel powerful, with energy pumping. When imbalanced, fire can spill over into other people's lives through the habit of needing to control or blame others.

Physically, imbalanced fire may show up as infection, inflammation, or migraine; or issues in the eyes, liver, gallbladder, stomach, or small intestines.

Those with excess fire in their constitution feel only as good as their last result, and their worth is often based on what they do or don't do. They are always looking to be *right*, get things *right*, or do the *right* thing. Within their trauma packets, their worth depends on being good or right. They often spend their lives looking for validation, which they receive temporarily when they complete a task.

Relationships can be difficult as other people can be seen as a means to an end result. They can lose their grounding by getting too fired up, and burn up the people around them, forgetting to stay in the Heart and trust that the Universe has their back.

Earth Constitution (The Bear)

Earth constitution is composed of earth and water. Note that water corresponds to the Sacral Chakra (#2), and earth corresponds to the Root Chakra (#1). We can view earth constitution as a bear, who likes to take things slowly, caring for her cubs while nibbling on the nuts and berries. She only gets fierce when guarding her cubs. Otherwise, she lumbers through life and slips into dormancy during winter.

On the mental body, when balanced, earth manifests as easy-going, consistent, and friendly. This constitution is generally kind and loyal to their coworkers, friends, and family. They are good at maintaining harmony in relationships. When mentally imbalanced, their mind feels dull, lacks activity, and seeks comfort through food or sex. They tend to resist most change, even if their mind decides it's best.

Emotionally, earth is happiest when gathering around food and family, and they find pleasure in these experiences. When imbalanced, earth can tend toward a heavy sadness. They may then cling to the physical realm for comfort—their belongings, dependency on their people, numbing with food—which creates a sense of emotional heaviness and being stuck in a state of depression.

On the energetic body, imbalanced earth shows up as heavy, stuck energy—inertia, like the inability to get off the couch and do something productive. However, once they get off the couch, they have enough energy and endurance for a task.

Physically, earth imbalance can show up as head or chest congestion, mucous, fluid retention or swelling, and excess weight.

When earth is in excess in the constitution, the person can overindulge in sex, food, or losing themselves in others. Often, earth will set themselves up as the *giver* in relationships. Because of their strong stamina, they can endure lots of giving and doing for others. Consequently, they eventually feel victimized because they've set up all their relationships with those who are good at taking or receiving. Many *givers* haven't learned to receive, and struggle in speaking their desires, thereby establishing an uneven exchange in their relationships. When this happens, they often feel sad, lost, and abandoned through these critical relationships, and will cope through numbing. With a lack of fire, they don't have the energetics to transform life situations and often feel stuck, falling into patterns of jealousy and entitlement (yearning for things to be different even though they haven't earned the change in circumstances).

Energetics and Trauma Packets

As we examine the energetic body from the Inner Alignment perspective of trauma, we look at the matrix of the elemental energetics (doshas) and the energy centers (chakras). It is through this lens that we can start to locate the trauma packets' physical locations and sensations. The emotions and mental beliefs show us what elements and energy centers are in excess or depletion. Observing these imbalances gives us precision in understanding the unique infrastructure of the inner trauma. This is critical for doing the depth of work necessary to heal the trauma packet and rewire the deep-seated and well-worn patterns of reactivity.

The energetic analysis also gives our clients an ability to see the trauma packet energetically. What we know from thousands of sessions is that the more someone understands their specific energetic imbalances, the more open they are to the possibility of healing and the effort required to rewire every layer of the body.

As you can see in the following picture, we can loosely correlate the elements to the energy centers. Again, we will simplify these concepts to convey a general understanding, but please note, most people have a combination of elements (e.g., air/fire constitution), so this analysis is highly individualized. Stress and trauma impact each person's chakras differently, so tendencies are much more complex than we are describing in the following summary.

Dosha and Chakra Mapping

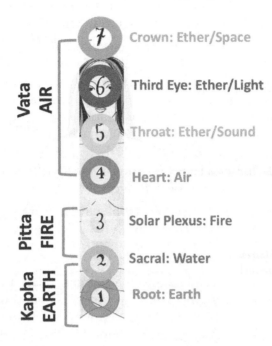

Vata / AIR
Pitta / FIRE
Kapha / EARTH

7 — Crown: Ether/Space
6 — Third Eye: Ether/Light
5 — Throat: Ether/Sound
4 — Heart: Air
3 — Solar Plexus: Fire
2 — Sacral: Water
1 — Root: Earth

Air constitution (vata) correlates with the air and ether chakras: Heart, Throat, Third Eye, and Crown. As we look at where someone with air can get imbalanced, we assume there's excess air, and there's some weakness in the lower chakras (Root, Sacral, or Will). Reducing air and strengthening fire and earth in the lower chakras is critical for creating some balance to ground that excess air. While trauma packets can show up anywhere in the body, at any layer, we would be attuned to those lower chakras for creating balance at the physical, mental, emotional, and energetic layers. People with imbalanced air in their constitution usually have trauma packets stored in the Root Chakra (i.e., grounding to this earth and creating stability), Sacral Chakra (i.e., maintaining harmony and connection with friends or family), and/or Will Chakra (i.e., staying motivated, having courage, or feeling worthy).

Fire constitution (pitta) correlates with fire and water, Will and Sacral Chakras. When fire gets excess-imbalanced, it will show up in the upper belly with symptoms of chakra or dosha imbalance—controlling, being right, blaming, anger. Those with excess-imbalanced fire will often have trauma packets in the

Heart Chakra. Their work is to strengthen their grounding and stability (Root connection), and develop the Third Eye and Crown Chakras to start collaborating with Divine Source.

Earth constitution (kapha) correlates to the water and earth elements, Sacral and Root Chakras. In excess, earth can get too heavy, dull, or lethargic. Their work would be to open up the fire and air aspects on the physical, mental, emotional, and energetic layers of the body. Earth will often have trauma packets in the Throat, Heart, or Will Chakras, and their work is to stoke their fire, connect with their desires, and express their needs and boundaries. Opening their spiritual chakras (Third Eye and Crown) is important work.

Here's how this looks when a client presents with little t trauma in these areas of the body:

Mandy With Excess Air

Mandy has imbalanced air in her constitution. She spent her childhood clinging to her busy parents, wanting to be carried and held. She had sensory issues and trouble retaining information in her mind at school. She loved art, music, and playtime, but tended to spend more time by herself because her classmates were wild and unkind at times. She was sensitive and seemed to need more care than the other kids. Because of this, her parents started to feel like *There was always a problem with Mandy* and *She needed too much help* and *She was too emotional* as a child. This small t trauma created trauma packets within her of feeling like something was wrong with her. Soon, *I'm bad and unloved* was developed in her belief systems. She developed anxiety and often felt ungrounded energetically.

When she got her first job, she couldn't seem to figure out her role and responsibilities. She asked a lot of questions, needed extra hand-holding, and couldn't please her boss. Eventually, she got fired and fulfilled the belief that she was unimportant. From that point on, she changed jobs every year or so, creating the same flight response pattern of self-doubt and perpetuating the instability. This created ongoing panic attacks and severe anxiety.

Here's the thing about Mandy: She was air constitution as a child—a little butterfly that needed some help grounding her nervous system—but her parents were fire constitution. She

86

was a butterfly being raised by lions. Naturally, she would be creative and expressive, with a lack of fire in the mental body to keep up with all those other fire kids in school. She needed more grounding: more repetition of skills to ground thoughts; physically grounding her body to her parents' bodies and the earth; and grounding emotions through the care and help of those around her so she could eventually do it herself. Instead, with repeated messages from her parents about how she should be able to do things on her own (a projection from a lion parent), she created a whole auto-associated trauma packet of vibrations, thoughts, and emotions relating to being unloved, broken, and needing *too much*. She then created her whole life around those trauma packets.

Some with imbalanced air may find themselves numbing all that sensitivity with alcohol or marijuana (to ground). Sometimes they will find a spouse to serve as their pseudo *external* Root Chakra, to help with the bills and provide stability. Or they might generate imbalance with too much fire and overachievement so they never have to feel ungrounded or unstable. However, in the end, air doesn't have the stamina to maintain overachieving, so they burn out quickly. All of these are work-arounds that create further imbalance, because we can never balance our inner world with external people, things, or achievements.

Kaia With Excess Fire

Kaia is pure fire constitution. As a child, she played sports, got good grades, and obeyed all the rules. Her fire mom raised her around achieving and getting into the best college, and she did her best to please her mom. But her mom never showed up to her games, never gave her that hug to let her know that she loved her no matter how Kaia did in school. Because Kaia was so independent at a young age, her mom wasn't around much, as she assumed she could take care of herself. As a result of feeling unloved and uncared for, Kaia searched for a partner to fill that void so she could finally feel loved.

The unloved trauma packet lived loudly in her Heart, and she attracted a wife who would eventually create that same unloved pattern with her. She was a good partner, but she too was an overachiever, and Kaia began to feel even lonelier and more unloved in her marriage. As the years went on, she kept climbing the corporate ladder to prove her worth, but never felt a sustained sense of worthiness. She began feeling more and more unworthy of true love from her spouse, which created her fight response and led to more disconnection.

Because of her overfocus on doing and achieving, she neglected her own self-care. She did so much at work and at home, and kept herself on the hamster wheel without tending to her own needs. She judged her body and wouldn't even glance at herself in the mirror because she didn't like the way she looked. She couldn't bring herself to truly love herself which, projected outward, meant that she could not receive love from others. Fire constitution depression emerged when she gave up on love, creating a sense of powerlessness.

Victoria With Excess Earth

Victoria was raised by earth parents, who moved slowly and put a strong emphasis on family and the creature comforts of life. Victoria's parents were so caring that they met her needs before she even knew she had them. She, in turn, learned to be a caregiver to others, giving gifts and providing assistance whenever needed. She became a nurse, tending to the needs of others at work, caring for her kids and husband at home, and serving her church community in her spare time—a true fawn response to life.

Over time, she felt that nobody ever helped her. She began to notice that her friends and family depended on her but she had nobody to lean on. Even if others were there to help, she would never ask for help because she would be too much of a *burden* on others, too selfish. In time, she found herself depleted from meeting others' needs, so she would numb with Netflix, ice cream, and wine. The numbing caused excess weight, making her feel more abandoned, which led to a deep state of hopelessness and earth depression.

General Trends

Many people with trauma have a weak Root Chakra and some level of air imbalance due to a lack of grounding and stability in the home.

Those with fire-imbalanced (narcissistic) parents tend to have fire built up in the Will Chakra (burning stomach) with a corresponding lump or squeezing in their Throat Chakra because they could never truly express themselves when overpowered.

Those with earth-imbalanced (enabling) parents tend to fear discomfort, and have a lack of fire to define their desires, speak their truths, or have confidence to put themselves out there in life.

Those with air-imbalanced parents will often lack grounding in the Root Chakra and feel helpless, unsafe, and vulnerable.

[Note, if you're a parent, you might be freaking out because it becomes clear that our own imbalances have a direct effect on our children. Before you get lost down that rabbit hole, remember that love is the most important ingredient here. Connection to your Heart and a willingness to get back to love is key. More on this later.]

As you can see, this matrix of energetic understanding of the layers of the body can help us paint the picture of childhood, and develop an understanding of what got lost in someone's natural inner balance. Recognizing this matrix paves the pathway to healing. (More information on doshas and chakras in my book, *Awaken Your Potency*.)

Notes for Healing the Energetic Layer

At the energetic layer of the body, the chakra imbalances will indicate where the trauma packets have embedded into the layers of the body. The trauma packet must be healed at the intersection point of the layers, which will release the main block at the chakra. Once this is done, the dosha elements can come back to natural balance. To heal this layer, the following must be addressed in the healing process:

1. Identify the main chakras experiencing imbalances through an examination of the negative emotions, thoughts, behavioral patterns, and physical or energetic sensations in the body.

2. Once the imbalance is identified, follow the sensations to heal the chakra imbalances within the

trauma packet through the Inner Alignment Soul Retrieval process.

3. Once healed, rewire the thoughts, emotions, and energetics to the newly healed trauma experience in the trauma packet by developing the balanced expression of the chakra. (Note that rewiring the chakra prior to trauma packet healing will not be effective because trauma packet thoughts and emotions will always be the base vibration in the body.)

4. Balance the doshas through lifestyle changes to develop more energetic capacity in the element that is deficient.

Chapter 6:
Mental Body Layer

We live in a society that over-values the mental body and undervalues the awareness, energetic, and spiritual bodies. As such, people think they *are* the mind and its thoughts. Because childhood trauma is often misunderstood, most clinical therapy attempts to change thoughts and behavior. Many believe that they can help clients to simply start thinking in a new way and that will heal the underlying problem. This omits the fact that the redundant daily thoughts originate from a space deep within the body, not the mind, and are an effect of a deeply held pattern that spans every layer. While understanding the mind is important, the thoughts that originate from trauma packets are not easily changed, due to their origin being inaccessible to the mental body.

Thoughts, Beliefs, and Habits

Joe Dispenza, best-selling author of *Evolve Your Brain: The Science of Changing Your Mind,* always teaches so beautifully on the way our thoughts create our reality. He says that you think about 65,000 thoughts in one day and about 90% of those are the same thoughts as the day before. The same thoughts will always lead to the same choices. The same choices will always lead to the same behaviors. The same behaviors will always create the same experiences. And the same experiences will always produce the same emotions. Those same emotions dictate our biology, our neurocircuitry, our neurochemistry, and our neurohormones. Even your genetic expression stays exactly equal to how you think, how you act, and how you feel.

He says that how you think, how you act, and how you feel is your ego-personality, which creates your personal reality. The belief paradigm through which you filter the world will be limited to those consistent 65,000 thoughts that rule your mind. This belief paradigm gets hard-wired into the neural networks in your brain and becomes a habit that is created through auto-associated body memory. This means that the habit is wired into you and can habitually repeat itself without any conscious thought. Any part of the habit can trigger other aspects on the other five layers of the body.

Remember when you learned to ride a bike? Your brain and body had to synchronize many movements together so that all those parts could move in coordination with each other. As soon as the body memory wired in the movements, the body memory could activate without having to think about it.

A habit is a redundant set of automatic unconscious thoughts, behaviors, and emotions that is acquired through frequent repetition. It is formed when you've done that set of things so many times that your body knows how to do it as well as your mind. Therefore, if you're thinking the same thoughts as the day before 90% of the time, demonstrating the same behaviors 90% of the time, and embracing the same emotions as the day before, then those auto-associated networks get anchored into automatic expression, without having to think about your thoughts or emotions. They fire automatically because they are patterned in. For example, every time I come home from work, I think the house is a mess and I get emotionally irritated. I begin to auto-associate coming home from work with irritation. Before long, I will get irritated as soon as I start the drive home, whether the house is a mess or not.

This ego-personality and its related habits become your identity, and by the time you are mid-life, they become a set of memorized behaviors, emotional reactions, unconscious attitudes, beliefs, and perceptions that function like a subconscious computer program. As Joe Dispenza says, about 95% of who you are by the time you're 35 years old is a memorized state of being.

Fear-Based vs Love-Based Belief Systems

The mental layer of the body governs our thoughts and belief patterns, how we think about our world.

A thought is a flow of ideas that can lead to a conclusion so that we can make sense of, interpret, represent, or find patterns in our reality. Each thought produces electrochemical processes that program our bodies to repeat these processes.

As we collect associated thoughts and put them together to make sense of the world around us, we develop belief systems. These belief systems become narratives of how relationships work, what love is, what it means to do productive work, and who we are in relation to others.

Most of these thought patterns, or neural networks, in the brain are formed by the age of seven years old. So, many of us are living with brains that were wired with thoughts and belief systems that were formed as young children. We are thinking about life from a mental infrastructure whose scaffolding was built when we were toddlers!

Some children are raised in families whose experiences, thoughts, and belief systems were based in safety, love, empowerment, truth, and connection. We would call these expansive or Heart-based belief systems. Children raised with these beliefs are most likely wired in a way that sets them up to have potential for positive inner thoughts, productive relationships, and successful work habits.

For example, Matt was raised in a family where his parents tucked him in each night, held him close with love each day. When he was struggling, his parents were there to help him through each stage, supporting him without enabling him. When he started dating, they guided him on how to show up for his partner, and what love looked like in relationship. As an adult, he was able to have hard conversations with people he loved. He sought out mentors to teach him how to stay in his Heart in corporate life. Matt felt capable of giving love and sharing his Heart in the world. He knew how to receive care and support and had a belief system that he was worthy of receiving that from others. This belief system allowed him to filter the world for a partner and job filled with support. When that care and support was not present, it served as an indicator signal, and a *not a good fit* alert would sound. This indicated that it was time to seek a more fitting situation.

Some children are raised in more trauma-based families whose experiences, thoughts, and belief systems are based in ungroundedness, fear, victimization, abuse, judgment, and avoidance. We would call these **limiting** or **fear-based belief systems**. These children's brains are most likely wired in a way that set them up to have difficulty in relationship with self and others. As adults, they have confusions and distortions that block long-term happiness.

For example, John was raised in a family where his dad was an alcoholic and spent most of his time angrily criticizing John. John internalized his dad's anger and decided it was because he was a *bad kid*. His mom was mostly depressed, but went through the motions of taking care of John. His mom didn't like herself, so it was hard for her to truly express love to John. She did her best, but John still grew up feeling like, *If I wasn't born, my parents would've been happier*. He felt like an inconvenience, and assumed this in every romantic relationship he had as an adult. He subconsciously filtered relationships based on this *I'm bad* world view, and married someone who was angry and criticized him (like his dad did). This relationship felt familiar and fit his world view of not being good enough. He loved his wife as best as he could, but always felt that if he was different, she would love him more. His beliefs of not being good enough were fortified in his marriage, so he continued to attract more situations where this filter fit his reality.

In summary, our mind's belief systems create our internal reality. This inner personal reality creates our personality and affects our entire experience of the world. The way we think builds neural synaptic pathways that trigger our unique body chemistry, affecting the way we feel and dictating how we act in most situations. Through the law of attraction, we will continue to attract similar situations that match our world view, our belief systems, and governing thoughts (i.e., *I'm bad* will attract situations for me to feel like *I'm bad*). Therefore, understanding our mental body is a critical step in the interwoven six-layered body.

Animal Brain vs Thinking Brain

Neuroscientist Paul MacLean formulated the Triune Brain model, which is based on the division of the human brain into three distinct regions.

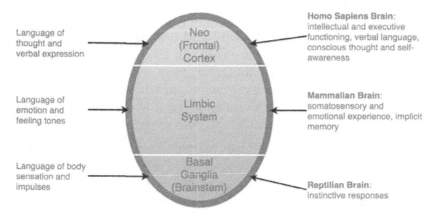

The Triune Brain model suggests that the human brain is organized into a hierarchy, which is based on an evolutionary view of brain development. The three regions are as follows:

1. **Reptilian or Primal Brain** (Basal Ganglia): Exists in reptiles (like lizards and snakes) and governs the instinctive responses, body sensation, and impulses.

2. **Paleomammalian or Emotional Brain** (Limbic System): Exists in more advanced animals like dogs and cats and governs emotions and feelings.

3. **Neomammalian or Rational Brain** (Neocortex, including Frontal Cortex): Exists in humans and governs complex thoughts, speech, executive functioning, conscious thought, and self-awareness.

Inner Alignment simplifies this by grouping the Basal Ganglia and the Limbic system as the Animal Brain (equivalent to a dog), and the Neocortex and particularly the Frontal Cortex as the Thinking Brain (exclusive to humans).

Survival instincts related to trauma responses come from the Animal Brain, and conscious thoughts and activity come from the Thinking Brain. When a trauma occurs in childhood, the child responds from the Animal Brain to maintain safety and attachment. The experience is later processed through an underdeveloped Thinking Brain that has very little understanding of how love and relationships work, so the experience gets frozen in the body with the primitive Animal Brain survival response. This survival response gets auto-associated to the trauma packet and becomes a well-practiced pathway for recreating the primitive emotional and physical response. Five-year-old thoughts may be attached to the trauma's Animal Brain experience, which will likely not be rational or based in adult reality when it is processed through the Thinking Brain later.

In other words, during trauma, the Animal Brain processes the experience in pure survival brain response. The trauma packet of speaking up for myself to my mom at six years old is built with very primitive feelings and thoughts, and then gets stored that way. *Mom equals not safe. Speaking my voice equals bad. Telling mom how I feel equals scary and sad.* When the trauma packet triggers later in life, it regenerates all those primitive thoughts and vibrations. The Thinking Brain then continues to wire very primitive thought structures that support the trauma packet's Animal Brain experience.

Our Thinking Brain is not fully formed until we are well into our 20s, and in cases where there is significant childhood trauma, it can be much later. Our experience of trauma in adult life may be processed and stored very differently than experiences that happen as a child. Thoughts and experiences developed in adulthood get built on top of the foundation, or within the infrastructure, developed in childhood. If the foundation from childhood is wobbly, then adult beliefs will be unsteady as well.

Death Fears

When a trauma packet holds specific belief systems about whether someone is worthy—safe, lovable, valuable, or deserving—the person creates a cause-and-effect relationship around this specific flavor of unworthiness. They develop a *tiny mad idea* (TMI) of how the world works with respect to the specific chakras affected by the trauma. Their whole life revolves around the TMI. For example, *If I do well in school or work* (Will Chakra), *then I'm worthy of someone's love and attention* (Heart Chakra). This TMI is stored in the trauma packet and from it, belief systems are formed.

Within this TMI is a very intense and deeply rooted *death fear* that lives at the center of the belief. The death fear vibrates loudly in the trauma packet because it is connected to the Animal Brain's survival instinct. Success at school gets wired into the mental and emotional bodies from the Animal Brain survival mechanism, so that not doing well at school feels like the threat of death. As an adult, the rational Thinking Brain *knows better*, but the body literally feels like it's going to die later in life if, for example, success at work is not achieved.

Death fears get seeded into the trauma packet during the original trauma, and are replayed consistently through childhood and therefore woven into the auto-associated network of thoughts, emotions, and body chemistry. This is how the deeply embedded fears can wreak such havoc in seemingly benign situations of day-to-day adult life. Feedback from a boss can feel like a deathly scolding from a dad because it is surfacing a death fear from a young age through the trauma packet reactivation.

Subconscious, Conscious, and Superconscious Mind

It's important that we build the capacity to know whether we are approaching life from the conscious mind with thoughts and beliefs formed from adult thought processes, or from a trauma packet that was built in childhood with the simple Animal Brain processes. When a trauma packet is built from the Animal Brain, it will not have a complex thought process, e.g., *Criticism equals death*. It will not have a higher perspective with expansive beliefs. When we are aware, in the present moment, and working from a more conscious Thinking Brain perspective, we can evaluate and override the subconscious thoughts that were built from an underdeveloped prefrontal cortex. For example, *My boss gave me feedback and I feel like I'm going to die, but I can see that I'm OK in this present moment, and there are other jobs if this one doesn't work out.*

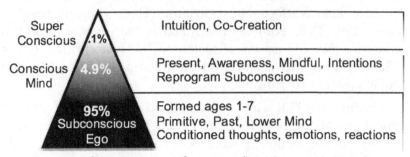

Super Conscious .1%	Intuition, Co-Creation
Conscious Mind 4.9%	Present, Awareness, Mindful, Intentions Reprogram Subconscious
95% Subconscious Ego	Formed ages 1-7 Primitive, Past, Lower Mind Conditioned thoughts, emotions, reactions

There are three layers of the mind (see diagram above):

The **subconscious mind**, or the ego-mind, operates from the past, steers toward negative thought patterns, and serves as our autopilot to keep us safe. We spend 95–99% of our time in the programed thoughts, emotions, and reactions of the subconscious. This is where we access old trauma packet thoughts, built from the Animal Brain. The ego-mind lives in fear-based, limiting belief systems, so it tells us that we are *not enough*; to find true happiness and feel good, we must find it from the outside world. We can observe the repeated patterns in our relationships as we trigger our subconscious mind and churn the same thought processes and emotions that we downloaded in our formative years.

The **conscious mind** lives in the present moment and requires our mindful awareness to keep it engaged. We spend about 1–5% of our time in conscious awareness from the Thinking Brain through the awareness body. Conscious mind is where we can experience happiness, playfulness, and relaxing peace in the present moment. The conscious mind is critical for stopping negative thought patterns, rewiring the brain toward our intentions, and changing our behavior. From this conscious mind, in the present moment, we can reevaluate our limiting, fear-based thoughts and belief systems and begin to wire in more expansive, Heart-based thoughts and belief systems. Gathering present-moment data is a critical part of this conscious mind rewiring process. Working with the Thinking Brain to create the case for rational thinking is important when the brain was originally wired through trauma-based situations. We will talk more about the conscious mind in the awareness layer chapter.

The **superconscious mind** is a mindful connection to soul and Source that provides us with a higher perspective through intuitive wisdom based in love, unity, and interconnectedness. Most people spend about .01% of life here, but by raising our consciousness we can strengthen our superconscious connection and intentionally create a more purposeful existence. This can also be referred to as *higher consciousness*, and we can access it through bliss body connection. Many people in society don't know the opportunity for this connection exists, and if they do, they haven't consistently practiced accessing this part of their higher consciousness. To do so requires us to raise our consciousness beyond the current physical reality, by connecting into the theta wave state of the brain to attain an elusive state of peace, creativity, and bliss. Those who are raised in a family that lives in survival mode, through fear-based thoughts and beliefs, may not have the luxury to consistently access the superconscious mind due to the need to focus on physical realm safety. Survival requires the lower chakras (Root, Sacral, and Will) to be active and the Animal Brain to be dominant. Consistent states of peace, love, and bliss are accessed through the upper chakras (Heart, Throat, Third Eye, and Crown), an active heart brain and toned vagus nerve. We will further discuss the superconscious mind with the bliss layer of the body.

In summary, the subconscious mind regurgitates thoughts from the past, the conscious mind generates thoughts in the present moment, and the superconscious mind uses the present moment to access higher dimensions of thinking. All three aspects of the mind can be projected into future moments. This is where personal power comes from: projection of thought from the present (versus the past) into future thoughts.

Subconscious Ego-Mind and Fear-Based Belief Systems

Since the subconscious mind is programmed at such an early age, many confused or irrational thoughts get wired in before we can use our rational conscious mind to reevaluate them. Whether someone has big T or little t trauma, belief systems can be developed with many fear-based distortions, with death fears at the root of the auto-associated neural network of thoughts, emotions, and behavior.

Once we think these irrational or distorted thoughts a few times, and filter our world through them, they become our operating belief systems—a thought matrix of how we think the world works. We assume that these thought matrices are reality, and surround ourselves with people who share the same or complementary belief systems that confirm our distorted reality.

Since these belief systems were built by the ego-mind, they are based in fear. They tend to *feel* imprisoning, and constrain our quest to experience more joy, peace, and expansiveness in life. We can feel that they lack truth, love, safety, and the wholeness of who we really are. Because this is a common limitation of the human mind, many irrational belief systems get passed down from generation to generation and become the person's *truth*, when in fact, they have no basis in reality.

Below are a few common erroneous belief systems that are deeply ingrained in many people. Please note: The following belief systems (marked with *) may not apply in the same way to those in minority groups who experience oppression from societal structures, such as the mentally ill, people of color, gender minorities, and the homeless.

Scarcity Mentality (vs Abundance):

Many people have a fear that there's not enough, they are not enough, or there will never be enough of what they need or want. *There's not enough time. We don't have enough money. This job isn't enough. My contribution isn't enough. I'm not enough.* If we think there's not enough, what do we create through the law of attraction? Situations that prove this scarcity belief system.

Scarcity mindset is common in Western society, and creates an *every man for himself* experience of life that leaves almost everyone involved feeling like nothing is ever enough. Even in the presence of abundance, we will project *not enough* into the future, or we will suffer about how short-lasting the abundance is. This belief system can create a perspective of suffering that feels like you are always underwater.

In reality, the Universe is abundant. There is enough of everything! Love: Yes, plenty to go around. Food: Yes, lots of it. Success: Everyone can have it! With an abundance mentality, you can attract whatever you have the courage to desire. Abundance mindset is accessed through the conscious mind in the present moment. The awareness body broadens our view to notice the possibilities we cannot see in scarcity mindset. The bliss body creates the space of allowing, to invite in all we feel worthy of receiving (providing we've cleared the trauma packets in the way of the bliss body connection).

Powerless Mentality* (vs Empowerment):

Those who hold a strong powerlessness belief system have the feeling that they can't get what they want—in situations, relationships, jobs, or with their bodies—because they cannot access their power in the present moment, or because they think someone else has more power than they do over their current circumstances. *I am powerless in the presence of this illness*, or *My work life is miserable because of my boss*, or *My marriage sucks because my husband doesn't do for me*, or maybe *I'm stuck in a situation and it's someone else's fault*. They feel disempowered and unable to shift situations, and begin to feel like a victim of self or others.

Unfortunately, through the law of attraction, the more disempowered we feel, the more we attract disempowering situations in life. This belief system is also based in fear and lack of understanding of responsibility and empowerment. It makes us completely powerless because we take our own responsibility and potency out of the equation and hand it over to others.

In reality, we have the potency to change every single aspect of our lives, especially the ones that don't work for us. We attract everything based on our vibration. Once we heal our trauma packets, we can choose our emotions and vibrations. We have the choice to continue old thought patterns, or empower ourselves with rewired thoughts in the present moment. The Universe is responding to what we are putting out there, so if we don't like what we are attracting, we must realize that we have attracted it in the first place—responsibility! With responsibility, we can begin to shift our vibrations and desires to attract something new. Whether we're experiencing an illness, an unhappy partnership, or an unfortunate situation, we can always make an internal shift to find joy, peace, happiness, and empowerment in the situation... even if the shift is noticing what we're thinking, and having the desire for a more positive outlook.

Often, we are not a victim in present-moment circumstances. We have free will and the power to choose our relationships, jobs, living situations, etc. However, we *feel* victimized because of the noise of the trauma packets stored and replaying in our bodies. As children, when that bad thing happened, we were dependent on others for our safety, and therefore victims of a terrible situation. That *was* true, but because it still replays in our bodies, it feels like it's *still* true. Our conscious mind, our awareness body, allows us to broaden our perspective and decide if that victimization is in fact still true. Most of the time, it's not, and we can make present-moment changes to command our power back to ourselves in the present moment.

Entitlement Mentality* (vs Earning):

Due to childhood patterns and belief systems, some people don't see how they are active players in everything, co-creating with the Universe, exerting their will with precise action to earn what they want in life. Instead, they feel jealous or angry that life isn't working out the way they want, and entitled to having someone else fix it. This belief system can be based on expecting others or the Universe to meet their needs without them having to put in the proper vibration, or precise effort, to attract what they desire. Instead of seeing and doing what it takes to earn what they want, they believe that others should accommodate their needs.

Again, this is a belief system based in fear and lack, which attracts more fear and lack. When we take ourselves and our responsibility out of the equation, we lose our power to attract, and shift from an entitlement mentality straight into a victim mentality.

In reality, we must earn what we want in life through precise vibration, effort, willpower, action... and acceptance of what the Universe is providing in response to our vibration. We are not entitled to our children behaving 24/7, because they are children and children are not perfect. We are not entitled to an effortless job situation, especially if we chose to throw our life purpose out the window. We are not entitled to a happy marriage if we married for fear-based reasons or haven't done the work to create good communication and relationship skills. Life takes presence, engagement, mindfulness, and a consistent effort to evaluate what we want versus what we are getting and adjusting accordingly.

Control and Knowing Mentality (vs Acceptance):

Many of us want to feel in control of the situations in our lives so we can feel safe or secure. *If I can just control... the outcome of my kids' grades in school* or *the way this presentation will be pulled off* or *how this person will react to a situation... then I can alleviate the fear I have around it.* This is backward, of course.

The reality is that the only thing we can control is our reaction and response to external circumstances. We can do our best and roll with what life serves us, accepting what is happening in the present moment and recognizing that we never really *know* anything. The need to control or *know* is just our mind's way of trying to feel safe because of the death fears that are hanging out beneath the surface. Control is an illusion.

Ego-Mind Judgment and Projection

Sigmund Freud said that people have a tendency to project their subconscious thoughts onto others. The ego-mind uses psychological projection as a coping mechanism to deal with the negative emotions that lurk in the subconscious mind. We all project negative judgments onto others and believe instead that *others* are thinking those thoughts about *us*. Freud gives an example of a woman who is having a marital affair and accuses her husband of having an affair; or a man who has a bad habit of stealing and assumes that others are always trying to steal from him. The process can be even more subtle than that. For example, *If I have low self-esteem and I don't like myself, then I project that you don't like me either.* Or, *If I don't look people in the eyes, that means I'm mad at them, so I assume you are mad at me if you don't look me in the eyes.*

The ego-mind has a bad habit of driving us straight into negative thought and judgment and projecting this trauma packet-induced negative judgment on others. We use judgment to prove ourselves or others unworthy in some way: *I'm bad, not valuable, unloved. You're bad, not valuable, and unlovable.* If we let our ego drive for too long, we get stuck in those negative thoughts, which gain momentum and can be destructive in our lives.

When the subconscious limiting thought patterns reveal themselves in our lives, we often go straight into self-judgment and lose all potential for conscious awareness. When we judge ourselves, we avoid the underlying issue because it makes us feel bad. We form blind spots where we don't acknowledge parts of ourselves, and we cover them up however we can. In Inner Alignment, we see these negative thought habits as shadow qualities. Many people have blind spots with their shadow (where they simply can't see the behavior) or they overemphasize their shadow, which can create a fear response (fight/flight/freeze/fawn) and paralysis in thought and emotion. For example, Zara is a little loose-lipped and has a fear of hurting people's feelings. She often feels like she is offending people; her mind loops about the things she said and whether others are going to be upset with her. As a result, she avoids people after interactions. This overemphasis on her shadow creates a flight response and fear paralysis in her mind.

The ego-mind's propensity for negativity is pervasive if the conscious mind, or awareness body, is not active. Since these are deeply embedded habits of thought and behavior originating from trauma packets, it takes a deep desire to become more conscious and mindful of this negative autopilot.

Mental Body and Trauma Packets

In the first stage of awakening the mind to a new consciousness, we become aware of the automatic subconscious thoughts that comprise our ego-mind's thoughts. We understand that these trauma packet thoughts were programmed into our mind, brain, and nervous system before we had a working understanding of cause and effect, before our mind could even process reality from an adult perspective. We begin to see the limiting beliefs from our childhood—scarcity, powerlessness, unworthiness—being the primary thoughts and beliefs systems that govern our daily lives. With this, we start to develop a desire to think differently, to build new beliefs and thought paradigms so that we can release the weight of these trauma packets.

As we become aware of our current mental body wiring, the conscious mind and awareness body activate. We start to notice when our subconscious is feeding us outdated thoughts that aren't consistent with how we want to live. We have moments of clarity as the conscious mind activates and chimes in, but the clarity gets overridden by the trauma packets stored deep within. Those auto-associated patterns that get triggered by our inner thoughts and feelings, or external relationship triggers, override the moments of conscious mind and present-moment clarity. The trauma packets are like an anchor that continues to pull our consciousness below the surface of the water into the depths of fear. To keep clarity and conscious mind is like constantly trying to keep your head above water, while you have dead weight pulling you down.

In the next stage of awakening our mind, we begin to rewire our rational Thinking Brain with more adult-focused thoughts. (This is one of the gifts of talk therapy, as it helps develop new thought patterns around current or past situations.) These new thoughts tend to be more expansive, filled with potential and possibility. More expansive thoughts practiced on a consistent basis allow the person to spend more time in the conscious mind. The awareness body helps to alert us when we've dipped into a lower vibration—a trauma packet-induced pattern.

Maybe we build a spiritual belief system and dabble with the law of attraction to start to understand how our thinking governs our reality. We push ourselves to try on more positive emotions. We build the muscle for feeling good. With new thoughts and feelings and actions, we work with the neuroplasticity of the brain, creating new thought patterns with corresponding positive emotions. We spend time meditating to access the superconscious mind, the theta wave brain state. We work to free our minds from the repetitive patterns. We do yoga to bring ourselves back to present-moment mind.

Then, most of us plateau and find that the old, programmed thoughts and vibrations tend to take over again. Since the trauma packets are the loudest thoughts in the body, old thought patterns become pervasive weeds that take over the garden within a week of autopiloting through a busy project at work. Then it feels like we are back to square one, with a garden overgrown with weeds, a mind cluttered with outdated limiting thoughts.

Why is this? Because no matter how much you retrain your rational thoughts, the trauma-related thoughts and vibrations are enmeshed so deeply within, at every layer. Even when you *know better* because you've created all this value in your life, the unworthiness prevails. No matter how much rewiring of the mental body you do on the conscious level, the body memory of these belief systems holds the unworthiness consciousness and will continue to govern what you think and feel.

Bridging Conscious Mind to Trauma Packets

In Inner Alignment, we find that you can change your beliefs in the conscious mind and rewire the Thinking Brain, but those new beliefs don't penetrate the beliefs that live within the trauma packets. If a trauma packet becomes reactivated, and all the auto-associated six-layered responses are initiated, then the expansive beliefs are essentially inaccessible. You can rewire your mind through conscious belief system building, but without rewiring the beliefs *within* the trauma packet, you will find yourself continuing to ignite the limiting beliefs when the trauma packets are triggered.

For example, Linda has read every Wayne Dyer book, listens to Abraham-Hicks on repeat, and lives her days with intention. She believes she is a competent, successful woman, who deserves to be happy and find love.

She has a fire/earth constitution, so she has good stamina, a healthy body to accomplish the many results she desires, and a strong intellectual mind. Her Root, Sacral, and Will Chakras are strong, which means: she feels safe, grounded, and financially secure (Root); she has a great group of friends and strong relationships, and is gifted at creating client networks (Sacral); and she is a successful businesswoman who puts in tremendous effort and achieves great results with clients (Will).

She desperately desires a loving partnership, and while she has reprogramed her mental body to believe she is worthy of the love, she feels unable to create this for herself. When it comes to matters of the Heart and getting the love she wants from men

(Heart), and seeing the potential for this in the future (Third Eye), she is blocked. Her Heart Chakra carries old trauma packet thoughts of *I'm not lovable when it comes to romance*, which stems from the trauma packets of how she felt after her parents' divorce. (Her father moved out of the house because he was having an affair, and her whole world fell apart. Her Heart literally broke in half. From that point on, she barely saw her dad, and when she did, she had to share him with his new wife and children.)

The Heart Chakra trauma packet lives at the center of her chest and feels like a stabbing pressure that repetitively squeezes her heart. Even though she knows she is lovable, that pain is still filled with thoughts of *I'm not lovable* and *A loving man doesn't exist*. Emotions of sadness overcome her and she tends to shed many tears around this issue.

However, her rational and conscious mind knows better. She knows that her friends have found love, so it's not impossible. She has created so much value in her other relationships as a caretaker, and those people love her, so conceptually, she understands that it's possible to find a loving partner. Unfortunately, there is no bridge between her conscious expansive beliefs and her trauma packet beliefs. No matter how much she goes to therapy to talk about the issue, practices positive affirmations (mental body), feels her sad feelings (emotional body), meditates (bliss body), and practices heart openers in yoga (physical and energetic body), her trauma packet, centered in her Heart and filled with thoughts of unworthiness around love, continues to be the loudest vibration with respect to romance.

Any layer of the body can trigger the trauma packet to the surface. A thought about dating can surface the auto-associated despair emotions and sensations. The emotion of sadness can bring up the auto-associated thoughts of unlovable thoughts. Seeing a happy couple can activate the trauma packet. When the trauma packet gets triggered, Linda will cycle through a repetitive negative thought momentum, replaying old stories and beliefs from the past and projecting them onto her future male relationships. When she is absorbed in the trauma packet, her *romance pain body* gets activated. (More on this in the next section.)

Notes for Healing the Mental Layer

At the mental layer of the body, the work is to shift out of the survival-based Animal Brain and subconscious mind to build a new belief system that fully accesses the conscious mind (awareness body) and superconscious mind (the bliss body). To heal this layer, the conscious mind must be systematically built in the healing process, which means:

1. Building awareness of the auto-associated, trauma packet negative thoughts, beliefs, behaviors, and habits that live in the subconscious and are projected as reality in present moment. It is critical to recognize in real-time that these death fear thoughts are outdated and do not apply to the present-moment adult experience.

2. Accessing the trauma packets through Inner Alignment Soul Retrieval to heal the original experiences from which the thoughts and beliefs were built. Weave expansive thought paradigms into the old experience with profound awareness anchored into the child consciousness, shifting the child self's survival Animal Brain consciousness into adult understanding and perspective. This will expand the trauma packet thoughts into Heart-based beliefs.

3. Practicing the new, expansive thoughts and beliefs throughout the day for two months to build the neural pathways in the brain to sustain the thoughts planted in the trauma packet through the Inner Alignment Soul Retrieval process.

4. Staying connected to the sensation of thoughts in the body to continually build positive thought connections and neural circuitry. Becoming aware of old auto-associated thoughts and vibrations (such as scarcity, powerlessness, entitlement, and not knowing), and replacing them with experiences that gather data on abundance, personal power, and safety in the present moment.

Chapter 7:
Emotional Body Layer

The emotional layer of the body is tightly bound with the mental and energetic layers of the body, so it is challenging to delineate it as separate. In Inner Alignment, we make the delineation so we can identify the underlying death fear emotions that create tumultuous waves, affecting the energetic or mental body. While thoughts can affect emotions, emotions can trigger thoughts and energetic imbalances.

We all experience fear. Fear can be generated by the mental body and chemically wired into our cells. It can also simply live deep within the emotional body, within the trauma packets and the cellular memory, and trigger from the body memory. No matter where fear originates, the resulting negative emotions can take on a life of their own and create a severe impediment to overall satisfaction in life.

Those with childhood trauma are often literally wired to experience a lifetime of negative emotion, unless they make some major changes on every layer of the body. If we look at society in the state that it's in right now, this becomes very evident. A search of general mental illness statistics shows that mental health patterns are set up in childhood, with *half of all lifetime mental illness cases start by 14 years old*, and *three-fourths by 24 years old*.[2]

In addition to the prevalence of mental health issues, mental health practitioners are often using band-aids to treat the effects of anxiety and depression without addressing the root cause. Approaching the anxiety and depression at the mental or emotional layer of the body without addressing the underlying six-layered cause in the trauma packet can prolong unsuccessful treatment for decades.

Working with Negative Emotions

To access the root cause of negative emotions, we need to understand what lives beneath the negative emotion within the trauma packet, and what creates the automatic triggering of emotion that seemingly takes over life.

Fear vs Love

When we examined the mental body in the last chapter, we delineated fear-based and love-based belief systems. As such, when we work with the emotional body, we approach it very simply through the lens of emotions that are based in vibrations of *love* versus those based in the vibrations of *fear*. We would categorize emotions in the following way:

Love-based positive emotions are peace, contentment, hope, excitement, happiness, playfulness, gratitude, joy, inspiration, caring, nourished, easeful, calm, and carefree.

Fear-based negative emotions are sadness, depression, embarrassment, guilt, shame, frustration, anger, rage, nervousness, worry, anxiety, panic, hopelessness, despair, grief,

---

[2] Kessler, Ronald C, et al, "Lifetime prevalence and age-of-onset distributions of DSM-IV disorders in the National Comorbidity Survey Replication," Arch Gen Psychiatry. 2005 Jun;62(6):593-602. pubmed.gov.

boredom, aloofness, selfishness, loneliness, helplessness, and disconnectedness.

One would assume that positive emotions based in love may create good-feeling vibrations, and negative emotions based in fear may create bad-feeling vibrations; however, whether the emotions feel good or not may depend on whether they feel *familiar*. If a child grew up in a family where Mom only acted loving when she wanted you to do something, the emotion of love may feel bad, heavy, or burdensome. You may not be able to access a feeling of love in the Heart. If a child's family operated from a place of emotional disconnection, then when the child grows up, a warm and caring environment may feel foreign and uncomfortable. If a child spent most of their time in sadness or depression, feeling content as an adult may feel boring or empty.

When positive emotions feel foreign and uncomfortable, and negative emotions feel familiar and comfortable, we call that *cross-wired emotions*. Most of us with childhood trauma have some level of cross-wiring, where negative emotions feel good because they are familiar. For example, crying to sad music feels comforting (because that's what I'd do to feel better in my teens), or punishing myself for bad grades feels good and motivating (because the fear makes me feel fired up to do better). A positive emotion can be cross-wired as well: nourishing myself feels lazy and wrong (because when living on a farm, you never got to sit down), or peacefulness is scary (because I'm waiting for the other shoe to drop when Mom comes home).

In addition to the presence of certain emotions in our childhood, the absence of positive emotions may also affect brain development. Without the presence of positive emotions during the brain's formative years, we may lack the physical infrastructure and neural circuitry to sustain positive emotions. Living in the space of love needs to be learned through loving relationships. Without this loving foundation, it is very difficult to build the pathways, because the circuitry and chemistry has no reference within. It requires a connection to the Sacral and Heart Chakras. If we are living in the head, where the limiting beliefs of the automatic subconscious ego-mind feed on fears of the past, we are going to be feeling more negative thoughts and their associated negative emotions. If we are living in the Heart, with expansive belief systems, we hope to feel more positive emotions.

Wisdom of Negative Emotion

Society seems to believe that we should be in a consistent state of happiness. People feel like there's something wrong with them if they are not accessing consistent states of joy. If happiness is the goal, then we are probably going to find ourselves disappointed at least half of the time. What if happiness is not the point of life, though? Life is full of happy moments, yes, but also full of loss and grief, disappointment, and frustration. There is a full range of emotional states that we may find ourselves experiencing, and if we don't have a bias toward *only* positive emotions, we may find ourselves more resilient in the times of difficulty. The truth is that life can be hard, and being in a human body, with a human ego-mind, can be challenging.

If happiness is not the point of life, if it's not the end goal, then what is? Emotional resilience and steadiness… staying completely anchored in the eye of the storm, where we are connected to the Heart, to the earth, to Divine Source… fully allowing the *weather* of thoughts and emotions… observing without judgment or attachment, and thereby remaining in a place of resilience and reality. Within a tropical storm (cyclone), the calmest space is right at the center. The same is true with life; we can stay grounded in our Heart center (*I am grounded in who I am, I am with myself*) while the storm swirls around us, no matter what weather shows up in the doshas—**earth**quake, **wind**s, wild**fires**. We keep the center calm and still despite what waves are moving through. We release emotional resistance to the storm around us. By witnessing the storm *outside* of us, we do not confuse ourselves with the storm.

What we resist persists. If we push against negative situations and storming thoughts, we stay engaged with them. If we allow them to move in and through us, then they too shall pass. Instead of assuming there will be no storms, we can expect changes in the weather. We have the choice to resist the storm and keep it here longer, or release resistance and let it move through.

112

Emotions serve as our **inner guidance system** to navigate life and these storms. When we see these emotions through the lens of our chakras, it gives us depth to what the range of emotional feeling and expression might be: safety, connection, willpower, love and compassion, truth, clarity and direction, intuition, and spiritual connection. Emotions can guide us toward these important keys to learning and expansion on this human and spiritual path in life. Emotions are like the game of hot-and-cold. When we feel a grounded positive emotion in the Heart, we are close to Heart center, and closer to what's true for us. *Getting warmer!* When we feel fear and negative emotions, we are losing that steady connection in our Heart. *Getting colder!* Using the emotional guidance system to glean signals is key to understanding what the sensations mean.

Negative emotions help us discern our desires and truths. *I feel angry when someone cheats on me.* Well, should I work that emotion to feel neutral and unaffected, or let that emotion be a signal that something is not right here? That anger is a signal for a boundary and a need for truth expression. *Hey, you cheated on me, I don't want that in my relationships!*

Negative emotions can tell us when we followed our ego and ignored our soul's truth. When I hated my job consulting for the International Monetary Fund, the negative emotion was a signal that I wasn't using my gifts! I chose money and status over the whispers of my soul, so the negative emotions were like a barometer of alignment with my truth.

Negative emotions can also tell us when our relationships are imbalanced. For example, if someone is consistently giving and caretaking, and feeling sad and disappointed that nobody shows up for them, then there may be a need for communication and renegotiation of the relationship exchange. Instead of numbing that emotion, we can glean the wisdom of misalignment to help transform situations that don't work.

Here are examples of balancing for emotional well-being:

Mark is angry at everyone around him. His fire has become imbalanced, and the wisdom may be to slow down and listen within. More stillness. More grounding. Less doing and more being. If he had tried to work the effect of that anger by doing anger management classes, he may not have gained the inner wisdom of *why* the anger was showing up. Now his work is to release the doing in his habitual life and experience more being.

Nola has anxiety when she is around her in-laws. Instead of thinking she should feel happy around them, she goes into her Heart to find out what's going on. In doing so, she realizes that she feels pressured by them to be someone she is not. She's not comfortable with who she is around them because they want their son to be married to an unrealistic ideal. Instead of popping an anti-anxiety pill, she connected to inner wisdom that may require her to express her feelings, and set some boundaries. Now her work is to build the courage (Will Chakra) to speak her truth (Throat Chakra) around her in-laws.

Rob has depression and feels especially shut down around his job, but changing jobs hasn't helped because job issues keep showing up. As he leans into the sadness and grief, he realizes that the professionalism in his work environment is sterile, and there's no heartfelt communication or connection. His sadness is revealing his desire to be in a more Heart-centered career, where human caring has a space at work. Instead of going to therapy to talk about the sadness, he went within to connect with his true desire. Now his work is to determine how he can create a Heart-centered work environment for himself.

We can think of emotional weather as ocean rip currents (riptide or undertow). If you're being taken by the tide, the last thing you want to do is swim against it. Resisting the current wastes your energy and puts you at risk of drowning. When a current comes, you have to let yourself go straight *into* it, to flow with it until you can swim out the other side. The same is true with the negative emotions we experience. Running from them, resisting them, or trying to get rid of them creates resistance (because *what we resist persists*). That said, getting swallowed by the waves of negative emotion and allowing ourselves to stay underwater doesn't work either. That creates rage, depression, and persistent anxiety. If we resist emotions, we risk getting swallowed up by them. If we let go completely and go fully into the emotion, we risk getting pulled under permanently. So, what's the alternative? The alternative is to feel the emotions deeply and fully, and process them through the layers of the body, receiving their wisdom. With a rip current, you let the current take you until you can swim out the other side. Same is true for the emotion. We allow the vibrations to rise up, we feel them by going straight to the center of the vibration. We can acquire wisdom when we have the courage to move through the emotions. Once we've gleaned the wisdom, we can release the negative emotion and hop back into the Heart.

Society avoids negative emotion, but most negative emotion sources down to a fear that needs to be processed. By developing a level of comfort around exploring our fear, we can become curious about uncomfortable emotions. Instead of practicing the old stories *around* the childhood emotions, we can move straight through the fear, so that, through law of attraction, we don't attract more of the same.

The Pain Body

Most of us who have a history of childhood trauma are living from trauma packets of the past in fearful negative emotions. The accumulation of fear and negative emotion over time creates a body of negative energy that has a low vibration, because it sources down to a death fear living deep within the trauma packet. There is a momentum that occurs with this low-vibratory emotion. Negative emotion brings on more negative thoughts, which trigger additional negative emotions. This creates a snowball effect in our lives.

In Eckart Tolle's bestselling book, *A New Earth*, we are introduced to the concept of the *pain body*. He describes a pain body as an accumulation of painful life experience that was not fully faced and accepted in the moment it arose. Tolle says these accumulated experiences create an energy form of emotional pain. Energy forms of pain attach to other energy forms, and in time, an emotional-energy entity consisting of old emotion is developed. It lives in human beings, and it is the emotional aspect of egoic consciousness. Excerpted from Eckhart Tolle's *A New Earth*, pages 145–161:

> "The pain-body awakens from its dormancy when it gets hungry, when it is time to replenish itself [on] the most insignificant event as a trigger... something somebody says or does, or even a thought. Suddenly, your thinking becomes deeply negative.

You were most likely unaware that just prior to the influx of negative thinking a wave of emotion invaded your mind—as a dark and heavy mood, as anxiety or fiery anger.

All thought is energy and the pain-body is now feeding on the energy of your thoughts. But it cannot feed on just any thought. A happy, positive thought is indigestible to the pain-body. It can only feed on negative thoughts because only those thoughts are compatible with its own energy field. The vibrational frequency of the pain-body resonates with that of negative thoughts, which is why only those thoughts can feed the pain-body.

The usual pattern of thought creating emotion is reversed in the case of the pain-body, at least initially. Emotion from the pain-body quickly gains control of your thinking, and once your mind has been taken over by the pain-body, your thinking becomes negative.

The voice in your head will be telling sad, anxious, or angry stories about yourself, about other people, about past, future, or imaginary events. The voice will be blaming, accusing, complaining, imagining. And you are totally identified with whatever the voice says, believe all its distorted thoughts. At that point, the addiction to unhappiness has set in.

It is not so much that you cannot stop your train of negative thoughts, *but that you don't want to*. This is because the pain-body at that time is living through you, pretending to be you. And to the pain-body, pain is pleasure. It eagerly devours every negative thought. In fact, the *usual voice in your head has now become the voice of the pain-body*. It has taken over the internal dialogue. A vicious circle [is] established between the pain-body and your thinking.

Every thought feeds the pain-body and in turn the pain-body generates more thoughts. At some point, after a few hours or even a few days, it has replenished itself and returns to its dormant stage,

116

leaving behind a depleted organism and a body that is much more susceptible to illness. If that sounds to you like a psychic parasite, you are right. That's exactly what it is."

Tolle's description of the pain body describes how trauma packets can overtake emotional well-being at any moment. While it's described as an emotional-energetic-thought compound, we know that the neurosynaptic wiring in the brain and cells can influence the response on the physical body systems. This brain wiring can create a sympathetic nervous system response, affecting the heart rate and blood pressure, breathing pattern, hormone secretion, etc. Like trauma packets, the pain body is an emotional wave that influences all layers of the body. While it seems to come from nowhere, it actually comes directly from the accumulation of emotion in the old trauma packets.

There is a subtle difference between trauma packets and pain bodies. A trauma packet is the original frozen experience that has thoughts, emotions, energies, and consciousness attached. Over time, associated behaviors and reactivity patterns grow from the activated trauma packet. These reactivity patterns, behaviors, and habits, combined with their associated interference energy (e.g., entity attachments, lineage karma, others' energies) can activate a pain body reaction that stems from the original trauma packet.

As the statistics state, most emotional issues are formed in childhood, so it would make sense that pain bodies start with childhood trauma and accumulate similar experiences throughout life. Pain bodies can go dormant, but the trauma packet serves as the underlying infrastructure for the emotional pain body to trigger and reactivate.

Trauma Packet Emotion vs Present-Moment Emotion

Pain body emotions that originate from accumulated trauma packets are different than normal emotions that occur from present-moment life circumstances. With each emotion, it's important to discern whether there is a trauma packet reactivated, or an emotion triggered from the present moment. An old trauma packet, with lingering emotion and a corresponding pattern, could look like: *Every time my spouse forgets to check in with me before going to the store, I feel enraged, even though I know I shouldn't feel that way.* Whereas, if you are currently experiencing an issue or trauma, your emotional guidance system is signaling something within you like: *I'm feeling sad because my dog is dying, and I'm confused as to whether I should put him down.*

Many of our daily emotions are old trauma packet emotions overlaying present-moment situations. The mind may think that the emotions apply to the present conditions, but most often, our emotions are re-enacted from an unresolved trauma packet. For example, Joe is triggered when his middle daughter gets defiant, more so than when his other daughters disregard what he says. Why the discrepancy? Well, his middle daughter activates his *mother trauma packet* due to her similarity to his mom, which results in his heightened emotional response. When reacting to his middle daughter, his nervous system feels like he's fighting for survival, screaming to be heard and seen, just like the many times in childhood with his mother. Is this about his middle daughter? No, it's about his mother, because it's triggering his mother pathway in his brain, body, and behaviors. An old *mother pain body* has taken over and caused interference in his relationship.

If the emotions aren't a signal from a present-moment situation, and they're just causing pain body waves from triggered underlying trauma packets, the goal is to learn how to stay in awareness in the present moment and steady in the Heart, despite the emotional storm. Discerning what's relevant, whether there's a lesson or message, is critical to discern what to do with the emotion. When we identify an emotional pain body, we can learn to feel steady in the Heart even when an old vibration shows up. With the example above, Joe would need to be aware that his mother pain body is triggered, so he must be vigilantly anchored in his love for his daughter so that he doesn't re-create the pattern in his lineage.

Past-generated emotion requires deeper work through Inner Alignment Soul Retrieval and rewiring the six layers to unpack the vibrations living deep within so the pattern can change.

Present-moment emotions need to be felt and discerned on every layer of the body so we can move through the series of thoughts, emotions, and vibrations to get the inner wisdom.

Fear Reactivity Responses

Emotions can trigger pain body thoughts, and thoughts can trigger corresponding emotional pain bodies, until a body of energy has enough momentum to wreak havoc on someone's life. These pain bodies can play out patterns of destruction no matter how the person responds to the accumulated emotions.

Depending on how childhood influenced the energetics (chakras and dosha imbalances), thoughts and beliefs (limited beliefs systems), neurosynaptic wiring, and emotional pain bodies, each person will respond to the fear differently through a patterned fear response. To the same stimulus, people will have varying responses: fight, flight, freeze, or fawn. For example, a mother yells at her daughter to clean her room...

If the daughter is wired with a fight response, has a strong Will Chakra, and is mostly fire constitution, she may slam her door, say *I hate you*, put her headphones on, and get prepared for what she will say during her punishment that night.

If she is wired with a flight response, has a weak Root Chakra, and a lot of anxiety with air constitution, she may go to her friend's house for safety.

If she is wired with a fawn response, has a lot of energy in the Sacral Chakra, and has an earth constitution, she may clean her room, tidy up the rest of the house, and make dinner for her mom (so her mom calms down and she can feel love again).

If she is wired with a freeze response, she may stay in the room with her mom in a dissociated state, watching it all like a movie.

With any of these fear responses, there is little connection to that still, safe space in the Heart. These are survival responses that stem from the Animal Brain and keep us in a state of reactivity. Living life from a place of fear reactivity will keep us in patterns of reactivity that become so deeply wired that we won't be able to move away from the outdated patterns later in our adult relationships. There is little peace when we have these emotional behavior patterns, set up from childhood, that keep us in a state of adult emotional reactivity.

Whether we have a habit of fighting, flighting, fawning, or freezing, the goal is to get to the root of the issue by dismantling the response in the trauma packets. Once healing occurs in the trauma packet, and awareness is built, we can witness these patterns and choose a new pattern from the space of the Heart. Only when we are living and responding from the Heart can we have authentic, loving exchanges and relationships with those around us.

Neuroscience of Emotional Pain Bodies

Let us review the neuroscience of emotions, so that we can be sure to understand the neurochemistry of a continued pain body reaction.

When we have feelings of frustration, sadness, shame, hopelessness, or anxiety, each separate emotion releases its own flurry of neuropeptides. Those neurotransmitter peptides surge through the physical body and connect with their corresponding receptors. The emotion peptides that you release the most will determine the structure of the receptors in the cell. Therefore, if you have a pain body flight reaction that feels like anxiety all day long, you send out anxiety peptides (or hormones) and the cell will restructure itself to receive as many anxiety peptides as you send out. If a cell has been exposed to anxiety more than any other emotional chemicals, then when the cells divide, the new cell that is produced will have more anxiety receptors. Likewise, the cell will also have fewer receptors for peptides that its mother/sister cell was not exposed to as often, which means fewer happy hormone receptors. Triggering a specific anxiety pain body (or flight fear reaction) throughout the day is literally programming your cells to receive more anxiety chemicals in the future. This lessens the number of receptors for positive emotion peptides in the cells, making you more inclined toward negative emotions and the anxiety pain body.

Every cell in the body is replaced about every two months, so it takes two months of bombarding your cells with positive emotion peptides to create a new body chemistry and new cellular structure so you can create the receptors to hold the positive emotion chemistry. However, you would need corresponding belief systems to create the neural pathways to support a more positive thought and emotion structure. Once this structure is developed in the brain and cells, the body will be flooded with those positive neurotransmitter peptides.

To simplify, we must step back and look at how this impacts those who have a cross-wired response to positive emotions. If positive emotions feel bad or foreign, or if you don't have the belief system to maintain positive emotion neurotransmitters, how could you spend two months in a constant state of happiness to rewire your brain and body?

If your six-layered body has heavy trauma packets with auto-associated thoughts, emotions, sensations, and energy that triggers automatically and keeps you in a subconscious, past-focused state of mind, how can you shift out of depression that has anchored into your body? How can you stop panic attacks that take over your body at will? The entire system would need a consistent influx of positive emotion neurochemistry for two months to shift out of negative, fear-based emotions.

Energetics of Emotional Pain Bodies

While worry and anxiety, sadness and depression, and anger are emotions that everyone feels from time to time, there are emotional tendencies based on a person's energetic body. Doshic differences and chakra imbalances play a big role in the way emotions are expressed.

A pain body can originate from a trauma packet buried within a specific chakra, and therefore have specific emotional tendencies related to that chakra. Within the Root Chakra, there is a feeling of survival-fear. Sacral Chakra carries shame, guilt, and abandonment emotions. Will Chakra can often carry anger and resentment. Heart Chakra often carries a sense of loss, grief, and sadness. Throat Chakra will have feelings of disappointment around not being seen or heard. Third Eye and Crown Chakras can feel a sense of being stuck and hopeless.

A pain body can show us what energetics are out of balance so we can regain our alignment in our lifestyle. Sadness and depression can be a sign of too much earth within the layers of the body, so more fire may be needed. Anger and rage can be a sign of too much fire in the body, so more cooling and grounding earth may be helpful. Anxiety and panic can be a sign of too much air in the body layers, which indicates a need for fire or grounding. That said, these dosha generalizations are often an oversimplification of doshic nuances when it comes to pain body reactivity.

Doshic emotional differences are important because, for example, the way we work with depression in air constitution is different than how we would work with depression for earth constitution. Below you will find a description of how anxiety, anger, and depression can manifest for the doshas. Of course, this can vary significantly based on the combination of what is occurring on all layers of the body.

Doshas and Emotions

	Air	**Fire**	**Earth**
Anxiety	Looping mind on worst case scenario Lots of movement in head and chest	Thoughts about what I can't control Burning / tight in upper belly	Freeze and Numb
Anger	Quick burst -Yell Move through quickly (Cyclone)	Blame/ resentment P-Rage, Manipulation VP-Yelling (UP) PK-Resentment (Down)	Resentment Entitlement for giving
Depression	Disconnection Disassociated	Stuck in anger Give up	Heavy sadness Hopeless

In general, those who study Ayurveda will learn that **anxiety** is due to air imbalance, but in Inner Alignment, we find that anxiety occurs differently for each constitution. Anxiety in air constitution will often feel like a fluttery movement in the chest, with incessant worst-case scenario thoughts and paranoia. Anxiety in fire constitution will often occur as burning, tightness, or nausea in the upper belly, with thoughts around that which must be controlled or completed (e.g., chores, projects, to-do lists, other people's responsibilities). If anxiety occurs in earth constitution, it is likely a freeze response with ruminating thoughts of being *stuck*, with no possibility for change in the future.

Typically, in Ayurveda, excess **anger** is categorized as fire imbalance, but every dosha experiences anger differently. Anger in air constitution can start in the upper belly and move quickly to the throat, resulting in an outburst of yelling without thinking first. They then shift quickly, forgetting about the anger and moving on. Anger in fire constitution often burns in the upper belly. They can resort to manipulation to get others to fit into an expectation, and if expectations aren't met, they can resort to control, rage, or narcissistic tendencies. Anger in earth constitution may start as burning or pressure in the upper belly that moves downward. Thoughts of entitlement usually fester and become buried resentment. They will often not openly voice the anger for fear of hurting someone, so it gets buried and builds until they get fed up.

Typically, in Ayurveda, **depression** is categorized as earth imbalance, but we find that depression occurs in each constitution very differently, depending on the pain body reactivity from the trauma packets.

Depression in air constitution can feel like heaviness or emptiness in the chest. The sadness may be related to grieving, as they lack the love for which they hoped. It can also come from a place of needing to disconnect because their nervous system feels fried, or the emotion was too much for them. In this case they may disconnect, isolate, or dissociate due to overwhelm.

Depression in fire constitution can be felt as burning in the upper belly or pressure in the chest. Feelings of sadness are often around thoughts of unmet expectations, a sense of loss of control, or grieving (or giving up on) what was desired.

Depression in earth constitution is typically felt as heaviness or pressure in the chest or lower belly. Either the mind is dull and lifeless, or it is consumed with thoughts of powerlessness, abandonment, and unmet needs for connection. There is often a fear of getting stuck in the heaviness and spiraling into hopelessness.

Pain Body Behavior Patterns

As we have examined, the doshas and chakras can influence energetic tendencies, and these tendencies will often influence how trauma packets play out pain body reactivity.

If dependent on others for love, those with earth constitution will fawn to avoid abandonment and maintain connection. In doing so, they remain disconnected from their truth and prioritize others' needs before their own. This is an old pattern developed in childhood for love and safety. They created a habit of the *caretaker role* early in life, as stored in the trauma packet, and then repeat these auto-associated trauma patterns through adulthood. The pain bodies that contain these specific abandonment death fears keep this trauma packet active in primary relationships. Their strong Heart and Sacral Chakras, paired with weak Throat and Will Chakras, can indicate these consistent patterns.

Fire constitution may have a fight response, which leads them to patterns of doing what's right or getting the task done to prove their worth. This often sets them up for the *perfectionist role* in life. Trauma packets usually contain childhood experiences of being rewarded for doing things well or right, and punishment for being wrong or bad. With a strong Will Chakra, and often a weak Root, Heart, or Crown Chakra, the person is wired to prove their worth and value through results in the physical realm. A person with their world view based upon the validation they receive from others will only feel as good as their last result.

Someone in the flight response with air constitution will keep moving around situations, continuing to stay busy to maintain a feeling of *freedom and individuality*. Typically, this is done to maintain their safety because of a weak Root, Sacral, or Will Chakra. If they don't have a grounding, steady connection to others, or the power to finish things, they keep moving and seeking new experiences to keep themselves engaged in life. However, this tendency leads them to avoid situations that make them feel inadequate. The need for connection in the Heart Chakra keeps them performing acts of kindness for others, which easily and quickly depletes them.

People often ask how they can change these emotional patterns that are so deeply embedded into their six-layered bodies. They may try to balance their chakras, thinking this will change the emotional pattern. Energetic body shifts may help temporarily, but because of the neural chemistry of emotion, they won't hold long enough to shift to the other layers of the body. The energetic rewiring prior to healing the trauma packet can feel like swimming upstream, because the dosha, chakra, and neural chemistry is embedded at the root of the emotions.

It's critical to work underneath the pattern, within the trauma packet, to dismantle the distorted foundation upon which these emotional, energetic, and behavioral patterns were built, while simultaneously building healthy trauma packet vibrations. Once the trauma packet healing rebuilds the inner deficit (of safety, connection, worth, love, or expression), the old patterns don't need to be maintained anymore, and the person can be rewired into a new way of being.

Notes for Healing the Emotional Layer

At the emotional layer of the body, the work is to develop the capacity to feel and discern the full range of emotion, and learn to navigate the emotions skillfully.

To heal this layer:

1. Identify and build awareness around the trauma packet-induced emotional patterns that are limiting soul expression, including: repetitive pain bodies, cross-wired emotions, fear reactivity (fight, flight, freeze, fawn), and the roles set up in life around those emotional patterns. Get to know the sensations, thoughts, and emotions to begin to discern how and when the trauma packet emotions activate, so that one can discern between old trauma packet emotion and present-moment emotions.

2. Access the trauma packet emotions through Inner Alignment Soul Retrieval to heal the original experiences from which the emotions and fear reactivity were built. Allow the child's emotions and expression in raw form to validate the emotions. Bring the child self into a space of safety, love, and connection (or whatever was missing emotionally) so they can experience what their Heart has been yearning for, and begin to know what the feeling of the chakra expression feels like. This will expand the trauma packet vibrations into Heart-based emotions,

allowing this to become the base vibration in the trauma packet.

3. Counterbalance the habitually imbalanced emotional pattern (anger, depression, anxiety) through energetic body balancing (e.g., reducing vata/air, increasing pitta/fire).

4. Counteract the fear response through the contrasting patterns (e.g., balance a flight response with fight, through the Heart-balanced fire of truth).

5. Develop awareness in the pain body response through awareness at any point in the reactivity pattern.

6. Gather data on shifting into new relationship roles and the new emotions that come with them (e.g., caregiver learning to receive).

7. Develop the capacity to decode emotional imbalances to determine the source, and act accordingly (e.g., determining whether anxiety is caused by lifestyle, choices that go against the soul's desires, old trauma packets, or interference energy).

Chapter 8:
Awareness Body Layer

When we are connected to the awareness body, we are more centered in the conscious, present-moment mind. From this space of the *what-is*—i.e., what is actually happening in the present moment versus that which is replaying from the past via trauma packets and the subconscious mind—we have the opportunity to make new decisions. We can build new neural pathways in the brain (new thoughts!), create new body chemistry (new emotions!), and pave new patterns of behavior that are more connected to the space of the Heart's truth. Awareness body connects the four lower bodies—the mental, emotional, energetic, and physical bodies—to the soul, Heart, or bliss body. The awareness body gives us the ability to observe ourselves from a higher viewpoint so that we can access Heart wisdom from a more evolved perspective.

Awareness body is the bridge:

- From the small ego-mind to the superconscious mind, Divine Mind, or higher consciousness;

- From past-based reactivity to present-moment conscious free will; and

- From being stuck in old beliefs and emotions to creating new ones.

People awaken the awareness body in different ways. Often, the difficulties and challenges that arise in life will give us a *swift kick in the butt*, opening our eyes to what we couldn't see before. For me, several personal issues took me into a deeper awareness of myself. Getting kicked out of the house at 16 years old woke me up to what it took to survive in the world as a child. My health decline in my 20s awakened me to my physical health and built awareness of what I put into my body. My third daughter's potentially fatal metabolic disorder woke me up to the preciousness of life and gave me gratitude for my family in every moment. My friend's early death awakened my spirituality to the other side of the veil. Several wake-up calls shook me out of the ignorance and slumber in my everyday life and forced me to look at the conditions of my behavior, my thinking, my emotions, and my soul in a new way.

Sometimes, a sudden divorce or death of a loved one can lead us onto a path of introspection and deep inner inquiry. Perhaps this time of difficulty is important for us to wake up to the deeper aspects of life, inner transformation, and love?

For some, the awareness body can awaken and go dormant again as soon as someone returns to homeostasis, a sense of satisfaction or comfort. However, for many of us, when we awaken this awareness body, we can never go back to sleep. We embark on a journey of exploration, questioning, and soul expansion. We become seekers on the path of awakening and curiosity. This curiosity and questioning come from the space of our awareness body.

Presence and Innocent Perception

There is a lot of mindfulness and spirituality information available these days about the importance of being *present*. One barrier to presence for most people is the effort involved in staying in the present moment, i.e., simply paying attention versus playing out old habits. We are often ignorant to the fact that we spend our time reacting from automatic reactions from the past overlaid on the present moment. We often get confused and think that the trauma packet situations are actually happening presently, but in fact, we are blanketing those thoughts, emotions, and vibrations on top of our current relationships. To be present, one must pause, introspect and see that old thoughts are being overlaid on the current situation. One must be able to see the what-is of what's happening in the present moment, versus the re-enactment of an old trauma packet vibration that *feels* like it's happening in the present.

Most people spend life chasing pleasure and avoiding pain—an activity of the Animal Brain, which keeps us out of the awareness body and on the hamster wheel of reactivity and fear. For example, for those aware of what we eat and how it affects our body, it can be confusing to think that someone could drink soda or smoke cigarettes. The Animal Brain leads people to these body-craving habits, and therefore, the awareness body isn't *online* for those behaviors. Even when there is some awareness, many people don't have the skills to change the behaviors because the auto-associated wiring triggers the response before awareness activates. They don't notice until after the pleasure-or-pain cycle has completed. For example, Jessica doesn't notice that she has overeaten until she feels her belly aching after dessert. Her body awareness doesn't come back online until *after* the auto-associated binge cycle has completed.

Often, people who are waking up spiritually, working through trauma packets, and starting to come back into their alignment, automatically start dropping unhealthy addictions without even focusing on stopping. This happens naturally because, once the awareness body awakens, it brings an attunement to the physical body and a sense of innocent perception: *Hmmmm, what am I eating? This actually tastes like chemicals. It doesn't feel good in my body.* Or *I don't feel connected to myself when I'm drunk.* The awareness body gives us the ability to look at old patterns with a new set of eyes, so we can live from a place of present-moment, Heart-based, conscious choice, versus habitual Animal-Brain reactivity and impulsiveness.

Eckart Tolle talks of presence in his *Power of Now* teachings and makes the concept of conscious awareness very simple:

"Be where you are. Look around. Just look, don't interpret. See the light, shapes, colors, textures. Be aware of the silent presence of each thing. Be aware of the space that allows everything to be."

He teaches that in this state of presence, we can be the witness or observer of our thoughts, minds, and actions. This develops our ability to see ourselves beyond the small self that is stuck in reactivity, from a higher perspective. In this higher perspective, as the observer, the mental body is not as active, so we're not judging, worrying, or searching for our next high. We are simply being in the moment with whatever shows up.

Byron Katie helps us look at things from the perspective of questioning every thought that the subconscious mind or trauma packets throw at us. Her book, *Loving What Is*, provides guidance on how to un-enmesh from our ego-identity, our mental body, so that we can know that we are not these old thoughts from our trauma packets. She says:

"A thought is harmless unless we believe it. It's not our thoughts, but our attachment to our thoughts, that causes suffering. Attaching to a thought means believing that it's true, without inquiring. A belief is a thought that we've been attaching to, often for years."

This concept suggests that inquiry, an innocent perception of the present moment, is necessary to release identification with thoughts. Katie teaches ways to create distance and questioning of our thoughts so we don't buy the old stories and thought paradigms that were constructed at such a young age. Her process of *The Work* is a set of questions that builds the awareness body, allowing the higher perspective to be accessible.

These masters of the practice of presence show us how to come back to the simplicity of the present moment. Only when we do this can we access our higher states of consciousness, or the higher dimensions within us.

The process of shifting into present awareness is the transition from the mental body (which is wired with distorted thoughts, belief systems, and body chemistry) to the awareness body. The activation of the awareness body is the ability to zoom out and observe the current situation from the simplicity of what is happening in the present moment (the what-is) without the encumbering trauma packets or neural circuitry distortions. Building present-moment consciousness through the awareness body bridges us to Heart consciousness (the bliss body).

Awareness of Automated Fear Responses

Since most people are operating from the Animal Brain, which is wired for survival and runs on fear, they do not usually approach life from the place of awareness body. Fear-based thoughts are wired into the brain, support fear body chemistry (depression, anger, anxiety), and keep the mind in a state of fear response (fight, flight, fawn, or freeze). When this autopilot is set in motion, people spend decades replaying the old vibrations, not even noticing the repetitive nature of their life, not even noticing that they've been limited by this same issue since childhood.

The first step out of the repetitive pattern requires *noticing* what is happening. Noticing that this thing keeps happening in every [insert situation here: romantic relationship, or work situation, or weight loss attempt]. While the mental process of linking it to childhood can make the ego-mind feel safe because it *understands* the issue and where it came from, this often doesn't change the course of the repetitive difficulty in life. The mental body analysis-paralysis doesn't actually create the healing needed. It only provides a band-aid, because the ego-mind tells itself it *knows* and can temporarily feel safe in the knowing—until of course, the issue is triggered again.

Stepping out of the vortex of automatic thought and emotions, out of the pain body while it's raging, is an act of the awareness body pulling you back into the present moment, back into a witness or *audience* of the dramatic theatrical play that the pain body is carrying out, rather than a character *in* the play. The ability to zoom out of the vortex of this pain body attack allows us to take back our power in the moment.

Practicing awareness, as the observer or witness of the mind, in every moment of every day strengthens this consciousness so that in the event of a pain body takeover, the awareness body is a strong muscle that can activate more quickly and stop the vicious cycle. Without awareness body, the well-patterned fear response behavior typically triggers very quickly—fight, flight, fawn, or freeze—and before you know it, you've enacted an old childhood pattern. At some point in the reactivity, you can *notice* the pattern enough to know that you are currently re-enacting an old behavior that doesn't serve you anymore. Neutrality through the awareness body can give you the pause, and the *choice point* to make new decisions, so that you can break the habit of automatic re-enactment. While this doesn't heal the underlying trauma packet that created this reactivity, it can create new patterning through conscious awareness.

Awareness body allows us to feel the vibrations in the body without merging with the deeply held story that automatically plays from the trauma packet. It may not stop the auto-play, or the auto-associated six-layered response to the triggered trauma packet, but it allows us to get some space from the vibration of the death fear. During the pause, we can access the Thinking Brain, which can help us tune into whether the lion is coming to kill us or not. The body may feel like it's in imminent danger, but the awareness body helps us process real-time data to evaluate whether there truly is danger. Most often, there is no danger present.

Awareness allows us to know we *are* safe even though we don't *feel* safe while the trauma packet replays. By holding awareness to the death fear vibrations in the physical and energetic bodies, and simultaneously keeping the Thinking Brain and awareness body active with the wisdom that there is safety in this present moment, we give ourselves the choice point. We give ourselves the ability to choose to merge with the automatic pain body response, or simply stay in the present moment, deeply connected to the body, as hard as it is to resist the well-worn pathways of reactivity. Even if we inevitably merge into the old pattern, awareness helps us recover more quickly. Instead of getting lost for months or decades, we can recover back to present-moment safety in minutes, hours, or days. In our work, we call this *recovery time*.

This is how the awareness body gives us our power and freedom back. Conscious awareness helps us feel like it's possible to overcome future bouts of pain body attack—anxiety, depression, rage—so that we carry less fear into our relationships and life situations.

This strong sense of awareness is about as far as most current healing and mental health modalities can bring us. Most people who come to me ask: How can this awareness lead me to not having to feel this way anymore? The answer lies in the Inner Alignment Soul Retrieval process, which heals the trauma packet and unlocks access to the bliss body so that the soul can be felt again.

Awareness Body and Law of Attraction

As we've discussed, in any given moment, our mental body is most likely importing past thoughts into the present moment, essentially forcing us to live in the past by pulling 90% of the 65,000 thoughts we thought yesterday. This is automatic, non-present-moment thought momentum.

The law of attraction states that like attracts like. If we are afraid of abandonment, and regurgitate trauma packet thoughts around past abandonment in the present moment, then we are more likely to attract abandonment situations from our future moments. We are thinking abandonment thoughts, which practices abandonment fear neural pathways in the brain. We are feeling sad abandonment emotions, which sends off corresponding hormones. We are energetically vibrating abandonment, so we reverberate that energy in the present moment. Every future moment will be more of the same, because like attracts like.

With the power of the awareness body, we can manifest our future desires by practicing them in the present moment. When we anchor ourselves into the present moment, there is innocent perception (less negative thought and judgment) and pure awareness in noticing the what-is. In this space of presence, we have the option to start envisioning what we desire, importing *future* thoughts related to our intentions into the present moment. Instead of automatically importing past trauma packet thoughts and vibrations, we become more empowered to practice the future vibration of our desires. Doing so allows new vibrations, thoughts, and emotions to be imported from the desired future state into the present moment. Practicing these intentions, desires, and visions—and creating their vibrational momentum in the present moment—enables us to attract what we want in life through full activation of the awareness body. This can only be done if someone is ready to activate the awareness body in *every* present moment. Again, this takes incredible stamina to stay awake to the present, and is much more difficult if the trauma packet continues to regurgitate the past.

The image below illustrates the use of the imagination to import future thoughts into the present moment, instead of automatically importing and repeating the past.

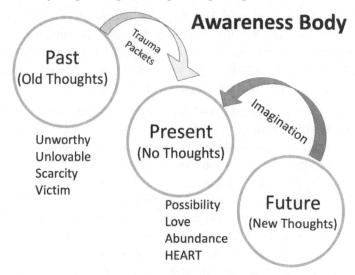

Dimensions of Consciousness

As we discuss this concept of awareness body, it's important to look at our consciousness from a deeper spiritual perspective. To do this, we'll lean on Barbara Hand Clow's book *The Alchemy of Nine Dimensions*. From her work, we can break down our awareness body from a spiritual perspective on the dimensions of consciousness. Those on the spiritual path have heard the New Age spirituality delineation of 3D versus 5D, where it has been said that 3D, third-dimension consciousness, is dense and physical (not spiritual) and we're moving to 5D, fifth-dimension consciousness, which is spiritual and love-based. This is a bit of an oversimplification that distorts the truth of the importance and depths of us being connected to *all* of our dimensions of consciousness always.

Clow shares that there are nine dimensions of consciousness, and honestly for me, some make more sense than others.[3]

Dimensions of Consciousness

9th Dimension—Black Hole
8th Dimension—Divine Manifestation
7th Dimension—Light Frequency
6th Dimension—Sacred Geometry
5th Dimension—HEART/CHRIST CONSCIOUSNESS

Upper Dimensions

4th Dimension—Collective / DUALITY CONSCIOUSNESS
3rd Dimension—Physical; PHYSICAL BODY

Middle Dimensions

2nd Dimension—Microorganisms; Earth Crust; TRAUMA
1st Dimension—Iron Crystal Core of the Earth

Lower Dimensions

The **first dimension is the iron crystal core of the earth,** which sets our physical homeostasis and holds the consciousness, wisdom, and records of everything that's lived on earth. The iron crystal and its rhythms correspond to the iron crystals within our blood, and therefore connect us to the first dimension through our physical embodiment. Since the first dimension connects us to the earth, it is the tether *under* our Root Chakra.

The **second dimension is the earth's crust,** which holds the microorganisms that make life on earth possible. This microbial life and balance correspond to the tiny living microorganisms that inhabit our body (skin, blood, gut, etc.). When this is in balance we are connected to the earth and have harmony in the microbial balance within our bodies. When disharmony occurs through disconnection from the resonance of the earth's crust,

---

[3] While this information can be hard to grasp, and may not resonate with those who feel it is too *out there*, I will give you some concepts to consider and suggest you skip this section if it doesn't resonate. Just note that trauma lives in the second dimension.

dis-ease occurs. This can occur on any layer of the body. For example, the physical body can have a microbial overgrowth or infection, the emotional body can get stuck in a dense depression, and the mental body can get overwhelmed in fear. Trauma, with its mental and emotional density, can get trapped in the second dimension of our bodies. This is where trauma packets live within us, which is why illness can stir trauma, and embedded fear can stir illness. Because trauma lives deep within the crevices of our second-dimension consciousness, it is more difficult to access and therefore more elusive in healing. (It can't be accessed through the mental body, which corresponds with the fourth dimension of consciousness). In my opinion, the second dimension connects to the Root and Sacral Chakras (though Clow would say it connects to just the Root Chakra).

The **third dimension refers to the physical things and beings that exist on the earth within space and time** (our physical body, plants, animals, water, air). There is pure physicality of these things within linear space and time, e.g., where you are with relationship to the direction of sunrise or sunset, days, and seasons. The third dimension just *is*. There's no thought or judgment around a tree shedding its leaves; it just does it. No collective mourning around the squirrel dying in the woods; it just decays and gives life to new vegetation. I hypothesize that the third dimension connects to the Root and Sacral Chakras as well.

The **fourth dimension is the collective consciousness, the mental realm that lives in duality consciousness**. This dimension corresponds directly with our minds and how we relate to others' minds. This is the playground upon which we communicate and share concepts with others. It is also where judgment, negative thoughts and emotions, and collective trauma vibrations live (slavery, scarcity consciousness, unworthiness, bad or wrong person). Society's belief systems, thought paradigms, and collective mental activity live within this dimension. Think of CNN or Fox News broadcasts that set the tone of fear, right or wrong, or good or bad. Organizations such as churches and schools that dictate morality and the *right* way to think and live. This dimension corresponds to the Will Chakra.

Trauma experienced through the interplay between people occurs in the fourth-dimension collective mind, and gets stored in the second dimension deep within, close to the body, and inaccessible to the mind. Trauma happens through fourth-dimension interactions, thoughts, and emotions, and can get trapped deep within the *crust* of the body.

To expand ourselves as humans, our work is to unplug our identity from societal beliefs (fourth dimension collective consciousness). Then we can anchor to the lower dimensions to ground our bodies to what-is and transcend into higher-dimensional connection and thinking.

Most people get lost in the overfocus on third and fourth dimensions, the body, and the collective and individual ego-mind. It's not that the third and fourth dimensions are bad or wrong. The overfocus on these dimensions is imbalanced because the upper dimensions (fifth through ninth) of Divine consciousness often haven't been developed, and the lower dimensions (first- and second-dimension connection to earth) haven't been anchored, honored, and transmuted.

The **fifth dimension is Heart consciousness**. Some may also call this Christ Consciousness or Unity Consciousness, which is less connected to the religious aspects of Christ and more focused on Divine consciousness in human form and thought. I see it as practical implementation of Divine into human thought and activity. Living from the Heart, accessing Divine Love, Power, and Wisdom through anchoring into the Sacred Heart within us. This is a powerful space within, an incredible consciousness, that we've seen demonstrated through the lives of the Ascended Masters who have walked this earth, spanning traditions, like Buddha, Christ, and Krishna—enlightened beings that held the higher dimensions of consciousness and lived life with this love as leaders. While the fourth dimension, the collective, distorted the Masters and their messages, we can individually connect to these upper dimensions for our own connection to Divine Wisdom and Love.

The fifth dimension opens the Heart and gives us access to all the upper dimensions. Through this Heart connection, we can access our intuition, overcome fear and negativity, and create harmony across connection to other dimensions. The fifth dimension is connected to Heart Chakra, and opens the awareness body portal to the bliss body. At this chakra, we connect our lower chakras (Root, Sacral, and Will), which help us navigate our connection to the body, earth and other humans, *and* our upper chakras (Heart, Throat, Third Eye, and Crown), which connect us to our Heart's love, truth, purpose, intuition, and Divine consciousness. The Heart is where heaven and earth meet within us.

The **sixth dimension is the sacred geometrical form** that sets the basis for all forms on earth. On a physical level, we anchor these forms into our human experience through walking labyrinths, visiting temples, or doing ancient movements that hold poses of sacred form (yoga, tai chi, Qi gong, sacred dance, etc.). Anchoring these forms into our body keeps our third-dimension physical form aligned with the upper dimensions. With conscious intention, we can align our bodies to these sacred shapes. Have you ever noticed how doing physical yoga can awaken someone to the Heart? Or how present you feel after tai chi?

Opening the Heart activates our connection to these geometrical forms. Starting to gaze at the Flower of Life form, Fibonacci spiral, Metatron's cube, or the platonic solids can activate this connection. We start to see that there are no straight lines in nature, just curves and sacred patterns, like at the center of an apple or a twisting tree. The sixth dimension is connected to the Throat Chakra.

The **seventh dimension is sacred sound waves**. Sacred sound connects us to Divine consciousness. This sound actually generates the sacred geometrical form. It can be generated through music, chanting Sanskrit, sound bowls, tuning forks, and gongs. We can witness the phenomena of sacred sound creating sacred geometrical patterns. For example, we can witness music or sound as it creates patterns in water, or the sacred sound waves that create the unique shape of snowflakes. The seventh dimension is connected to the Third Eye Chakra.

The **eighth dimension is the organized field of Divine Light that gives us access to the Divine Mind.** It is the space from which we access our Divine Consciousness; it manifests through our connection to our Divine Mind. The eighth dimension is connected to the Crown Chakra.

The **ninth dimension is the black hole that connects us to the Galactic Center**. This is accessed above the Crown chakra and connects us to frequencies of pure bliss. As we access Divine Mind, we attune to extremely high ninth dimension frequencies to accelerate the lower dimensions of ourselves. By doing so, we can attain full awakening, enlightenment, or samadhi (union with Source). These connections will help us evolve the planet and humanity with innovations, new paradigms, and ascension. This connects us to the Source of Divine Source, beyond our bliss body.

Integrating All Dimensions

If I were to guess how the dimensions correlate to the koshas, I would say that the physical and energetic bodies connect to the first, second, and third dimensions. The mental and emotional bodies correspond to the fourth dimension. The awareness and bliss bodies correspond to the fifth through ninth dimensions.

Most of us are stuck in the third and fourth dimensions of the physical and mental realms. In these spaces, one person wins and another loses. There are wars, scarcity, victimization, and power struggles. Life is about survival. When we can move into the space of the fifth and higher dimensions, we are able to move into higher states of consciousness, where love and Divine connection become the priority.

That said, we can't just live in the upper dimensions, or in the higher chakras, because this creates imbalance with the physical survival balance of life. Living in the upper dimensions, disconnected from the lower dimensions, is not the solution, though many have been trying to do this in spiritual communities. We often see individuals in spiritual communities connected to higher consciousness, but due to an imbalanced and unhealed second dimension, they inadvertently play out trauma patterns with others. Many priest- or guru-led communities have fallen due to this type of imbalance (e.g., power or sex scandals). The trauma packet's shadow remains lurking in the crevices of the body, in the second dimension, if someone is only on the path of connecting to the upper dimensions. In time, these will show up to be healed, creating a crisis if the lower chakras and dimensions have been denied. We must be on a path of connecting to *all* the dimensions of ourselves.

With respect to the awareness body, it's important to notice the space from which you are operating. Are you operating from trauma vibration, disease, fear, and illness (imbalanced second dimension), and replaying old scenarios for the last decade? Or are you maintaining connection to love, sacred form, and Divine perspective? Are you in survival mode, bouncing around in duality with an imbalanced fourth dimension? Or have you shifted your awareness body through innocent perception, connecting to the loving abundance and co-creation available to you?

If this sounds too spiritual or complicated, perhaps go back to the simple question of whether this present-moment thought stems from love or fear. Is this action from the Heart and anchored in love, or is it from a death fear or pain body pattern from the trauma stored in the body?

The dimensions are critical as we begin the discussion of how to heal these trauma packets that are exiled away, out of reach from present-moment consciousness, inaccessible even from the awareness body. The awareness body can see the *effects* of the trauma packets if you allow yourself to notice what's happening in the present moment. It can sense the fear or duality that keeps us plagued with the issue. Awareness can connect us to the body so we know we have a pain body, or to know we're in a vibration of a death fear. While the awareness body can't clean up the trauma packet on its own, it can get us closer to seeing the effects of what's stored deeply inside us, within the second dimension of consciousness.

Notes for Healing the Awareness Layer

Building the awareness layer of the body is like building a muscle to stay in the what-is of the present moment. This allows access to all that is happening within the other body layers, across all dimensions of the self. The work to create healing through the activation of the awareness layer is as follows:

1. Develop present-moment awareness of each layer of the body that lasts throughout the day: how the body

feels, what thoughts are present, what emotional or energetic weather is moving in and out of the body. Establish this awareness without judgment or a need to change anything. Simply be in the what-is without resistance or fear of the present moment.

2. Through Inner Alignment Soul Retrieval, address the trauma packets that anchor consciousness to the past. Navigate into the second dimension to access the original vibrations at every layer and bridge the higher dimensions into the original experience so that loving awareness and adult consciousness penetrate the frozen experience. This allows the big picture to loosen the micro-view of the trauma experience.

3. Rewire daily experience of thought and emotion to the higher perspective built in the trauma packet. Recapitulate life through this expansive viewpoint.

4. Build the ability to experience life from an integrated dimensional interweaving, simultaneously creating space for earth awareness; personal fear and trauma vibration; inner and outer physical reality; collective constructs and distortions; Heart consciousness; and the higher spiritual Divine intuition, visions, and knowing. The end goal is innocent perception and neutrality through higher perspective and understanding, without duality.

5. Develop and attract future visions, goals, and desires by accessing the multi-dimensional reality (the laws of attraction and resonance) by resonating in the vibration of the future experience and attracting future experiences in the present moment. Gather data on the spiritual power that can be accessed through being connected to all aspects, all dimensions, of self.

Chapter 9:
Bliss Body Layer

When I tell people that bliss is their base state, they usually don't believe me. They feel fear, anxiety, depression, and frustration, but not bliss. The soul, or Heart presence, is there, but at some point in our lives, we lose access to it. Other vibrations become louder than the subtle, peaceful bliss vibration that softly hums underneath all the noise.

The noise becomes the new normal, so we begin to identify with it. It's like the moments after you leave a loud indoor concert. You don't realize how loud it was until you experience the absence of the noise. At first, it even feels like something is missing because the noise became the norm. Same is true when the energetic, mental, and emotional noise stops. At first it feels like boredom or emptiness, because the focus is on the absence of noise. However, once the attachment to the noise is released, we can begin to hear the subtle hum of the bliss body. Our access to this part of ourselves only exists through the doorway of the awareness body in the present moment. The ability to still the mind and emotions allows the awareness body to bring us to the what-is in the present moment, so we can attune to the subtle bliss within.

What creates the noise that keeps us so disconnected from our bliss body?

- Emotions create tsunamis of chaos.

- Energetic imbalances block life force.

- Negative thoughts create fears within our minds.

- Animal Brain is always telling us we're going to die.

- Nervous system is in a constant state of reactivity.

- Limiting belief systems create distortions on how we perceive the present moment.

- Pain bodies take over our awareness.

- Trauma packets reverberate through all layers.

There is so much swirling within our body layers that we simply can't feel the inner bliss that's wired into our bliss body. The process of Inner Alignment is the journey to still the waves of the layered body, bring wholeness back, and reconnect to the sweet nectar of bliss that lives within.

Soul Fragmentation

Because traumatic events from childhood (big T or little t) create and store trauma packets within our being, these trauma packets are, in a sense, *stuck on repeat*, replaying themselves in the second dimension of consciousness. The part of us still stuck in that situation from the past is essentially fragmented off, perpetually reliving this negative experience. The replay of this fragmented part pulls life force from the body while the issue reverberates in the lower dimensions of our consciousness.

It's like when you have too many windows open on your computer. They continue to pull energy in the background which steals the memory or energy from the current task, making the application freeze. Same is true with various trauma packets that are using up energy and psychic space in the background—old, fragmented parts fighting for their lives deep within you—while you go about your benign daily tasks, chronically drained and emotionally reactive for no apparent reason.

Let's say an adult has a trauma packet with a fragmented eight-year-old part who is still afraid to come out of her room after being scolded by her mom. She feels confused, unloved and abandoned. This younger part of the adult has confusion around love and safety, not knowing how to speak her truth and get what she needs in her home. The adult self is unaware that the eight-year-old self is fragmented and frozen in that space, struggling to get the love and safety that she needs. This fragmented part makes an incredible amount of *noise*, keeping waves in the mind, emotions, and nervous system, and depleting energy reserves until the adult can't really feel the subtle hum of the bliss body. Thoughts of *I'm unloved* and emotions of sadness and loneliness stir up the present moment, but the present-moment self is unaware of the cause of those vibrations. The adult may be able to put together a concept or story of being unloved, but has no ability to permanently calm these waves or settle the noise through intellectual understanding.

In this sense, the trauma packet has created separation, or a fragmentation of the soul essence. A vibrant little girl lost a part of herself in the scolding she experienced that day, and she hasn't felt the same since. A part of her that was light, free, and completely open to the inflow of love was fragmented off to a space of loneliness, sadness, and powerlessness. This fragmented part will continue to stay in that shattered space until the eight-year-old can heal and reintegrate back into her wholeness.

This is how our clients describe soul fragmentation. They lost a part (or several parts) of themselves over the years. Sometimes they feel like they're watching their life from outside themselves, without connection to their body, emotions, or the feeling of their Heart. Often, they feel lost, abandoned, and confused, despite having a great life or a good spouse. When we accumulate enough trauma, we start to feel really porous, broken, and detached from our ourselves. Those parts of ourselves are stored in the body as trauma packets that have chipped away from our wholeness and created an inability to fully feel ourselves. This makes it feel impossible to access love

145

and joy, because those are the vibrations of the soul... and the trauma packets create too much chaos to actually feel the subtle vibration of the soul.

When we leave a part of our soul in those early life events—feeling disconnected, vulnerable, and unsafe in this world—we are often unable to connect to others. This leaves present-life relationships (family, romantic, parent, child) feeling painful or blocked. Connection to Divine Source is thwarted because you have to feel your soul to feel your connection to the Divine.

There's no wonder why, when we look out into society today, there seem to be so many lost souls. A tremendous degree of soul fragmentation has gone unhealed.

This soul fragmentation has a significant domino effect, as it spreads like wildfire down family lineages. Through epigenetics, the energy and DNA of trauma is passed down through the generations. Spiritually and karmically, these family patterns become ingrained and normalized. Mentally and emotionally, we have fragmented souls raising children in a way that creates deeper and deeper fragmentation in their offspring; lost and fragmented souls raising lost and fragmented souls. In our work, we address this as *family lineage karma*. A family lineage usually passes down these accumulated pain bodies until someone in the family heals and begins to clear the lineage.

Because we can't make sense of our trauma packets, nor process the corresponding fear vibrations out of our bodies, we start to go into separation from ourselves. We create energetic and psychic walls around the traumas and try to muffle the vibrations so we don't have to feel that anymore. The vibrations become a different sound—muffled but loud, hard for us to detect, but all too consuming.

Often, we try to cut ourselves off from the loud vibrations in the body, but that becomes a temporary band-aid that creates longer-term damage, like disconnecting the annoying dinging signal of the low-gas alert in the car. You can make the sound stop beeping, but it doesn't change the fact that you're running out of gas. By disconnecting the sound, you put yourself and the car in a more dangerous situation. Same is true for muting the effects of soul fragmentation. You can try to think new thoughts, or take antidepressants to numb the emotion, or drink coffee to create some faux prana, but this doesn't get to the root cause of the noise. Until the trauma packets are healed, the vibrations will continue to get louder and penetrate deeper into every relationship and aspect of life.

For example, if we cut ourselves off from our low belly heaviness, where our sexuality resides (Sacral Chakra) because the sexual trauma feels so awful in there, we might muffle the noise, but we lose access to all the good of that space within. We lose zest for life, connection with others, and the ability to create and manifest. We lose the intimacy and the sexual connection. With every inner blockage and attempt to muffle, we start to feel painfully disconnected from ourselves. The vibration of fear is the loudest vibration in our body, so the feeling of love (or self-connection) begins to feel out of reach. It gets shadowed by the fear and trauma vibrations.

Our work is to heal the underlying trauma packets so we can reconnect with those fragmented parts of self again, to create peace and harmony in those old experiences and feel whole once more.

Accessing Bliss Body

Jill Bolte Taylor wrote the book *Stroke of Insight*, and outlines an incredible perspective for us to consider with respect to the bliss body. She explains her experience as a brain anatomist while having a stroke on the left side of her brain. She went in and out of moments of what she called nirvana (bliss body connection) when her left brain was shut down from the stroke. She saw her hand as a pixelated wave of light and was delighted by it. Joyful and peaceful. Yet, when her left brain would come back on board, she realized she was in danger, and remembered that she needed to get herself help. With left brain active, she could read numbers and think linearly to get herself help, but when it went offline, she would be back in the present-moment bliss of her right brain. When she finally arrived at the hospital, she would notice that when her left brain was offline, her right brain would magnify people's energy, thoughts, and emotions. With this, her level of sensitivity was awakened and her brain would process different types of energetic information.

If we take this further from her simplified description, we can deduce that the left brain, which thinks linearly, is there to keep us functioning and operating in space and time. However, most people are living from a trauma packet-induced state of survival mode. With left brain always active, it's very difficult to access the part of the brain, we can call it *right brain* here, that connects us to a very expansive, blissful state that only exists in the present moment. With the hyperactive left-brain linearity keeping us anchored to the third and fourth dimensions of consciousness, we can't access those upper dimensions (fifth through ninth) of the Heart and Divine Consciousness (superconscious mind) states through the right brain activity.

It makes sense that DMT, Ayahuasca, and other plant medicines, which activate certain parts of the brain that process energetic and spiritual information, have become popular in spiritual circles. Plant medicines have given people a glimpse of access to these areas of the brain that connect us to our spiritual wisdom. Personally, I think it's possible for us to access this consciousness without any substance, by clearing out the trauma packets, reducing the noise in our lives, and working ourselves into our bliss body on the daily.

Defining Divine Source

We can't discuss the bliss body unless we take on the subject of the Heart and the Divine, or soul and Source Energy. This is always a tricky subject because spiritual belief systems vary. Because I've worked with clients ranging from atheists to Mormons to yogis, I'm convinced that there are certain things that we can mostly agree upon.

There is a greater organization of this Universe. This is of a Higher Consciousness than any one of us alone can carry. The wisdom of nature, plants that heal, the sun that nourishes, fire that transforms, mountains that ground, and waters that purify. Perhaps for some people, nature is Source energy.

Some can see the spark of Light in other humans, maybe through the love shared among a family or through humanity. For them, this is their spirituality, accessing the love through human connection.

Others believe in a spiritual hierarchy of Ascended Masters who have walked this earth and mastered the human experience: Jesus, Buddha, Krishna, Quan Yin. Some believe in the Divine Feminine (Divine Mother) or Divine Masculine (Divine Father). Many believe in the Angelic realm, archangels, angels, and Divine beings. Others look to the realm of Divine Light or Divine Light Rays. Some believe in God.

No matter what the belief, there is often a sense of Divine Consciousness that is bigger than us, along with a sense of Divinity or Sacred within the Heart. My words for that are soul and Divine. The soul is a drop of the Divine ocean. The Divine ocean exists within each person, and our job is to still the waves so we can hear and feel that Divine Love, Wisdom, and Power.

If there's religious trauma, or a distaste for the historical aspects of religious distortions, people can have resistance around concepts of spirituality. In truth, many religions have lost the essence of love as the basis for spirituality and replaced it with rules and fear, which are the antithesis of Divine connection. Some traditions have created separation from self by creating notions that humans are inherently bad. Others have created fear around intuition or personal relationship with the Divine. Some have said that a leader or a book, and therefore the mental body, must tell us what's moral and good, which cuts us off from our own internal connection to soul and Source. Because of the distortions and fear created by the human ego within the fourth dimension, there are few roadmaps to re-establish connection to bliss body through the fifth dimension of the Heart.

No matter what's perceived as the Source of bliss within, our work is to access it and attune ourselves to it each day, in every possible moment. We want to still the mind, calm the emotions, and allow our energetics to connect to this higher frequency, while grounding it into our bodies and daily life. We don't need to go to the Himalayan mountains to access this bliss, but we do need a passionate desire and corresponding effort to reconnect within.

Sacred Heart Space

In Inner Alignment, we work with people from every perspective of spirituality. Many have lost faith and have had some level of religious trauma. Others are deeply faithful in a

Christian religion, but have fragmentation blocking the feeling of their bliss body.

With this, the goal is to simply *feel* the pure connection to the Divine within. If we bypass the mental body analysis of spirituality and cut out the intellectual concepts of duality (who's right or wrong, and what's fact), and allow people the connection to their Heart, they can access the inner knowing of this bliss body. Once this is connected, the rest is just words and mental analysis-paralysis; unnecessary thought that is secondary to the present-moment experience of Divine Source.

We all have a physical heart, so it's not hard for people to buy into the idea that love lives in the Heart. Accessing the fifth-dimension Heart Consciousness through the experience of love or peace in the Heart is a gateway to bliss body for many. That is the only governing belief system that needs to exist within the mental body when it comes to bliss body connection: a feeling of love in the Heart.

In our work, we can access this through the Sacred Heart, where upper dimensions of consciousness meet the lower dimensions of earth within us. Heaven and earth intersect within our Hearts. Within our Sacred Heart space, we can connect with our Divine Source, Ascended Masters, and Angelic or Light Beings, or simply sit in the safe refuge within us to access our bliss.

The Sacred Heart is an actual space within us, accessed through Hrit Padma Chakra, and it contains our Heart flame, the soul fire that keeps us alive. Most people can imagine sacred light or fire as Divine energy, or a representation of Divine energy. The Heart and the Heart Flame are accessible concepts that help to create the sacred connection to the bliss body. These concepts are universal spiritual truths that can translate into most people's belief systems, without creating inconsistencies or confusions.

The Seven Sacred Flames, represented by different colors for different Divine qualities, can allow for a unified intention within someone's spiritual belief system. The element of fire transmutes and changes situations, and as a representation of Divine energy, allows people to access their inner Divine power to transform their lives. In Inner Alignment, we access the Violet

Consuming Flame within the Heart. This is a three-fold flame that contains the Pink Flame of Divine Love, Blue Flame of Divine Power, and Gold Flame of Divine Wisdom. These three qualities provide a deep healing within, and the ability to transmute outer circumstances by clearing interference energy that distorts the truth of who we are.

Interference Energy

Let's examine what interferes with the subtle connection to bliss body. Often, we think that there is something blocked, wrong, broken, or bad about us, and therefore we aren't deserving of Divine connection. However, that is completely untrue. Every human on earth is deserving of the bliss connection that's already wired within, but there may be confusion around how to access the connection because of the noise or interference blocking it.

Interference energy can be any unseen vibrational disturbance that vibrates as fear and ultimately pulls us out of the safety and love or our Hearts. It exists outside of who we are as Divine beings. The cause and origin of these vibrational distortions vary. For example, they can be a discarnate being (a person who has died but who hasn't crossed over), entity or etheric parasite (energy that feeds off of fear or negativity in the energy field), lineage karma residue or program (e.g., scarcity or powerlessness patterns), or a simple pain body connected to a trauma packet. Typically, this energy has a low vibration that resonates with and feeds on our fear.

Since death fears live within trauma packets, those with heavy trauma packets often have significant interference in their energy field. Our clients with a history of suicidal ideation almost always have persistent interference energy in their field. Because the interference thoughts sound like their own ego's voice, the person is often confused and overwhelmed. Their work is to rebuild bliss body connection so the voice of the soul becomes solidified and louder. When anchored in their Divine Truth, they can face the interference distortions with strength and awareness.

The interference energy acts as a cloud that distorts the Divine Truth in every layer of the body. It causes phantom

151

physical symptoms, distorting thoughts, jarring energetics, and emotional overwhelm; twisting ours or others' communications, or stirring chaos in relationships and important situations. It creates negativity and drama, and pulls everyone involved out of their inner truth.

Unfortunately, perhaps due to all the horror movies that have simulated this type of menacing energy, people generally have fear of this vibrational interference in their or others' energy field. With this, it's important to stay connected to the Heart's love, the bliss body connection, to anchor into safety in the present moment. Doing so helps you identify that this energy is present and creating fear. Noticing and bringing your Heart's awareness to this energy will help send it on its way. Any resistance to it, or fear of it, keeps it engaged in the energy field and gives it power. It's important to remember, the interference is a mere speck in the energy field, an annoying mosquito, nothing to be afraid of when connected to our Divine Power.

To examine interference energy, let's look at the following:

Interference Energy

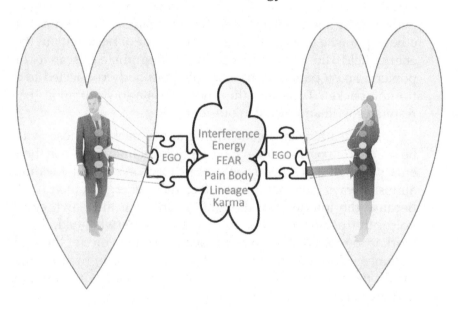

The woman (on the right) is me, in my Heart, connected to my bliss body through Divine Source connection. The man (on the left) is my husband in his Heart/soul connection. We each hold within ourselves some energetic imbalance that we are working on in this lifetime. My imbalance is a weak Root Chakra, and my work is establishing physical and emotional safety and grounding. His imbalance is excess energy in his Will Chakra, creating a need to know and control to feel his power. These predispositions to imbalance guide each of our ego-minds, which exist outside of our Heart/soul selves. My ego tries to create safety in experiences through proving I'm a good person. His ego works to be an expert at the top of every hierarchy to exhibit his worth for external value.

These aspects of the ego create chaos on their own, but in the presence of interference energy—pain body, active lineage karma, astrological alignments, or discarnate energies—either of our egos can lock into this cloud of energy. Once one of us locks into the cloud of energetic interference, if the other is *not* anchored deeply in awareness body and the Heart, we merge into the energy until it runs its course. When one or both of us engage with this interference energy, we lose perspective and reality gets distorted. We can only see each other through the distortions of the cloud. The cloud can make a situation look like something very different, based on the frequencies present in the cloud, much like a curved mirror that distorts the reflection of the object.

For example, we are currently raising three teenage girls. Two lions (fire constitutions) raising a pack of lionesses (fiery teens). Very often, these smart, strategic girls will try to manipulate us into doing what they want. One day, I was tired and worn down. One of my girls asked me to go somewhere, and I was irritated that she asked me to go there again. I said no, *again*. Later on, I realized that she asked my husband after I said no, and he said yes. I became upset with him for *always being good cop*, when *I'm always bad cop*. This is an old *I am a bad person* pain body that I carry from childhood. He got triggered into a pain body of powerlessness, an *I can't do anything right* pain body from his childhood. And we threw our pain bodies at each other for about an hour.

In this time, we literally couldn't see each other's Hearts. I couldn't see the man I loved. I could only see the *jerk that was letting the kids manipulate me*. He couldn't see the wife he cherished. He could only see a *witch who never supports him*. About 95% of our marriage is happy and harmonious, but when taken by the interference energy, neither of us could see that reality because we became engulfed by the distortions of the cloud. Our view of each other during that episode was through the distortion of fear. Each of our emotions, thoughts, and energies engaged with the cloud, through our ego-mind, in different ways. I went to the weak chakra and trauma packet remnants within me, and he went to the weak chakra and trauma packet remnants within him. The cloud hit each of us in a different way, playing out the fears that live in each of our subconscious minds.

This lasted until one of us noticed and felt the unseen cloud of interference. It just takes one to notice (awareness body) that we were playing out the old, engaging with an energy that was stirring the pot between us, magnetizing us into the cyclone of destruction. Awareness of the interference disempowered it. By seeing the other's Hearts again, we disempowered the interference energy.

We treat the interference energy like a storm that rolled into the house, never blaming the other for getting swept into it. Never assuming the other person *is* the storm. The storm is a separate energy, depersonalized. We are both responsible because we both got swept up in it. Personal responsibility exists with the recognition that neither of us *is* the interference energy, even though we each participated.

It may be tempting for the mental body to analyze what this energy is. I've spent a lot of time trying to figure that out, but I've found that putting attention to it draws it to me. By seeing it as a fly or mosquito, irritating but not scary, I acknowledge it without giving it power. Call it karmic patterns, a fear blob, an entity of negative energy, a disembodied soul, astrological pulls...or simply call it interference energy, that which interferes with connection to the Heart Consciousness and bliss body connection.

The work is to have an active awareness body to notice that there is interference energy, and pull our energy back into ourselves so we can see beyond the cloudy distortions. Once in the awareness body, we can access the love within our Hearts and use the Heart Flame, or the Violet Consuming Flame, to transmute the interference energy. To do this, we must ground ourselves in the present moment through the physical body (Root Chakra). Then, we can move out of the ego-mind mental body and into the Heart by activating the Heart Chakra. While seeing beyond how the current circumstances appear (Third Eye Chakra), we can pull in the Divine love that reaches beyond the interference energy (Crown Chakra). All dimensions of consciousness must be active for us to anchor into the present moment and access the higher truth in the present moment.

Bliss Body Resonance for Soul Residence

When we are fully connected to the bliss body, to our Heart, and resonate in the fifth or higher dimensions on a more regular basis, we create a safe and loving environment for the soul to thrive. A ripe environment for the love within to grow into every aspect of life. This must be accompanied by the awareness body's view of life beyond the physical realm, expanded into spiritual reality of Divine assistance. This builds the expansiveness of possibility, inner worth, and abundance of what comes through connection to Divine Source. While at the same time, we can maintain awareness of the deep, grounded connection to the earth, and energies that support us from nature. Connection to the heavens and earth that meet within our Hearts. Above, below, and within.

This is contrary to where most people are focused, which is outside of themselves, looking for others or things to bring that happiness or joy. Unfortunately, external sources, other humans and things, aren't where this bliss connection comes from. Temporary happiness from external sources never lasts because it can't sustain itself. So, we spend our life chasing it externally, when it lived within us the whole time. We're *looking for love in all the wrong places.*

If we're constantly dropping into death fears of scarcity and unworthiness, it's difficult for the wholeness of our soul to stay grounded in our bodies and maintain connection in the Heart with Divine Source. We get lost in the illusion of the death fear. We feel like we're going to die, and separate from the spiritual truth of who we are. There's a dichotomy between the death fear thoughts and emotions (fourth dimension) and its sensation in our physical body (second dimension), versus the lightness of spirit when connected to the upper dimensions. People will often disconnect from the physical body so they can stay in the spiritual space. Living in 5D (fifth dimension) and disconnecting from 3D (third dimension physical body). This is a coping mechanism that prevents wholeness. When they come back down into the body, there's an intolerance for the human condition, and often more fear of the physical experience of life.

Ideally, we're able to stay in our body (3D), connected to Divine Source (5D), and experience the collective storms (4D) for what they are in the present moment. We can concurrently feel the intensity of the mental collective fear while maintaining a strong connection to the spiritual reality of the situation. We hold the reality that the fear is uncomfortable in the body, while remembering that we can also maintain a connection to our Heart and pure love concurrently. Staying connected to both the fear in the body and ego-mind, while feeling the peace or bliss emanating from the Heart, with our feet on the earth...this is the goal of staying connected to all the dimensions of our consciousness.

One way to do this is to consider that we are all on the world stage, each playing a character in the play. We are all deeply connected to our own character's role in the theatrical production—wearing costumes, engaging the emotions, speaking the words, and playing the parts. Some of us remember that it's a play, and that we are free to experience emotions outside of the script, while others get so lost in the character re-enactments that they are disoriented by the production. Maybe they like it, or maybe it feels familiar; either way, they forget that there's a bigger picture.

It's important to stay in the awareness body, to stay consciously aware that we are all simply playing parts, and that there are directors, writers, and a backstage crew. Staying aware of the spiritual team, behind the veil or the curtains, is an important part of the production of life. To maintain this awareness is to maintain connection to all the vastness beyond this particular play. To recognize there are other plays, other producers and productions that may be less dramatic, and more peaceful. At any moment, we can connect to another vibration, or get some help from backstage. If we don't want to play the nemesis anymore, we have the choice point to take on a new character role. This awareness is critical for the feeling of expansive possibility, growth, and opportunity for change while in the depths of the storm. It could look like:

> *Wow, right now I'm playing out a dramatic scene with my mother. It feels terrible when I focus on my connection to her. She thinks I hold her happiness and I think that she holds my safety. Whoa, this is an intense exchange! Even though I keep playing this out with her, I know I can simultaneously stay connected to that which feels good. That which feels like love and safety beyond this play. I'd rather not be playing this out with her, but I can still feel connected to the big picture of this production. I can try on a new character role, or even a new play. There is limitless potential for how this can play out, and since it's improv, I can do whatever I'd like with this role, even if she keeps playing out the same script. I'm going to learn what the loving medicine woman character feels like... I'll try on those vibrations rather than the victimized child that I'm acting out right now. I'll import those future vibrations, and act out those emotions to see how that feels. All the while, staying in my Heart, feet on the earth, connected to the Divine as the Source of my love.*

Bliss body connection makes us more resilient to the interference energy that may storm through every layer of our body. The key is maintaining the connection to the Heart throughout our days, through the tough experiences, while a trauma packet is activated or a pain body is running its course. Otherwise, we get swept into the play, into the storm, and lose awareness of who we are, that we are safe and loved, and that we are extraordinary beings.

Love and abundance are our birthright. The more consistently we maintain this connection, the more we build a muscle memory to reside here. Life becomes more consistently joyful, peaceful, and beautiful. The Heart starts dictating how we feel in the presence of a trauma packet activated into a pain body. The pain body feels like noise rather than death, because the peace within is stable and grounding in the presence of the storm.

As we anchor to the Heart of who we are, our Divine nature, we can hold the resonance of our soul in every present moment. In doing so, we hold resonance with Divine Source energy and our soul can take residence in the body, deeply anchored in our sacred temple, the physical body.

Notes for Healing the Bliss Layer

The bliss body already exists within, so the work is to remove the distortions that block access to this part of self. To open access to the bliss body layer:

1. Through the Inner Alignment Soul Retrieval Process, access the trauma packet soul fragmentation to bring back the parts of self that have been separated or *lost* along the way. Reconnect these fragmented parts with the greater soul self so that wholeness is restored. Ensure that the connection with the Divine is anchored into every layer of the body.

2. Create a lifestyle that supports soul residence by reducing activities that create imbalance on the other layers of the body (e.g., alcohol or marijuana, self-judgment, fear response, or emotional imbalances such as chronic depression or anxiety).

3. Develop a daily spiritual practice that ensures soul embodiment and soul residence, and opens the flow of Divine Love, Power, and Wisdom into each moment of the day.

4. Gather data on the presence and assistance from Divine Source to build the belief systems and auto-associated patterns with the body to *look up* to the Divine for support, rather than looking outward to others.

5. Build an internal signal for when interference energy appears, to stay anchored in the Heart and avoid interference cloud distortions.

Section 2:

Pathway to Healing

Chapter 10:
Healing Trauma Packets

If the soul, or bliss vibration, is always there, how can we feel so completely disconnected from ourselves, from others, from soul, from Divine Source? How have we lost connection to what feels good?

These questions once plagued me. All the advice to attain bliss and happiness seemed so out of reach to most people. *Simply live in the present moment. Just surrender and let go. Practice gratitude so you can live there. Attain Samadhi. Transcend the ego.* Great concepts, but how do normal people do this? As we look around the world, there is so much suffering. Why? How does this incessant suffering happen? What can we do about it?

My exploration of this started quite young, since I had bulimia from 13 to 15 years old and was living on my own by 16. Having been on my personal growth path for over 30 years now, steeped in my spiritual path for much of that time, my personal healing process has been cobbled together over many years. Bits and pieces of me coming back on board with each tool I gathered and stored in my toolbox. Therapy helped me understand myself. Yoga connected me to my body. Ayurveda taught me how to restore balance. Profound soul retrieval brought me back to myself. Years and years of inner work stoked the fire of desire to be whole. It was a long and sometimes arduous path.

When I was 29 and simply couldn't bring myself to continue my soul-less professional work as a management consultant at the International Monetary Fund, I went searching for more formal training to help others, but nothing really provided answers for restoring the self back to wholeness: psychology degree, yoga teacher, meditation teacher, Ayurvedic Wellness Counselor, Shamanic practitioner. The yogic system made sense of the world, and teaching it inspired people and connected them to themselves, but nothing gave me the tools to help someone fully move out of depression to peace and joy. I craved the ability to bring people into their bliss and keep them there. I knew it was possible, even if the *how* didn't seem easily accessible.

I enjoyed helping people set goals and use the law of attraction to attain the goals, but sure enough, after some time, they would find themselves struggling and falling into the same old patterns. One day, when I was mid-session, I asked the Divine to show me how to help the person stop repeating the same pattern in his relationship. Next thing I knew, I was working in (what I later coined as) his trauma packet. Each time I would access this realm with this client, we would do work on the issue of the past and he would feel lighter and more joyful. I found that he wouldn't repeat the patterns in the same unconscious way.

It was through these early experiences of law of attraction goal-setting sessions that I started exploring the fear underneath the goals. I would do this deep inner process with everyone who sought help from me. Each time, I learned more about what could be shifted within a trauma packet to bring that person to a better vibrational space. I kept asking the Divine for guidance, and the process kept expanding. I noticed that the more skillful I became in shifting the trauma packet, the more profound and lasting the healing became.

In time, I could identify a ripe, present-moment issue in a client, trace it through the body, access the trauma packet, do some work in the situation, and retest the original trigger. Upon retest, I'd find that the reactivity was gone and the person could not access the same emotional response to the issue they had just an hour prior. Helping people overcome a lifetime of old stories and patterns was like witnessing a miracle each time.

Yet, over the weeks, I would notice that the person would re-habituate back to the old patterns, simply out of habit. The emotional charge was gone but they would revert to acting in old ways. I recognized that the trauma packet healing *held* for some time, but that they would eventually recreate the old issues if left to their own patterns, back to the way their brain and body had been wired.

Creating new habits was tricky, especially for those who had spent their life in the same fear response. No matter which one—fight, flight, freeze, or fawn—the response was deeply ingrained into their behavior. The pathway would trigger automatically if the person wasn't anchored in the awareness body. It made sense... it's hard to think outside the box you've been trapped in your whole life.

For the soul to stay deeply tethered in the body, we needed to anchor the vibrations that resonated with the soul. For example, if someone became deeply connected to their soul, and then their lifestyle led them to disconnection-based choices—eating poorly, getting high or drunk to escape emotions, engaging in relationship trauma patterns—then it became really hard for them to maintain that soul connection. The noise of the digestive system, nervous system, turbulent emotions, and incessant thoughts were louder than the subtle hum of peace within. This meant that soul-based living, through the rewiring of life habits, thoughts, emotions, and choices, needed to be anchored into the person's lifestyle to help them maintain the bliss body connection. Living in soul resonance created *soul residence*, full embodiment of the soul in daily life.

In observing that automatic neural wiring of the brain—auto-associated thought, emotions, and behaviors—I leaned on neuroscience to help anchor in the new soul-based wiring. Thanks to Joe Dispenza's work, these concepts were more accessible at the time I was searching.

Once there was evidence of clients' neural programming reverting back to the old patterns, I developed systems to create and rewire the new pathways needed to sustain new behaviors. I found that the rewiring needed to be established and implemented comprehensively so that healing could be addressed on all layers of the body, creating a similar vibration in daily life that now existed in the healed trauma packet. I found that if clients maintained the vibration developed in the healing session, every day at every single layer of the body, for at least two months—the time it takes for new neural pathways, new body chemistry, and new neurotransmitter receptors to form—they could literally rewire themselves to hold the newly healed vibrations more permanently. We did rewiring through deep one-on-one work for that period of two months, each day identifying as many old thoughts, emotions, and behaviors as we could and transforming them in real-time. It was labor-intensive but extremely successful, and consistently repeatable in the results despite the difference in cases and issues.

After graduation, clients would mention that the part of the program that facilitated their success was the loving and sacred space that we held for them. A healing team of authentic women who actively practiced everything that was being taught—soul retrieval and rewiring—and modeled it through every interaction. A team of people who connected to their bliss body every single day before interacting with anyone, where bliss body became the basis of their relationships. A team that loved each other and had an expansive ability to love every client who came in. It was as if, through working so closely with a healing team who lived in their Hearts, the clients learned through Heart resonance how to hold that vibration for themselves. The Heart connection was earned with each client through trust and authenticity, by walking the talk and modeling our very real path. It was earned by being available to them in real-time when they were struggling in reactivity. It was earned by seeing them as the Divine would see them, so they could feel seen consistently through the reflection of their soul.

In providing this to them, we found that we were healing old, wounded social structures that had been established while they were growing up with distortion in their family relationships. We were teaching them how to love themselves, how to treat themselves when they struggled. They were learning how to ask for help and how to receive the help when it was offered generously. We were re-parenting them and teaching them how to parent themselves.

Instead of becoming dependent on us to shine their goodness back to them, they learned how to build that within themselves. They became self-sustaining in their inner work, which reduced their fear of doing it on their own after graduation. The rewiring support that we initially provided was internalized and ultimately wired into their daily lives.

We've always heard that *God is Love* and *Love Heals Everything*. Well, this was sacred love in action, and it was the aloe on the wound of their childhood trauma.

In the following chapters, I will describe each aspect of the healing process we use to heal anxiety and depression resulting from childhood trauma, including:

- Inner Alignment Soul Retrieval to heal the layers of the body in the trauma packets;

- Rewiring each layer of the body to sustain the feeling of healing; and the

- Sacred container of love to hold this vibration.

Chapter 11:
Inner Alignment Soul Retrieval

The key to healing is to work with the trauma vibrations stored in the trauma packet across the matrix of the human experience to bring alignment back to bliss body vibration. This addresses **every layer** of the body (mental, emotional, energetic, physical, awareness) through each of the **dimensions of consciousness** (deep body vibrations, physical realm, collective ego consciousness, Heart consciousness), within the different **chakras** and **dosha** imbalances. This is not a simple approach to healing, but if done systematically, it releases lifelong, deeply held issues that often seem impossible to address.

The Inner Alignment Soul Retrieval process heals the root of trauma because it helps your child self, which is trapped and replaying old patterns, to connect with your current adult self to heal the separation that was established often decades prior. Doing so resolves the child self's issues, so you can reconnect with your adult self in the present moment in a more integrated way. Once this happens, you don't have to stay fragmented, with a part of you trying to prove your worth or get that love. You can relax, feel valuable, and be one with who you are now.

The fragmented self can re-merge with who they are in the present to claim their power, strength, and truth (or whatever was missing) in this moment, rather than spinning in old traumatic events. We can stop the replay once and for all, interrupting the negative feedback loop so that the emotional and mental noise (*I don't matter. I'll never be loved.*) can settle … so you can feel the subtle hum of your bliss body, through a sense of peace, freedom, love, strength, or whatever soul quality was missing.

Accessing and Healing Trauma Packets

To examine trauma packets further, we will go back to the visualization of the dimensions of consciousness. Let's look at Susan's trauma packet to demonstrate the dimensions.

Trauma Packets in the Dimensions of Consciousness

9th Dimension—Black Hole
8th Dimension—Divine Manifestation
7th Dimension—Light Frequency
6th Dimension—Sacred Geometry
5th Dimension—HEART/CHRIST CONSCIOUSNESS

Divine Source

4th Dimension—Collective / DUALITY CONSCIOUSNESS
3rd Dimension—Physical; PHYSICAL BODY

Issue with Husband

2nd Dimension—Microorganisms; Earth Crust; TRAUMA
1st Dimension—Iron Crystal Core of the Earth

Trauma Packet

Susan's trauma packet lives in the lower dimensions of consciousness (first and second dimensions). This is an old experience of her dad yelling at Susan for doing things wrong, and Susan not feeling loved by him. In this space, *doing things right* meant she was loved, and *doing things wrong* (i.e., in a way that displeases him) meant she was unloved. These bad and wrong vibrations reverberate through her on a daily basis. As an adult, she doesn't think about her dad, or that time she felt the depth of this trauma. In the present, when she feels her husband is upset with her, the old trauma packet gets loud. If he doesn't seem to like how she prepared dinner, or if she didn't do the task he requested, she becomes afraid of getting in trouble and not being loved. Her rational mind knows this is silly, that her husband loves her even if he gets annoyed in daily life, but her fawn response is strong. She is habitually doing for him so she can get love. While she may have analyzed her dad issue in therapy over the years, in the moment, the lack of love truly feels like it's about her husband and her survival in this marriage.

Accessing Trauma Packets

Current life triggers serve as the fourth-dimension portal into the trauma packet and are important signals to where the traumas live. Without them, we wouldn't be able to access the second dimension, inside the trauma packet. They're the alert, or flag, that's posted at the surface. While most of us rail against these flags, thinking *they* are the issue, it's important to see them as the portal to healing. If we know that most issues aren't even about the present moment, then we won't take them so seriously while they're happening. We can note them as the signal they are and see them pointing toward the deeper inner issue.

In order to follow the tether from the current life trigger (fourth dimension), to the trauma packet that lives in a very different space within us (second dimension), we must follow the physical body vibrations down into the cave (third dimension). The body serves as the bridge from the current issue to the trauma packet. If the physical body sensation is kept out of the equation for healing, the root cause of the current issue cannot be accessed. Without getting to the trauma packet that causes the sensations, we wind up circling the issue rather than addressing it. (This is why other modalities miss the mark. They stay in the fourth dimension, batting the issue through the ego-mind's desire to figure out how to make changes in the outer world. For example, increasing communication with your spouse on love languages so that you can feel less lonely, versus healing your eight-year-old fragmented self who felt abandoned by your dad.)

Typically, the relevant trauma packet under the body vibrations is not the specific memory that the mind would think. For example, the mental body might analyze that Vera's struggle originated when she was sexually abused by her mom's boyfriend. However, when we traced down to the trauma packet, the louder vibrations and most difficult part of that experience occurred when her mother *swept it under the rug*. For many, it's not the sexual abuse that creates the most noise, it's the betrayal of the caregiver who didn't provide love and safety or wasn't willing to advocate. This is why the mental body is ineffective in this deep work. What the mind *thinks* is living under the emotional reactions (after years of psychoanalysis) is not usually accurate. Accuracy comes from the vibrations in the body, which give very precise data to access the trauma packet.

Feeling the body is the *first* step toward healing. While other modalities understand this link between emotions and the body, the value usually stops there. There is an understanding that *feeling is healing*, but that's often a confusion in practice. Feeling the sensations somatically brings us back into the present moment in our bodies, which is good because that's the only place where life is happening. Often, however, people feel the trauma packet vibrations, re-activate the fear-based pain body, and are re-traumatized because they can't stop the old vibrations. If we go back to the metaphor of the trauma packets being a fire in the basement of the house, feeling the sensations somatically allows us to be present to the fire and the smoke within. Without the skills to put out the fire, however, people can get trapped in the basement with the fire, and inadvertently fan the flames through their fear and resistance. This creates further frustration, and a deep sense of feeling broken.

Staying in a trauma packet long enough to do what needs to be done is challenging for most clients. This is often a completely new space to explore within them. Connecting to an old experience while simultaneously being connected to the present moment is complex. Because most people on their healing path are so conditioned to analyze their issues with their mind (fourth dimension), they often slip back into the mental body, which is counterproductive. Redirecting from the fourth dimension back into the second dimension is like a delicate dance, gently flowing through productive trauma packet excavation without activating the mind.

The healer (a misnomer because we are not the ones actually doing the healing) leads the client into the space of the trauma packet very carefully. This is done by activating the client's inner journeying skills so they can first feel the body, and then see, hear, or feel the old situation that has lived in the trauma packet. This does not happen from the upper dimensions (fifth through ninth), nor is it a meditation or visualization process. The body reverberations open up the portal to the old situation, and then we shine a light on the situation to be *in* the old, frozen experience in the present moment. Sometimes the client hears a person's voice or words, and other times, they enter back into a visual scene. Either way, it's usually like a flat snapshot that takes form the deeper into the experience we go. It's not made up, or conjured from the mind's memory. It's simply an experience that arises directly from the body vibrations. At this point, present-moment consciousness is active, and the past consciousness is becoming awake and alive again. To me, it feels like the situation is frozen in time, and by shining the light of both of our awareness bodies (healer and client), we can enter back into the space that continues to reverberate such pain.

Accessing a trauma packet, simply entering into it, is a very sacred process. Sometimes, without even doing work within the experience, simply showing up as the observer of the scene can create a deep peace within that trauma packet. The healer and client awareness melts some of the pain by providing loving attention to the younger self in a way they haven't felt before. While one might think that re-entering into that space could re-traumatize someone, it's actually the opposite. The traumatization was created from the fear and separation that occurred when a child's need wasn't met or heard. Entering into the space of the old trauma actually creates a deep sense of relief because it reaches the space where the pain lives. It is incredibly healing for that younger self's pain to be witnessed with deep sacred presence, like they've been abandoned in that dark place for decades, and someone has finally shown up to help.

Anatomy of a Trauma Packet

Once we enter into the trauma packet, a certain amount of exploration is required at each layer of the body. This exploration is done with guidance and grace to keep the client in the second dimension, within the time and space of the trauma, so that the old dynamics and situational physics can be appropriately reconciled and mended.

Just as a scientist wants to avoid biasing the research data, the healer needs to stay a neutral observer in the trauma packet. It is extremely complex to lead a client through the dark cave and simultaneously blend in as a witness of the experience.

The healer is present to help establish an understanding, the what-is of the past experience, exploring the layers within the trauma packet. For example:

- At the physical layer of the body, what does the scene look like? How old is she here? Where is she? Who's there? What's happening? The healer asks questions from a space of curiosity to build the picture.

- From the emotional perspective, the healer establishes what is happening emotionally. How does she feel? What are others' feelings that are spilling into her space? Does she feel safe, loved, supported, connected, empowered, speaking her truth, connected to her Heart? And if not, what's affecting her?

- From the mental perspective, what are her thoughts about this? Is it what she wants? Is she overwhelmed? Does she think she should have more or less of something (safety, love, connection, truth, support)? Does she understand the big picture of what's happening? Is she confused? What is concerning her?

- At the spiritual awareness layer, does she feel supported and connected to herself, and to Divine Source? Or abandoned and alone?

From the bliss body, we know that if there's a trauma packet, she is disconnected from her Heart and bliss vibrations, which is why we're there in the first place. The healer will always work with the younger self until these bliss body vibrations are authentically and profoundly reestablished.

Again, the act of being with the client in this deep, dark, unexplored space is a sacred activity. The client doesn't usually feel re-traumatized in the space, and if they do tap into those old sensations, we are able to transition the vibrations very quickly to resolution. The fourth-dimensional mind is completely inactive, so it's not generating fear or resistance, and therefore not triggering the third-dimensional nervous system and auto-associated patterns that usually occur. We are simply in a slow, deep, second-dimensional space. It's a witnessing and re-experiencing of the past from a place of power, love, and wisdom, like we're taking a tour of our old family home, with all the players and situations, but without the fear and trauma vibrations. Fear cannot exist in the safety provided by the empowered adult self, accompanied by the trusted healer's presence.

Healing Trauma Packets in Soul Retrieval

The client's soul must heal many aspects at each layer to restore the trauma packet to wholeness in that situation. This process is led by the client's soul and intuition. Soul knows where to go, how to get there, what to do, and when it's done. Since a part of itself has been tied up in the past, tethered by the negative vibrations, the soul has a very clear perspective about what work needs to be completed. The soul knows how to heal itself.

The healer engages the soul to start guiding the resolution process. The healer has entered as a fellow explorer in the cave, shining the flashlight into the unexplored crevices. Once the client's soul explores enough, with some prompts from the healer, it can work in the situation to get that fragmented younger self what they need. The healer's role in this is to hold a loving, supportive container and provide questions so the soul can re-establish wholeness. This integration brings every layer of the body back on board, into the sensations of wholeness—physical shifts, mental thoughts and beliefs, new set of emotions to match what the soul did to reconcile the issue. The healer helps to weave a new fabric of the situation as the client's soul does its work. The process brings a neutral vibration into the trauma packet, releasing the old, painful vibrations. The trauma packet work is different for every healing session, as there is no roadmap. The healer walks the journey as the client's soul orchestrates the healing.

When the wholeness is re-established at each layer of the body, the healer can help bridge the transformed awareness of the second and third dimensions (deep vibrational body) with the higher spiritual dimensions (fifth through ninth). The integration of Divine Source energy into the trauma packet brings the bliss body, and therefore the blissful vibrations, into the trauma experience. Through the client's spiritual belief system, the Divine Source is able to penetrate into these lower dimensions, without the interference of the mental body (fourth dimension). For example, an LDS (Mormon) client may spontaneously feel the Heavenly Father wrapping His arms around the child. A yogi may feel Krishna's love, whereas a Christian may have a profound experience with Jesus's presence. An atheist may feel a deep sense of peace in the child self's connection to the earth. The opening to Divine presence is an absolutely critical aspect to facilitating full integration of this work since the client's soul leads the process and craves that spiritual connection.

Once the Divine presence has integrated and the younger self is harmonized back into a safe, loving, worthy space of the Heart, it's time for soul retrieval. The younger self no longer needs to struggle in an old situation. The situation is now reconciled. This younger self can merge back into its adult self, back to wholeness. This creates a sensation, usually in the Heart, that ripples throughout the physical body and feels like they've been put back together, back to wholeness.

The reintegration of the fragmented self through the Inner Alignment Soul Retrieval process feels like a homecoming. Many describe the feeling as coming back into themselves. Feeling whole again. Their Heart coming alive again. Sometimes it's a big sensation, and other times, it's very subtle and peaceful. Just about every time, it feels like witnessing a (re)birth, or a reunion. A miracle.

Once the soul retrieval has integrated, it is time to bring the mental body (fourth dimension) back on board to integrate the healing in the mind. Remember, the second and third dimensions experienced healing in the trauma packet, and then

174

we bridged the spiritual body (higher dimensions, fifth through ninth) into the healed trauma packet. What's left is integrating the fourth dimension, the present-moment mental body and all its thoughts and beliefs. We do this last because we want to keep the mind offline until the end. As the *new* trauma packet beliefs trickle into the mind, the thinking about the current life trigger becomes more expansive and non-reactive.

Each healing and soul retrieval is completely different from the next. This is why an experienced healer is critical to the process, to lead the journey without dictating it. The healer serves as a seasoned guide to help facilitate what is needed, and ensure the trauma packet is fully cleaned up so that this old vibration never shows up in the same way again.

Soul Retrieval Short- and Long-Term Results

Inner Alignment Soul Retrieval aims at attaining results, checking results, and tracking the cumulative results over time. This is why it's done weekly for eight weeks. We can check the efficacy of the issue that was transformed, and we can look at the growth trajectory over time to see if the healings are *holding*.

As discussed, after Inner Alignment Soul Retrieval process, a very blissful sensation ripples throughout the body. It generally feels light, peaceful, free, whole, and grounding. Once we feel certain that the upper dimensions have bridged higher frequencies into the trauma packet in the lower dimensions, we ensure that there has been a shift in the trauma packet thoughts, emotions, and vibrations. From this upper-dimensionally anchored vibration, we can check the original current life trigger to see whether it creates the same reaction, from the old vibration of the trauma packet.

At the end of session, as we replay the original trigger, we have the client try on the current life trigger from the new set of vibrations, through the fourth-dimensional mental body. When the client tries on the issue again, they recapitulate the current situation from the new thoughts, emotions, and vibrations in that corresponding trauma packet. What's typically left post-soul retrieval is a very neutral, what-is response to the situation, with present-moment consciousness and little-to-no emotional charge. In fact, in many situations, there is a deeper, more compassionate understanding of the situation. Often, the client will remember being irritated or sad, but can't conjure up the same emotions or vibrations. This is because the trauma packet can't trigger in the same way again. There are now new thoughts, new understandings, new emotions, and a deeper sense of safety and love (or truth and power), with Divine love as the basis.

These results translate back into day-to-day life beautifully, with less reactivity and an absence of noise. People will identify situations where they would normally react, and feel surprised that they are acting and feeling differently. Issues related to the trauma packet don't activate the fight-or-flight response in the nervous system, and the auto-associated thoughts and emotions don't fire the same anymore. This non-reactivity becomes the new norm so long as rewiring is practiced to anchor the new vibrations into the brain and body.

As you can imagine, after going through this Inner Alignment Soul Retrieval healing process eight times over two months, the root cause of automatic reactivity lessens significantly. The person can move from survival, scarcity, powerless, and unworthiness to a deep sense of wholeness, abundance, power, and worthiness.

Neuroscience of Soul Retrieval

As we work with the younger self in the trauma packet, there is new learning happening. New neural synaptic pathways are formed in the brain with *aha* moments around every corner. In many ways, it's like watching an infant experience something for the very first time. There is awe in the processing as it happens. We witness the client building a whole new inner infrastructure within the brain to comprehend this new way of seeing a situation that had been previously limiting and fearful.

The old, replayed trauma packet had once felt so unwaveringly stuck. However, the new experience in the trauma packet recapitulates, creating an immediate reorganization within the brain. The brain rewires a *new* way to think about the *old* situation. You can witness the old concepts, such as *I was never protected*, shift into a deeply safe space of inner protection. There is a rebuilding of knowledge, understanding, and beliefs in the trauma packet. This learning, and building of new neural pathways, wires more deeply in session because the ego-mind is inactive in the second dimension, like a child taking in the world with trust and very little resistance. The awareness body is actively bridging the person's consciousness to the bliss body in this experience. The bliss body provides a profound understanding that penetrates deep within, without many words attached, just an inner knowing. There are new sensations wired into the energetic and physical bodies, and these layers are also recapitulating to the new understanding and beliefs happening. There are new neural synaptic circuits, and a flood of new neuropeptides and hormones flooding the system... Feelings and sensations that have never been felt before. And when the mental body is brought back online, there is a deep and profound shift in the way the mind re-experiences the current life trigger (and past memory), which gets replayed and wired in as the client reprocesses in the weeks that follow.

Through Inner Alignment Soul Retrieval, all layers of the body are experiencing new vibrational data. A deeply integrated experience that is as impactful as the original trauma itself, because every layer of the body is intensely involved. Since the soul retrieval is as intense as the trauma, it makes a deep imprint on every layer of the body, allowing new ways of being.

Chapter 12:
Rewiring the Six-Layered Body

The positive vibration that occurs during and after soul retrieval penetrates every layer of the body with an intense state of peace and love. This experience imprints and can be as impactful as the original trauma experience. It creates new energetic and neural synaptic pathways, which can be accessed post-session, to allow the client to *ride the wave* of the new vibrations in the weeks that follow. The rewiring process systematically reinforces the new neural circuitry—new breathing patterns, energetics, emotions, beliefs, and awareness—to sustain these Inner Alignment Soul Retrieval experiences in the six layers of the body.

Many people on the healing path attempt this rewiring process prior to soul retrieval. (Daily affirmations of *I am safe* are practiced alongside yoga and breathwork.) However, without planting those vibrations into the second dimension (far away from fourth-dimension mental body, where affirmations are repeated), they usually don't penetrate to translate into daily life. The ego-mind spits out the affirmation, because the vibrational body doesn't agree. The mind practices the affirmation *I am safe* and the ego-mind and vibrational body respond, *Um, hell no! Not a safe bone in my body.* Rewiring prior to soul retrieval is like swimming upstream, so much effort with so few results.

After Inner Alignment Soul Retrieval, the deep positive vibrations are present, planted deep into every layer of the body, so that safety is the loudest and most real experience in the body. From there, rewiring work is simply keeping that momentum going long enough for the brain, nervous system, emotions, energetics, thoughts, and beliefs to grow that seed into a seedling (and eventually into a forest). Each moment of the day, that seed must be watered and tended to in order to prevent the erosion of the mind and emotional pain bodies.

This continuous rewiring work anchors the other five layers to the bliss body. When the thoughts, emotions, mind, energetics, and awareness are consistent with the bliss body, in the vibration of safety and love, then the soul can sustain what we call soul residence. When love is the basis of what you feel, think, express, and vibrate out, then the soul is like, *Oh yeah, I can hang here!* and it does. The soul starts navigating, no longer at the whim of the ego-mind. When the soul is in charge, life begins to flow, synchronicities happen, and the soul manifests with ease and abundant assistance from Divine Universe. The more joy you feel, the more joy comes. The soul momentum creates and manifests more to love. That's when life starts to feel juicy.

Let's take a quick look at how rewiring someone back to the awareness and bliss bodies is done more specifically. These practices need to happen every single day to create the shifts necessary over two months.

Physical and Mental Body Rewiring

After Inner Alignment Soul Retrieval, there is often freedom, peace, love, and inner connection. There is a deep reset back to the bliss body (upper dimensional) space that is anchored into the deep inner being (second-dimensional space), but the brain and body are still literally wired for anxiety and depression. The neural pathways are set up with an unworthiness trajectory, with corresponding hormones and neurotransmitters. The neurotransmitter receptors can only receive anxiety and depression signals. The receptors need to be bombarded with new, happy hormones for at least two months to reorganize so they can fully receive those happy hormones. Consistency in this process will help the client maintain the effects of the soul retrieval.

For example, if we healed the trauma packet of Susan being yelled at by her dad into a place of Divine safety and love, Susan's body will register these positive vibrations and replace the negative ones. Thoughts of unsafe become safe. Emotions of chaos and harm transition to love and calm. Energetics of heavy and tight are now loose and light. Physically, she goes from contracted muscles to more relaxed breath and nervous system. These new sensations will be easily accessed for a few days post-session, until the energetic momentum wears off and the old programming sets back in.

Anchoring the soul retrieval vibrations into the body requires their repetition within the transformed trauma packet, so the new vibrations can be wired into the automatic firing of the brain and nervous system. Instead of reverting back to fear, lack of safety, chaos, harm, heaviness and tightness, and contraction, she will need to reactivate the specific sensations from the healing session. Every time she reengages with the post-session bliss vibrations (safe, love, calm, lightness, relaxed), she builds the neural networks required to maintain that sensation. Throughout her day, she can re-experience the euphoria of the child self, forming new neural pathways in the brain. Corresponding neurotransmitters and hormones will consistently flood the body. The related neurotransmitter receptors don't exist yet within the cell structure, but after some consistent momentum and neurotransmitter flooding, she begins to feel the sensation starting and holding on its own as the receptors restructure to accommodate the bliss chemistry.

Ideally, the soul retrieval re-integration sensations can be replayed, re-thought, re-felt, and re-experienced all day every day in the weeks and months that follow. This way, the experience never leaves. The trauma packet isn't triggering like it used to, so a path opens to make these vibrations more and more auto-associated. Once the new thoughts, emotions, and energetic sensations become auto-associated, she can access them at will. This neural network will begin to fire on its own after about a month of consistent, mindful repetition.

The bliss seeds from the soul retrieval will only grow and thrive if the environment is quickly reconditioned to Heart-based thoughts, emotions, and energies. Otherwise, it's like installing advanced computer software into a typewriter, or putting a fish into a forest. Without the right conditions, those seeds of bliss can't survive and stay sustained. The soul simply can't flourish and live in a space that is filled with numbness, angst, and terror. Therefore, the days and weeks after Inner Alignment Soul Retrieval are vital for the environment to be conditioned for the needs of the soul.

Accessing the Breath Pathway

The mental body shift to awareness body, from ego or subconscious mind to conscious mind, happens through the **connection to breath**. Our breath is an incredibly dynamic aspect of us that very quickly works on every layer of the body.

On the physical layer, the trauma packet's breathing pattern is irregular, shallow, or rapid, and has an immediate effect on activating the nervous system—stimulating the fight-or-flight response (or dorsal vagal freeze response), and activating the autonomic processes of the body into a corresponding pattern. Typically, the heart rate and immune system increases, and stress hormones are released according to the stress response. Digestion slows down. The Animal Brain overcomes the Thinking Brain, creating reactivity to the stimulus for survival.

Because the respiratory system is the only system in the autonomic nervous system that can be both automatic *and* voluntary, the mindful regulation of the breath will impact the other systems of the body immediately via the communication sent back to the brain through the vagus nerve. The breath is most ideally activated in the diaphragm to stimulate the vagus nerve, which brings the ventral vagal branch of the parasympathetic nervous system into action. The conscious diaphragmatic breath can regulate the cardiovascular functions, normalizing heart rate and pressure. It can call off the release of cortisol and other stress hormones, reactivate the digestion, and restart the repairing processes of the body. The breath can switch the brain function from Animal Brain survival mode to Thinking

Brain. With the Thinking Brain active and breathing pattern regulated, more oxygen enters the brain and body, and an increase in heart rate variability creates resilience. This translates to more stability in the nervous system, and therefore homeostasis in the other body systems (endocrine, cardiovascular, digestive, immune, etc.).

Once the breath is regulated, it **bridges us into awareness body**, so we can *feel* the body in the present moment and have a broader perspective of what's going on within. This connection to feeling our body sensations activates conscious mind and gives back our free choice. It gives us the ability to choose a new pathway. A new thought. A new emotional state. A new connection. When we do this, we build the new neural pathways in the brain, and start bombarding the cells with new neurotransmitters so new receptors can be built. We start teaching the brain how to keep Thinking Brain active even when Animal Brain gets triggered in survival mode, all by simply connecting to the breath and the body in the present moment.

From the present-moment connection to the body, we *notice how a thought feels*, and consciously develop a new thought that feels better and more fitting. We notice when our thoughts have spiraled in a negative direction. When this happens, we now have the opportunity, through awareness, to say, *This is an old trauma packet thought that doesn't apply anymore.* Then we can turn the ship into a new direction with new thoughts based on the *now* moment. For example, the thought of *I'm fat* automatically shows up from old wiring when Vera looks in the mirror, and instead of letting it set roots in the mind and gain momentum, she notices it more quickly because it feels bad, and immediately finds places where that's not true (*I am full of beauty – a radiant being*) because those more positive seeds were planted deep in the inner being in the Inner Alignment Soul Retrieval session.

We begin **getting data** that contradicts the fear, which builds new, more expansive beliefs that fit the present moment (rather than the old trauma packet perspective). We begin to realize what's actually happening *now*, rather than overlaying the past on top of the present moment. While the well-worn thought of *I don't bring value* shows up, we notice it feels bad and incongruent to the soul retrieval beliefs that have been wired deeply within.

Then, we can immediately shift back to the more positive thoughts around value that were planted and experienced in the trauma packet, like *My value is inherent*. The mind can start to gather all the data where that old thought is not true, and gather counter-data for these thoughts, like *I can see my value everywhere*. The data collection process helps the mental body build the trust that the new belief is in fact reality. Since fear is often caused by a lack of data, the new data can relieve fear and allow the mental body to feel a sense of knowing.

Building Neutral Mind

From these new thoughts on *How I look* or *Where I see my value in the world*, we can start to build more data to create positive thought momentum, which wires in these thought patterns. We can use gratitude to build a more positive perspective, balancing out the negative thoughts by going about the day in gratitude for how worthiness in life feels. Practicing authentic thoughts and vibrations of gratitude and appreciation conditions the mind to create these neural pathways so they can more automatically run in the background. Again, since the seeds were planted in session, vibrations are already sprouting within to support those thoughts of gratitude.

Depending on the nature of trauma, people are usually slanted toward a negative mind, filled with negative thoughts about themselves or others, or in positive mind, which looks to only see the positive in the situation, ignoring the negative aspects. Either conditioned pattern of thinking is imbalanced. Thinking only negatively ignores all the positivity and beauty. Thinking only positively requires a deletion of the negative aspects of humanity and situations. Either of these imbalanced thinking patterns causes fear, anxiety, or depression, because they are not complete perspectives. Since they are incomplete, they feel full of fear, because again, fear signals missing data.

Ideally, we balance out skewed thinking by developing the thoughts that are absent. For example, if we typically only think negative thoughts, we live a life of negativity, which can create depression. To balance this, we start to notice these negative patterns of thinking and add the positive aspects through a more present-moment view of the situation. For example, if I think *I don't add value*, then I look at my current life and start to take note of all the value that I *do* actually bring. If the thinking is only positive thoughts, then we end up spiritually bypassing important data that's required for making decisions. We see this often when people stay in abusive relationships. (*He's a good guy, but he just loses his temper and throws things at me sometimes.*) In this case, we must build negative thoughts around the situation (*He can be abusive and destructive with me. That's not safe. And I don't like that.*), so that the reality of what-is can be present. This helps to address underlying anxiety or depression patterns that get embedded with the habitual positive thoughts that distort reality and create fear.

Balancing the mind, seeing both the positive and negative, allows us to shift into a neutral space in every situation. We call this balanced thinking **building neutral mind**.

Building neutrality into our thoughts keeps us out of the fear that's induced by mental body duality. Duality thoughts—right versus wrong, good versus bad, worthy versus unworthy—corner us into fragmenting the way we think about self and others. To categorize life this way, into good buckets or bad buckets, results in judgment, and judgment creates a deep sense of separation. *I'm beautiful* or *I'm ugly.* This creates separation from self. *She is nice* or *She is mean.* This creates separation from others. This thinking is not reality from the perspective of the awareness and bliss body. The awareness view of life is more open, without judgment, which allows for more expansive thought. Building a neutral mind—being able to see various aspects of a situation, including good, bad, and otherwise—is what loosens the duality thinking that got wired in from traumas and from being raised by unconscious adults. The reality is that nothing is ever fully good or bad. Most people and situations have both pros and cons, and we can stay connected to that truth without going into fear or separation with ourselves or the other person.

When we can't get to neutral mind because the ego has taken over, and Animal Brain is stuck in survival and reactivity, keeping the mind busy with a more positive activity is the best way to achieve neutrality. We can ground our thoughts by **practicing Sanskrit mantra**, as this occupies the mind, protecting it from wiring in the negative thoughts. Sanskrit mantras also work on the energetic body, activating energies within the chakras to create further balance and protection.

Rewiring Energetics

Each of us has a unique combination of energetics that dictate our experience of life. Understanding these energetics can help us feel less defective, less broken. Learning to work with the imbalances helps us feel empowered to do something about our mental, emotional, energetic, physical, and spiritual states. This allows us to forgive ourselves, take care of ourselves, and eventually, actively love ourselves.

We use the ancient Ayurvedic system to diagnose the imbalances and create self-care rhythms based on what symptoms are present. It is an easy method of self-understanding that helps rewire the way we relate to imbalance in every moment, every season, every situation.

Personally, Ayurveda was significant in building my self-understanding. It was the only system that could explain all the random symptoms for which I had visited many doctors without resolution. It reduced fear around my body by providing reliable data about what was imbalanced.

Energetic Awareness for Self-Understanding

As discussed, we can use this tradition of Ayurvedic Doshas in a simplified way so that people can categorize themselves as air (bird), fire (lion), or earth (bear). As they learn about the go-to emotions of their type, they can see that when they are more balanced on every layer of the body, they have fewer negative thoughts (mental body) and fewer negative emotions (emotional body), feel more connected to themselves (spiritual body), and have more energy (energetic body). A sense of empowerment develops as they learn that their negative expression is simply an imbalance that can be rewired and corrected over time. This awareness releases decades of self-hatred and resentment, which often builds after a lifetime of feeling broken.

Doshas provide an understanding of the positive and negative qualities (shadow) expressed through the ego-personality. When we do **shadow work** with participants, we explore the negative aspects of the doshas that are imbalanced so they can understand why they react a certain way in situations. This frees them from the duality of bad and broken thoughts—*I'm a bad person* or *I'm a failure*—and shifts them into *When my fire is imbalanced, it shows up as rage* or *If I get air imbalanced, I get paranoid thoughts* or *When I get depressed, earth has gotten too heavy within me*. In these cases, people begin to see that they are not their imbalance. Instead of feeling broken, this rewiring allows them to see what element is imbalanced on which layer of the body, and as a result, the steps to regain balance.

Doshas help us to be more realistic about our future potential. When we do **visioning and manifestation** with participants, we can be sure they embrace the qualities of their energetic make-up and inherent qualities, instead of setting goals that are conditioned from childhood. For example, a child who was laid back and gentle as an earth/bear constitution was repeatedly told that they should be a doctor to be successful. (This was a projection from a fiery dad's energetics.) That child went against every truth within his being and strived for the lion/fire goals that his parents set forth for him. Upon achieving that goal, he burned out and felt depressed. As an adult, in setting new goals aligned with his inherent gifts and desires, he could find a direction that's more natural for him. Wiring in acceptance of his natural tendencies is key for him to maintain energetic balance in his life.

Too often, the ego-mind is deciding the *shoulds* and expectations, rather than the inner voice that stems from our inner truths. We must be connected to our emotional body to listen to those inner truths. Those truths make more sense when we understand our energetics. Otherwise, the ego-mind makes our natural tendencies seem bad or wrong. The key is to know the difference between our natural tendencies and our imbalances. This understanding changes how we relate to ourselves.

When we **understand which main chakras are weak or in excess**, we can spend our life focused on creating balance in those spaces, and rewiring ourselves toward greater balance. For example:

- If I have excess energy in my Sacral and Heart (and weakness in my Will and Throat) Chakras, then I may be a bleeding heart, trying to save everyone from their own suffering, giving to others until depletion. So, my work might be to start receiving, opening to my own care, loving myself, replenishing my reserves, and learning to love others outside of giving.

- If I have excess energy in my Will and Throat (and weakness in my Sacral and Heart) Chakras, then I may be bossing people around, trying to control them by dictating what's right/wrong or good/bad about them. So, my work may be to strengthen my ability to connect with others, and learn how to be gentler and more loving with myself so I can be more loving and compassionate with those around me.

- If I have excess energy in my Third Eye and Crown (and weakness in my Root and Sacral) Chakras, I may have lots of ideas, creativity, and spontaneity and great spiritual connection, but my sense of emotional, mental, and spiritual safety may be lacking. So, my work is to strengthen my human relationships and heal the unsafety by learning to ground and find stillness in nature and the present moment.

Understanding where our work is within our doshas and chakras can be a tremendous help in understanding where we get imbalanced. This can lead to profound surrender to what-is, so we can move into self-acceptance and finally feel empowered to create inner balance.

Balancing our doshas will prevent the big emotional storms that can be brought on through life circumstances (e.g., imbalanced lifestyle, life transitions, seasonal changes, menopause, planetary alignments). An imbalanced dosha is like a house on a wobbly foundation. The slightest wind can tip it over (anxiety). Excess heat can create a wildfire within (rage). Too much cold and heavy snow can collapse the structure (depression). Prevention and maintenance are key to creating a solid energetic foundation.

When working these dosha and chakra concepts with clients, we catch the thoughts and judgments, the imbalances and shadow aspects, when they show up throughout the day so we can immediately rewire them while the issues are happening in the moment. This activates the awareness body in a way that keeps the person out of autopilot, auto-associated patterns. As soon as a pattern occurs, we catch it and correct it with the client, so that the patterns can be rewired in real-time.

Empath—Energetic Sensitivity

Many of us on this path are empaths, or energetically sensitive people. We take on others' energies and often can't discern personal vibrations from others' vibrations. *Is this my trauma packet or your thoughts about me that I'm feeling?* While some empaths can discern that they are taking on others' energies, thoughts, or emotions, most don't know how to process the energy out of the body and protect themselves from the sensory overload. An empath might either push through and hang around people and get energetically fried (fight response), bail on social activities out of overwhelm (flight response), or avoid people and isolate (freeze response).

These empathic tendencies actually contain our spiritual gifts, but it's tough to see this in an overstimulating world that doesn't define or value spiritual gifts. Once Inner Alignment Soul Retrieval starts to anchor the participant into a state of safety and peace, the empath gets a taste of the quiet inner connection that they've craved their whole lives. The trick is to wire this in, while simultaneously rewiring their confusion in the external overstimulation and chaos.

Our gifts of open upper chakras and energy fields, can often be distorted when we lack balance, self-care, and understanding. Open upper chakras create significant sensitivity in our senses—taste, smell, sight, touch, hearing, and psychic senses. Because our senses are open, and we don't know how to balance our lifestyle to manage the energetic noise, or decode the messages, we can often feel energetically bombarded by sounds, smells, light, and energies. We label ourselves an empath and then essentially hide from the world because we don't understand how to create balance, attune these spiritual gifts, and use them in a way that serves us and humanity. Avoiding people and groups is not the ultimate goal, so learning to manage our energy field is key to stay fully engaged in life.

Ideally, **empaths learn to mitigate excess energy** depending on where the energy is coming from:

- Other people's thoughts and emotions: Empaths can feel others' negative thoughts or emotions. Without tangible data or internal clarity, they don't know what's theirs and what belongs to others. If left unprotected, this open energy field can let others' energies in, without the empath knowing it happened, which can create chaos and overwhelm on every layer of the body. Learning how to cleanse and protect their energy field is important to rewire the way they interact with others' energies. It's also critical for them to know their own inner truth so that when others' thoughts and vibrations come, they can process them out of their field, confidently knowing what's theirs and what's not.

- Pain bodies: Learning how to create boundaries around others' pain bodies, and manage and diffuse their own pain bodies, can help the empath feel more in control of their own energies. This is essential rewiring that keeps them from merging with others' pain bodies and draining themselves.

- Interference energy: Empaths can feel discarnate beings and other energetic entities in or near their energy field. This energy can create anxiety that shoots straight into the nervous system, often showing up as panic attacks. Helping the empath decipher the origin of this type of energy (e.g., lineage karma programs, energetic parasites, a deceased relative, etc.) and empowering them with the tools to transmute it, helps the person rewire their energetic and spiritual bodies.

Once the empath can adjust their lifestyle to keep their nervous system grounded and energy field clear, they can start to tap into the gifts of their spiritual and energetic sensitivity. They find that they are gifted in connecting to the upper chakras' spiritual wisdom through intuition. The stillness within reveals artistic capabilities, psychic tendencies, healing skills, and other talents.

Rewiring Emotional Layers

As discussed, people are often cross-wired to feel negative emotions such as anxiety and depression as familiar and comfortable (or even just normal), and positive emotion as unfamiliar and uncomfortable. Cross-wiring can be difficult to rewire unless enough Inner Alignment Soul Retrieval has been done to plant bliss body vibrations deep within. Once bliss body vibrations are anchored in the inner being, the person can start to see the difference between vibrations that feel good because they are *familiar* versus those that feel good because they feel like love. That's a critical first step toward rewiring the emotional body—being able to register positive love-based emotions to feel good in the body, and negative fear-based emotions to feel bad—in order to begin the rewiring practice of generating positive emotions, and cultivating a desire to feel better.

Leaning Into Emotions

In childhood, we are told to not feel sad or mad, that our negative emotions have no place in the family. *Stop crying and grow up. Anger is bad.* We get the direct message that what we are feeling is wrong and we shouldn't feel the negative, so we push it down and separate ourselves from these negative emotions. In doing so, we fortify separation from self and abandon our inner truth of how we feel in every moment. The problem is that you cannot stop these emotions, so people may use defense mechanisms such as numbing, distracting, projecting, or suppressing to detach or deflect from their emotions, resulting in depression, anger, and anxiety. Helping someone get comfortable feeling emotions can be a significant rewiring activity, especially for those who have disconnected from their emotional body altogether.

Creating a relationship to the emotional guidance system is critical so that the Heart's communications can be decoded, understood, and acted upon. First, one must know that they are safe in the presence of uncomfortable vibrations and emotions. We've spent life avoiding feeling these emotions, because they are death fears that create very loud sensations deep within. Safety in the presence of these death fear sensations begins with the soul retrieval process, because meeting the death fears in the second dimension makes the experience feel less scary, like familiar territory. Once these old emotions are finally met during soul retrieval, they can be felt and processed in the body. From there, we can develop the deep understanding of the wisdom of negative emotion. While this is introduced through Inner Alignment Soul Retrieval, the person must continue to practice emotional awareness to sustain the ability to listen, feel, decode, and act upon the negative emotions that signal us toward or away from what our Heart desires.

Often, we experience anger paired with violence, and therefore interpret all anger as bad. We shut down the anger in the Will Chakra, which also shuts down the positive aspects of the Will Chakra, so we lose connection to our willpower, fiery truths, boundaries. We cut off our inner power. Instead, we can learn to peel the anger from the violence, and filter our anger (Will Chakra) through our Heart (Heart Chakra) straight to our voice (Throat Chakra), so we can feel and express those strong inner truths in every relationship. This is an 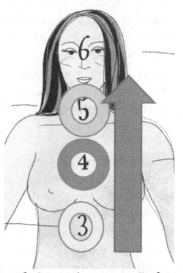 important rewiring practice for those with fawn, freeze, or flight fear responses, or those who have taken on the caretaker role in their relationships.

Rewiring our relationship to anger is a significant part of the healing process. So much of our work is emotional rewiring in helping people discern the underlying truth that anger brings: a deep desire, a strong boundary, an expression that came after the conversation but still needs to be spoken. Clients need the handbook for feeling anger and decoding its message, processing that fire through the Heart, expressing the truths, and acting accordingly.

Too often, the emotional signals are ignored and the messages from the Heart are missed. Sometimes, a negative emotion surfaces because the person's circumstance doesn't align with the soul's desire. Instead of numbing this signal, we can decode it to discern how inner alignment was lost. For example, my marriage starts to feel bad because *I'm the one putting in all the effort* for connection, and I feel resentful. Instead of letting that resentment build up (through a fear response of ignoring, numbing, distracting, etc.), I listen to the resentment to hear what the underlying Heart desire might be *(more connection!)*. Instead of ignoring or fueling the resentment, I listen to the underlying message of my Heart's desire. If my Heart wants more connection, then feeling resentful won't get me closer to connection. From that space, I can do the inner work to help myself feel more connected *with myself*. When I'm more connected to myself, I can attract more connection from others. I can communicate with my husband without expecting him to change. I can release the resistance to him, so that love can fill the space where resentment lived. This type of behavior modification needs to be rewired through daily connection to our emotions.

Learning to decipher whether emotions are the Heart signaling in the present moment to provide inner guidance, or are surfacing from old trauma packets, can be a process of re-learning how to relate to the emotional body.

Most people have a habit of automatically going into resistance to any negative vibration that feels uncomfortable, through numbing (drinking, food, marijuana), distracting 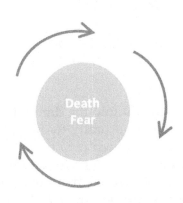 (staying so busy they can't feel), or checking out and disconnecting (scrolling social media). Avoiding feeling seems to be the most common thing to do when someone has negative emotions. When people do face these emotions, they do so in therapy where they talk *about* the fear, rather than spending time feeling and processing it out of them (i.e., looking at it from the attic, rather than putting out the fire in the basement). This keeps the habit of encircling the death fear, rather than moving through it. Talking about the death fear doesn't take you into it, it just keeps you looping around it.

However, after Inner Alignment Soul Retrieval, clients can begin to build a new relationship with their negative emotions. Instead of resisting the death fear vibrations, we lean *into* them. By **leaning into and feeling emotions completely**, we can determine whether this is an old trauma packet that needs to be processed, or if we are living out of alignment with the Heart and the emotions are signaling that something needs to change.

Once someone begins to work through deeply held fear during their Inner Alignment Soul Retrieval session, they can start to connect to their fear-based emotions with more confidence through their breath, moving from ego reactivity (fourth dimension) to body-based breath (third dimension) and into the deep inner body feelings of a death fear (second dimension). This allows people to move past the resistance and discomfort associated with death fears and create new neural circuitry of leaning into and moving through uncomfortable emotions. This helps the Animal Brain coordinate with the Thinking Brain to shift into conscious mind during a survival vibration.

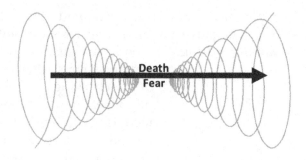

Leaning into the emotion fully, straight into the dimension where the emotions live, provides the opportunity to dissolve the sensation of death fear by moving through it to the other side. Once individuals allow themselves to move into, sit with, and feel the fear through a self-guided process, they develop confidence that they can cope and live through the worst-case scenario that they fear the most, that feels like death. Knowing they can handle the emotion gives them evidence that they can survive the death fear and the fear no longer holds them hostage.

Most of the time, we sense the death fear and avoid going near it. Moving through the death fear is like thinking there's a monster under the bed, and being willing to look under the bed to get the data. To do this, you move into the tightest part of the fear, allowing yourself to feel it so deeply, so it doesn't have a grip over you anymore. Once you sit in it long enough, you can keep moving through it and free yourself. This rewiring process is taught so the client can learn how to process through a death fear on their own.

Mitigating Pain Bodies

Pain bodies have a life and mind of their own that can activate negative emotions, seemingly out of nowhere, and trigger the mind and physical body into a pattern of reactivity. The interesting thing about the pain body is that when it's active it acts cross-wired. Negative thoughts and emotions feel good to the pain body, as it consumes them for its survival. If a person can't feel the difference between who they are as a soul versus the waves of their emotional body, they will think they *are* the pain body. They won't know the difference between the pain body's thoughts and emotions, and the soul's thoughts and emotions. Being merged with an emotional pain body can be not only exhausting and depleting, but incredibly destructive when merged with its thoughts. The problem is that most people don't know a pain body hit them until afterward, so again, awareness is key to rewire someone from automatic enmeshment with an emotional pain body.

The key to pain body prevention is to keep the body in a regulated state, in awareness body, so the base vibration is not conducive to pain body takeover. When the nervous system is calm, thoughts are grounded in neutrality, and the Heart is connected to bliss body, there is no feeding ground for the pain body to take hold and gain negative momentum. If the sensations of the body are still and present, in a place of love, when the pain body emotion starts to stir, it is easily identifiable in the early stages of activation. Like in a silent room, if a quiet murmur starts to sound, you will notice because it was previously silent. Or in the dark, if a light begins to flicker, you notice it because it was previously dark. Same is true when you have sustained a deep sense of awareness on the layers of the

195

body. The pain body is noticed when the emotional waves disturb the still placid waters.

This level of awareness is a little harder in actual implementation because few people stay so connected to their bodies throughout the day to notice when a pain body is lurking. Most people are caught up in the drama of life and fear reactivity, and have a lot of mental and emotional waves throughout the day, so they don't notice when the subtle vibrations of pain body fear start to creep in.

If there is not stillness and inner connection to bliss body, we can still build awareness around the different pain body patterns for early detection, so the negative spiral can be averted to mitigate significant destruction or depletion. If we link the concept of pain body to the Inner Alignment six layers, and to aspects of Cognitive Behavioral Therapy, we can break down our pain bodies, notice them more quickly, and learn to mitigate their destructive effects. This is the process we use to build mental body awareness to **break down the anatomy of our most destructive emotional pain bodies**. In Inner Alignment, we build pain body awareness through Reactivity Chain analysis.

Reactivity Chain

Vulnerability   Trigger   Body Vibrations   Fear Response   Thoughts Emotions   RE-actions   Consequences

To determine the stage of pain body, you must identify where you are in the pain body reactivity chain. Stages are:

1. Vulnerability
2. Trigger
3. Body Vibrations
4. Fear Response
5. Thoughts and Emotions
6. Re-actions
7. Consequences

For example, when working toward a deadline, I feel extremely pressured and stressed (*vulnerability*). My boss just came into my office and told me he needs a random project done before the end of the day, even though he knows I have another deadline (*trigger*). I feel immediate burning in my upper belly and fluttering in my chest (*body vibrations*). I start to feel like I'm going to explode (*fight fear response*). Then I ruminate on thoughts about how much I hate my boss as I feel angry and tell myself I'm not appreciated at this job (*thoughts and emotions*). I tell my boss he's inconsiderate for throwing this on me when I have a deadline at the end of the week (*re-action*). He takes me off the big project and now I can't qualify for a promotion (*consequence*).

1. Vulnerabilities

We all have underlying vulnerabilities that make us more susceptible to pain bodies, and these vulnerabilities could show up on any layer of the body. When the vulnerability is present, it is easier to slip straight into a pain body attack. A person's vulnerabilities are typically based on what's imbalanced in their energetic body (dosha or chakras).

On the physical layer, these vulnerabilities can vary, and include lack of sleep, drinking alcohol, taking medications, food intake, illnesses, level of employment, relationship status, personal responsibilities (like parenting, or taking care of elder parents). Emotional vulnerabilities can be any negative emotion that sets the scene for more negative emotion. Mentally, negative self-talk (*I'm ugly*), and negative beliefs about a situation (*My in-laws always judge me*), or negative self-thoughts of unworthiness (*I'm always screwing up*). Spiritually, vulnerabilities can be disconnection from Source, lineage karma (e.g., a pattern of divorce in romantic relationships), susceptibility to interference energy, or a lack of connection to the present moment through the awareness body (numbing or stuck in reactivity).

Energetically, we could look at vulnerability pre-dispositions from the dosha imbalance. For example, air constitution can become severely ungrounded from a lack of sleep, or restless from constipation. Fire constitution can be vulnerable if they are too hungry (hangry!) or experience obstacles when working toward getting a result. Earth constitution can be vulnerable during times of change, or when they've become too attached to a person.

Energetic vulnerability predispositions based on imbalanced chakras could be another variable. For example, an imbalanced Root Chakra may predispose you to reactivity around money scarcity, or lack of physical or emotional safety. Sacral chakra imbalances can be vulnerable to over-attachment to others for self-connection. Will Chakra imbalance vulnerabilities could be too much doing, feelings of powerlessness, or an unsatiated need for control. Heart Chakra imbalance vulnerabilities could be oversensitivity, caring too much, or lacking compassion. Throat Chakra imbalance vulnerabilities could be feeling unseen, unheard, or like one doesn't matter. Third Eye Chakra imbalance vulnerabilities could be an inability to see beyond a current situation (feeling stuck) or having many visionary ideas without the ability to implement. Crown Chakra vulnerabilities would be a deep feeling of disconnection from Source.

Whether the vulnerability is due to energetic (chakra or dosha) imbalance, physical imbalance, thoughts, or emotional death fears, the vulnerability sets the stage for pain body attack and reactivity.

2. Trigger

If we ignore the breeding ground created by the vulnerability, triggers result in reactivity. A trigger can be benign or serious, and can come from within (a thought, *I'm ugly*) or externally (someone else's judgment). Because of the ripe ground of vulnerability, a trigger starts the fall of the emotional dominos. If I'm tired from taking care of kids in the middle of the night (vulnerability), then all it takes is for someone to ask for *one more thing* (trigger). Or if I'm feeling unloved and sad (vulnerability) and a friend cancels plans on me (trigger), I can spiral into reactivity. If my air is imbalanced and I'm ungrounded (vulnerability) and spend the day at a party having small talk (trigger), I can be ripe for spiraling.

3. Body Vibrations

After a trigger, we experience specific body sensations associated with different pain bodies. These live deep within the trauma packets with death fear vibrations. Becoming aware of the sensations, can be a cue for reactivity associated with specific triggers. Body vibrations occur where the energetic and physical bodies intersect, and usually correspond with the chakra involved—for example, a sharp pressure in the upper belly (correlating to Will Chakra control issues) or a lump in the throat (Throat Chakra issues around not being able to speak my truth).

4. Fear Response

These body vibrations create a knee-jerk, automatic fear response. Either we want to *fight* with someone, take *flight* and remove ourselves from the situation, *freeze* by doing nothing, or *fawn* to manage the other person so we can feel safe. Each pain body can create a different fear response, but we typically have just one or two ways we respond when we are in reactivity. The response is based in fear, and the Animal Brain dictates the best response for survival. Recognizing our go-to fear response can be another indicator that we are in reactivity. If we catch it before the thoughts and emotions kick in, we can mitigate the consequences of reactivity.

5. Thoughts and Emotions

After the vulnerability, trigger, body sensations, and fear response come the thoughts and emotions. By the time we have negative thoughts and emotions, we are so far down the rabbit hole of reactivity that the momentum is difficult to stop. If we allow the thoughts and emotions of the pain body to feed on the situation, the reactivity steamrolls forward.

6. Re-actions

Instead of proactively and mindfully thinking and acting in the situation, we act as a result of all the dominos that have already fallen. Our reactions are how we respond in the outer world, due to the inner action of the vibrations, thoughts, and emotions. Ideally, we bring awareness to the reactivity chain prior to reacting so that we can rewire the automatic pattern of the pain body response and minimize negative consequences.

7. Consequences

There are always negative consequences to spiraling into pain body reactivity. Sometimes, the consequences are immediate reactivity patterns from others. Sometimes, it's the depletion we feel after being pummeled by the pain body. Other times, we deal with the accumulated effects based in law of attraction, i.e., if we spin out in resistance and reactivity, we get more situations where we resist and react. Nothing good usually comes from pain body reactivity, as it generally blocks our soul's deepest desires.

As we build awareness around our reactivity, we begin to see the patterns: common vulnerabilities, typical triggers, similar body vibrations. This awareness allows us to stop the reactivity earlier in the chain. Each time we slow down to observe, awareness body can activate sooner, minimizing the momentum of the reactivity and cutting it off earlier with awareness, so that the level of consequence and destruction is lessened.

To minimize the enmeshment with the pain body, we need to first notice that we are under the influence of a pain body attack. As discussed, most of the time we are so unconscious when we are *possessed* by the pain body that we don't even know that we lost present-moment consciousness. As discussed, staying connected to our awareness body through a daily practice of inner connection, connected to breath and body, allows for daily inspection of thoughts and emotions. It's much easier to notice the waves if we are steadied in a still lake.

Identifying what type of pain bodies show up on a regular basis can be effective in being able to prevent future reactivity. For example, knowing you usually struggle with authority, or that scarcity around money can be an issue. Knowing the conditions under which you tend to spiral into reactivity can be helpful in staying in awareness. Knowing your weak chakra aspects can be a signal to your typical vulnerability and triggers.

Ideally, we **address our vulnerabilities** to avoid the ripe breeding ground for reactivity. For example, if lack of sleep can create a lot of reactivity, then self-care around sleep becomes paramount every day, without exception. Or if you always get into a fight with a spouse after a few glasses of wine, then refraining from drinking may be wise when you're with your spouse. These may seem like common sense, but attachments to staying out with friends for connection, or numbing with wine to feel at ease, can often take precedence over preventing reactivity through self-care.

Knowing our triggers is another way to hold awareness and prevent reactivity. If there is a type of situation, discussion, or person that sets off reactivity, then extra breath, grounding, or centering may be required to stay in awareness body. Extra work may be necessary to reduce vulnerabilities before those types of triggers come up. For example, if I have a strained relationship with my boss, *and* I get tired and overwhelmed at 4pm every day, then I'm going to lay down for 15 minutes before going to my 5pm meeting with my boss, so I'm less angry and reactive. Or during holidays, if I always feel creeped out by my drunk uncle, I might sit on the other side of the dinner table to create space between us.

If we notice a reactivity pattern's fear response, we can begin to **balance the specific fear response** through awareness in the future. For example:

- If someone has a *fight* fear response, where they go straight to yelling at their spouse, then their work may be to implement an immediate freeze response, to create a pause in their chain of reactivity. Or they might create a fawn response to show love and care in the face of interference energy. They might also take flight and get out of the situation before they yell.

- If someone has a fawn response when they feel overworked and taken advantage of by their boss, they might need to develop an immediate fight response, to speak their truth and set boundaries with respectful strength anchored in the Heart.

- If someone has a flight response and wants to leave when they are not sure how to interact in a social group, they might need to develop a freeze response to keep themselves in the social situation so they can develop the skills to interact, or a fight response to fire up some courage to assert themselves.

When working with a deeply wired fear response left over from a trauma packet, we need to pave the pathway for new behavior. Awareness of the pattern is the first step because we need to see it to change it. Creating new patterns takes time and consistency, almost like teaching a person how to walk again.

When we work to rewire someone after Inner Alignment Soul Retrieval, pain body and reactivity chain awareness allows us to rewire new patterns of behavior that match a more grounded, peaceful, and centered way of life. After noticing and stopping pain body reactivity when it is happening, people begin to feel more empowered in day-to-day situations that used to leave them powerless and depleted. As the vibrations in the trauma packet shift and the six layers of the body begin to create new patterns of awareness, these auto-associated patterns begin to change, and new ways of responding in life become possible.

In our work, the end goal is not the absence of reactivity, because that's not realistic. We look at *recovery time*. How quickly can someone notice they are in a reactivity pattern, activate the awareness body, and find a new way through an old behavior pattern? The goal is to make the way back to love as quickly as possible.

Emotional Neutrality

Just as we work to hold neutrality in our thoughts, we also need to keep our emotions in a steady neutrality to keep the lake still.

In Inner Alignment, we call this **steadying the canoe**. Imagine standing on the top of the sides of a canoe. If the canoe tips to the right, toward your negative emotions, you fall into the

lake. If you tip too far to the left, toward your positive emotions, you lose balance and fall into the lake. To rewire the emotional body, we need to stay steady, rather than getting swept up in the negative fear or the positive excitement. (Yes, excitement activates the nervous system and throws off inner balance too!)

Steadying the canoe means that you don't lose your center, no matter what's happening in your external circumstances. Recognizing that the external world—jobs, homes, friends, partners, other relationships—is always changing. If our happiness depended on how the wind blew, or whether others were blowing fire our way, we would feel hopeless and powerless. However, if our center, our inner happiness, was built from a deep inner connection that depended only on us, and our connection to earth, Heart, and Source, then there'd be more steadiness all around.

Anxiety and depression are effects of imbalances on the six layers that often result from being dependent on the external world matching to our desires. This dependency on the outer to create inner happiness is why most people in our society are walking around extremely unhappy. Whether the person is chasing career goals, buying a bigger house, or seeking relationships to create inner satisfaction, they will remain unhappy in life in the long term.

Steadying the canoe doesn't mean you repress your negative emotions or temper your happy emotions. It means that your awareness body alerts you when you have become attached to the outer conditions to create your inner happiness. Once this awareness is wired into your inner process, you can zoom out to unhook from the situation long enough to regain your inner centeredness, through connection to your bliss body. To do this inner steadying, you must be willing to let go of the attachment to the external world to provide you happiness. You must acknowledge that the external world only gives temporary hits of bliss, never sustained, and always fleeting. When the awareness body notices the attachment, the willingness to unplug from the outer circumstances is key to steadying the canoe. Instead, we anchor back into our connection to our Heart for the positive flow.

For example, my husband was working less and we were having more quality time together. I was elated that we were spending time connecting more deeply. (Tipping the canoe with excitement for my attachment!) My emotional body was getting so much out of the connection that I could feel myself losing my inner connection. As I engaged my awareness body, I noticed that I had stopped my morning meditation to gobble up the time with him. I started to notice that I was letting go of connection to myself, to get the connection from him. Once I noticed myself tipping the canoe, I began my self-care practices to maintain my inner connection. The winds would soon be blowing in the direction of him getting busy, and I didn't want to feel resentment and disconnection because I had lost myself in my connection to him.

After a participant has done significant Inner Alignment Soul Retrieval, we are able to help them build this inner connection to the bliss body and be vigilant, through the awareness body, to maintain that connection whether life is giving them what they want or not. Staying steady in the canoe means we don't get swept up in positive or negative emotions because we are anchored in the loving bliss that lives within.

Rewiring the Awareness and Bliss Bodies

Where does happiness come from? WITHIN!

How do we access that? Through the HEART!

The connection to the soul, to Source, to the Divine, or to the state of I AM Presence is accessed through the Heart, specifically through the Sacred Heart within. The Sacred Heart actually exists within each person, and has a Heart Flame (or Soul Flame) that carries the Divine Consciousness to which we all crave connection.

So often, we look to other people to give us this Divine Love, Strength, and Wisdom. We get so lost in our lives without this inner connection, so we look for it externally, and can never seem to keep it when it comes from the external.

The whole point of our work in Inner Alignment is to get the nervous system and energetics settled so there's less noise; get the mental body into a place of possibility, abundance, responsibility, and trust, so it can be steadied to the Heart's desire; get the emotional body to a more peaceful space; and activate the awareness to notice when that steadiness gets lost… so that the participant can sink more deeply into their Heart, and live in the sweet nectar of inner bliss.

The Inner Alignment Soul Retrieval process plants the seeds of this bliss connection. After a session, the participant feels, sometimes for the first time in their life, a deep sense of love and inner connection. All the noise ceases, and for those moments, they are able to get a taste of what the bliss body feels like. From that point forward, they become a true seeker of this vibration. It becomes so clear that *this* sensation is the one they've been searching for outside of themselves. The deep awareness of what's possible gives them the inner drive to sustain this deep peace, love, and connection.

Bliss body is the source of happiness, deep inner joy that has no fear of loss. The external world lines up to create only temporary happiness. Bliss body has unlimited bliss vibrations. The only work is to maintain connection to this part of yourself. Just as you take a shower each day to keep your physical body clean and have meals each day to keep your physical body fed, the same maintenance is necessary to keep the other layers from getting too noisy to feel the bliss body. Our daily rewiring practices help us anchor the bliss connection within ourselves, tapping into this well of bliss each day to keep the mental and emotional waves still, and the bliss connection strong.

We have this bliss connection as children, full of our inner essence and fully connected to the present moment. I think of this often as I think about my children when they were young— pure joy in the present moment, trust in the world and nature around them. This is our default at birth. However, through big T and little t trauma, we slowly lose that connection because the noise and wiring of our trauma packets obscure the presence and bliss.

After Inner Alignment Soul Retrieval, the work is to wire the participant back to bliss body, and to empower them to re-establish this connection if they lose it, so they can sustain these vibrations when they finish soul retrieval work.

Breath Awareness Serves As The Bridge

The awareness body serves as the bridge between the four lower bodies (physical, energetic, mental, emotional) and the bliss body. In the previous sections, note how the activation of awareness is what helps the person come back to what's happening in the present moment so that they can overcome the limiting, fear-based thought, emotion, behavior, energies, and imbalances. Without awareness, we stay merged in the negative thoughts, pain bodies, energetic imbalances, and attachments to the outer world to bring happiness. With awareness, we can bridge ourselves back to our inner world, where our power lives.

As discussed, **connection to breath in the present moment** is the primary tool for quickly and effectively anchoring us back to the *now* at every layer of the body. Breath connection does this by directing all our senses to the sensation of the breath. Diaphragmatic breath calms the nervous system, which settles all the other systems in the body. Breath regulates the pranic life force and allows us to direct it in a way that settles or stimulates us with more high-vibrational energy. By focusing our mind to the present moment on our breath, the mind detaches from the external hamster wheel and reconnects to the Heart within. With that refocus, the emotions take a break from the incessant trauma packet waves and allow us to feel the present moment more deeply. Mindful breath brings presence, which activates our awareness and releases resistance in the present moment. This presence gives us the opportunity to access our Heart.

Entering the Sacred Heart

Once awareness is achieved, one can access the bliss body through the Sacred Heart. Entering into the Sacred Heart is mentioned in many different spiritual traditions. In yoga, the space is called the Hrit Padma Chakra (slightly below the physical heart; in between the heart and spine). This is the space where heaven meets earth within. In Christianity, the devotion to the Sacred Heart is widely practiced, where the Heart of Jesus is viewed as a symbol of *God's boundless and passionate love for mankind*. In Shamanic Seven Directions Ceremony, all six directions—east, south, west, north, above, and below—meet at the seventh direction of the Heart, with the Heart as the hub of the wheel.

In our culture, we refer to the Heart in dynamic ways. We say it is the source of love and truth, *Speak from your heart*, or *Love comes from the heart*, or *He has a big heart*. We talk of the heart as a location, *Home is where the heart is* or *Living in the heart*. We talk about the heart having intelligence and leadership, *Follow your heart* or *Get to the heart of it*. There are many references to the Heart because the Heart is where we access love, and love is what everyone on this planet wants more than anything else, even though they follow their external attachments to try to find it.

Through several traditions, I found the concept of **entering into the Sacred Heart,** which intrigued me and eventually became a core practice. Deep meditation in my Sacred Heart allowed me to access just about anything I needed, or was grasping for, in the outside world.

Arriving in the Sacred Heart feels like *home*. It is a touchpoint back into the Heart of who you are, without the confusions or distortions of who your ego thinks you are. It is *refuge* from the chaos of human thoughts and emotions, of the incessant unworthiness that arises from the subconscious. Many people experience the Sacred Heart as a cave with the Sacred Flame burning, however, each person's Heart space is unique to them.

Entry into the Sacred Heart takes time and practice. You can't enter with false pretenses, egoic desires, or through the mental body. If at first you don't succeed, you can allow the desire to fire up within you until you gain access. Accessing the Sacred Heart is an important pathway to establish the connection to bliss body. This is not a one-and-done process. To maintain bliss body connection, we can commune with the Divine within the Heart as frequently as possible to maintain the connection, and continue wiring the inward search for love, so that the externally focused ego-mind doesn't drive the search for love outside of self. This needs to be rewired and practiced regularly to maintain inner connection.

Within the Sacred Heart, we can:

- Access the Divine in form, such as Ascended Masters within our spiritual belief structure (e.g., Christ, Krishna, Divine Mother/Father), Angels, or Archangels, or simply access the Divine Light;

- Receive healing, inspiration, wisdom, strength, peace, forgiveness, or joy from the Heart space itself or from the Divine;

- Transmute the pain, karma, or blockages through use of the Sacred Heart Flame; and

- Use forgiveness prayers (such as lineage forgiveness or *Ho'oponopono* prayers) to cut karmic cords and release accumulation of karma.

In Inner Alignment, we work with and further **develop each participant's personal spiritual belief system** so they can draw on spiritual assistance. For some, it is important to lean on an Ascended Master (e.g., Buddha, Shiva, Saint Germain, Christ) or Divine Beings that corresponds with their tradition. Working within a spiritual belief system helps to move the beliefs from mental body into every other layer, so this Divine connection becomes more real and tangible, with two-way communication. In the absence of a spiritual belief system, we help build a simple set of beliefs based on the client's Heart connection.

We also introduce the process of **working with the Divine Light** through the Seven Sacred Flames, and more specifically in the form of the threefold Violet Consuming Flame[4], which carries the frequencies of Divine Love, Power, and Wisdom. Violet Flame transmutes interference energy and karma, re-establishes connection to Divine Source, and produces miracles based on the person's connection to the Divine I AM Presence within. Participants become wired to use the Sacred Fire and gather evidence that when they ask for this assistance, it *always* comes. Gathering the data in this way allows the Heart to act with confidence when the ego-mind doubts the efficacy of this approach. The mental body needs data and evidence to make future decisions and allow for new thoughts and beliefs. With data and evidence of Divine assistance, the ego-mind doubt can be more easily overridden by the awareness body in the future. This rewiring is absolutely critical for opening participants to their spiritual power in every single situation in life. The Divine works for the highest good of all involved, so this win-win pattern is important learning for the mental body that lives in win-lose duality.

---

[4] Please note that the Violet Consuming Flame used in Inner Alignment is simple and streamlined (different from what can be found on the internet).

Spiritual work done within the Sacred Heart space can be very profound, wiring in a sense of deep care and love from the Divine. This strengthens the Third Eye and Crown Chakras and wires in the capability to see beyond current life limitations, while also activating the Heart and creating safety and connection in the Root and Sacral Chakra embodiment of these loving vibrations.

Power of Heart Desire and Manifestation

One of the more significant aspects of the awareness body is the connection to soul desires, the activation of these desires within, and the immediate response that happens from the Universe when someone allows the desires to flourish within them. While most people live in fear, practicing the vibration of what they *don't* want, they could live in alignment with their Heart, in the space of love, possibility, and trust... and attract their desires into their life through the universal spiritual law of resonance and law of attraction.

Rewiring someone back to their potential, and the practice of these possibilities in their vibrational body, is critical to shift out of defeat and hopelessness, and into the space of co-creative potential with the Universe. Unfortunately, those with anxiety and depression often don't have awareness of how potent they are or how easily they can change their current vibration to attract new circumstances. Learning how to live from this expansive potential activates the Third Eye and Crown Chakra capacities. This must be done while staying grounded in the reality of cause and effect so the lower chakras, which help implementation and execution of desires, can be balanced with the upper chakras' capacity to dream up what's possible.

To facilitate this, the participant needs to **connect with their Heart's deepest desire**. If this desire is outside of themselves (external relationships), then it's critical to move into the vibration of what it would take to attract the external circumstance. For example, if someone deeply desires a loving partnership because they feel lonely, they won't be able to attract true love from a place of inner disconnection and loneliness. The attachment to a partner to make them happy will create further resistance. They'll have to develop the capacity of loving self first. Once that self-love is established, they let go of needing someone else to love them. With a neutral mind and balanced canoe, the person can practice the vibration of loving self and receiving love, until the Universe moves mountains to respond to that new expansive vibration.

The opening of the Third Eye Chakra allows for the vision to take seed, and the access to Crown Chakra allows Divine assistance. This takes Heart vision, magnetization (or attraction), and Divine assistance.

The **Heart's vision** is emitted into the field as an electrical current from the Third Eye Chakra. This vision of the manifested state of the Heart's desire is practiced as pure potential that creates the mold, template, or infrastructure of the manifested state. If done in a state of lack or wanting, this vision will create more wanting. If done in a state of ego's external attachment, it will create more attachment. However, if done with a deep inner fulfillment, with external conditions as a cherry on top, then the aligned vibration can attract the desire.

The **Heart magnetizes** the conditions to create the manifested state. To generate the best frequency for this magnetization, the emotions, thoughts, and vibrations of the manifested state must be consistently maintained to produce the environment to easefully allow the Divine Universe to fulfill the desire. This is a dance between desire and letting go, trusting and allowing the Universe to work its magic without being attached. Under this, one must have a deep sense of neutrality, gratitude, and acceptance of what-is in the present moment. This frequency allows the Universe to fill the mold or template of the vision with the vibration or Light particles that fulfill the desire.

Leaning on Divine assistance provides a clearing of the fear and resistance that block trust. In our work, we use the Violet Consuming Flame to ensure that the interference and blockages are removed (such as karmic patterns, others' energies, and personal fear in thoughts or emotions).

The shift from fear and limitation to one of possibility and Divine assistance requires data gathering. Rewiring pure potential into thoughts, emotions, and spiritual awareness takes time and data. When you asked for help from Jesus or the Violet Flame, did you get what you desired? If not, where did you lose your vibration? Continuing to gather the data that *when you ask you shall receive* is important to counteract the doubting and skeptical ego-mind. Just because the mind doesn't understand it, and science hasn't yet proved it, doesn't mean that spiritual power doesn't exist. It exists so powerfully once it's built from within, with the correct mental and emotional alignment. This ability to co-create from the Heart is learned and built over time.

These concepts of abundance and manifestation are used toward the soul desire for healing. Inner healing is one of the highest manifestations we can work toward. When we set out to heal, the Divine Universe moves mountains to help us. We can set a vision for what our healing looks and feels like, set the conditions for this vibration to manifest, and work with the Violet Consuming Flame to assist in clearing the way. Once this empowered way of living is rewired into the layers of the body, the person doesn't feel limited by outer circumstances because they have the data that they can change those circumstances, with miracles provided daily.

Linking the Body Layers to the Heart

Many people cannot access the Sacred Heart pathway to the bliss body at first because the other layers of the body are creating too many waves, too much noise, which distorts the subtle vibration and attunement to the bliss body. In this case, we begin to rewire the lower four bodies (physical, energetic, mental, emotional) to the bliss body through a different pathway of the awareness body, which leverages the physical and energetic bodies.

Inner Alignment leans on the eight-limbed yoga system as an ancient tool for inner connection: breathwork, yoga postures, inner ethics and observances, inwardness, conscious focus, meditation on the Heart, and merging with the Divine Consciousness. This is a tried-and-true path for rewiring back to the divinity that lives within.

We have developed a yoga posture sequence called **Meditative Flow** that traces the sacred geometrical patterns of the body, to activate the physical and pranic connection to the Heart. This sequence settles the mind and emotions and cracks open the Heart, so the participant can access bliss more effectively and consistently. This Heart activation gets auto-associated with repetition, and wires directly into each layer of the body. While the physical body makes sacred movement, the breath synchronizes to move the energy through the pattern, which provides a gateway into the Heart. This takes just seven minutes a day and sets the stage for practices that can rewire the other layers of the body.

The Meditative Flow sequence activates the sacred geometrical pattern by tracing the energetic body's Merkabah, activating and pushing energy within the Toroidal Field, and moving the spiritual kundalini energy up the spine to the upper chakras as the midline is traced. The flow grounds the energy to the earth, activates the Heart, and awakens the spiritual connection. As a result of this activation, there is an instantaneous shift into bliss body through the fifth and sixth dimensions.

This full-body shift into bliss body can be at the same time euphoric and peaceful, active and still. With the Inner Alignment Soul Retrieval developing the seeds of this vibration during session, this Meditative Flow can cultivate the connection in the morning, so the work is stay connected to the awareness body throughout the day. Doing this allows a person to observe when the bliss sensation has been disrupted (and at which layer), and make the commitment to restore this vibration as early as possible.

Recovery Time to Bliss Body Connection

As discussed, we are not looking at perfection in staying in bliss body. We look for **recovery time**. How long, after the bliss is disrupted, do you notice and get back to the bliss vibration? We all tip our canoes, sometimes every day (or hour!), but do we stay in the low vibration for minutes, hours, days, months, or years? This recovery time is the most important aspect of the rewiring process.

So often, people will go into guilt, shame, or self-punishment when they haven't been able to stay connected to their Heart, when their shadow self has reared its head. This secondary reaction to the vibrational drop is often what keeps someone *stuck* in a vibration much longer than necessary. If we take the secondary reaction to the fear off the table, and recognize that those patterns keep us in separation from self, we can evaluate whether that self-pointed guilt, shame, anger, or overwhelm is helpful or creates a barrier for recovery.

These secondary reactions usually come from a confusion that we *are* the negative thought, emotion, or action. Instead of seeing ourselves as the fear, it's important to create some space from the source of negativity. Perhaps there are lineage karmic patterns at work here? Perhaps there's an accumulation of energy showing up as a pain body? Perhaps some interference energy is present? Often, when we get caught up in self-blame, we must remember that who or what caused the issue is less relevant than who notices it, what vibrations are triggered within, and how lost in the interference distortions each person got. Recovery back to the awareness in the Heart, back to love, is what matters most. With this, we can move into self-forgiveness and active self-love.

Chapter 13:
Love As the Basis

Everyone on this planet wants love. They may have been cross-wired, or have limitations on how to receive it or give it, or have confusions about what it is, but make no mistake, we all just want to be loved and feel a deep sense of safety in these loving connections.

Current addiction theory says that the root cause of addiction is *lack of safety and connection* in relationships, which stems from childhood experiences. This is consistent with the central theme of attachment theory, which is that primary caregivers who are available and responsive to an infant's needs allow the child to develop a sense of security. The infant or child knows that the caregiver is dependable, which creates a sense of safety for the child to then explore the world.

Many people are walking around without a deep sense of safety and connection in their relationships. Relationships are based in dependency (*I'm not complete without you*), or with love as a currency with conditions (*I will love you if you give me attention*). Real love—deep, consistent love—is elusive to many people, mainly because they are still searching for it outside of themselves.

Getting the Love We Need

Ideally, we get love and safety in childhood, and our parents help us build this within ourselves. With this, we can branch off and sustain this love within our Hearts throughout our life. However, those who never had consistent love in childhood will continue, as adults, looking for someone to provide it for them. And those who received *too much* of that external love and safety (beyond developmentally necessary) will also continue looking for someone to continue providing it for them. Much of humanity is still searching for Mom or Dad's love from the external world, through the behavior of reactivated trauma packets.

In Inner Alignment Soul Retrieval, we meet the need for love within the old trauma packet, where the deficiency originated. Once the need is met, the person is able to create new experiences of receiving and exchanging love in daily life. These new experiences wire in the capacity to experience love in new ways. Some of the most important rewiring occurs in the energetic body, within the chakras. Love is anchored by clearing the Heart Chakra to receive love, the Crown Chakra to open the spicket of love that is ever-flowing from Divine Source, and the Root Chakra to establish the sense of safety within. This is a self-sustained system of getting the love we need from self and Source, whenever it is desired.

Once this self and Source love is established, then we have a basis for building that loving network around ourselves. This external network is an important reflection of the love within ourselves. We must first feel it within in order to fully receive and experience it externally. Most people have the process reversed. *If someone loves me, then I'm lovable*. Instead, the truth is that, *When I feel lovable, I will be able to attract love from those who can resonate with the love I have for myself.*

With that, how does one learn to receive and give love from the space of a deep connection to themselves? Well, it can't come from isolation or disconnection, limping through life broken and alone. If it wasn't taught and wired in childhood, it must be taught and wired during the healing process.

Personally, love and connection were modeled to me by those who received the essentials in childhood:

In high school, my best friend, Jen, was raised in a family that knew how to establish love and connection; they had strong Root, Sacral, and Heart Chakras. She was able to provide that for me during those tough high school years after I was kicked out of my house, by showing up for me in generous ways. She would take me into her Heart and care for me when things were confusing. She would inconvenience herself by convincing her parents to allow me to come over (even though I was living on my own at 16 and threatened their wholesome environment). Later, when I moved away, she sent her brother to come visit me to make sure I was safe. I had never experienced this support before. All the previous love I had experienced had obligation or strings attached, i.e., something I would have to pay for later. Jen's love was unencumbered. I soaked it up and studied it from 16 until now at 46 years old because it was like aloe on my wound. It taught me so much, at a time when I desperately needed it.

In college, another best friend with a solid childhood, Sally, taught me non-judgment and unconditional care. We ran the church programs together and worked collaboratively. We suffered and cried together. We loved and held each other, and built a deep spiritual intimacy with another.

In my marriage, my husband's solid childhood helped to teach me about love. He showed me how to have tough conversations. I could be an idiot but still receive love. He modeled forgiveness, and how to not run when things became hard or confusing. He cared for me when I couldn't care for myself. He held the mirror, without judgment, so I could strive to be more loving, more generous with my love.

Jen, Sally, and Matt were my models of love. They created the physics of love in my mind, through my Heart, in my nervous system. Without their love, and the wisdom and uniqueness of their Hearts, I wouldn't have a clue how to create that in my community or in my children.

When love is a concept, it feels elusive. When love is an experience, it gets woven into every part of our being, and that's when true healing begins. We all must heal through love. When healers have integrated themselves into their own safety, and can tap into their own well of inner love (loving self, and receiving love from Source), they are ready to hold the space for deep healing in others.

Implementing Love in Healing

We've discussed the main aspects of healing childhood trauma in detail—Inner Alignment Soul Retrieval to heal the root cause by working in the trauma packets, and rewiring of the six-layered body to maintain the bliss body connection created in the Inner Alignment Soul Retrieval process. While the processes are critical, healing in this system is only possible if it is conducted in a deeply loving space the entire time.

This love must penetrate every single aspect of human interaction to establish a secure and safe connection one-on-one and in group settings, with regulated nervous systems, and embodying *love in action*.

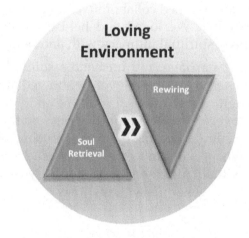

For example, once Susan received love in her abandonment trauma packet, her rewiring needed to be supported by an incredibly loving community, where this reality of love and safety actually existed. If she was trying to rewire herself to *I'm safe* and *I'm loved, and I can screw up, and my failure doesn't mean the death of me in my family,* then her environment needed to support her Heart being the basis for all interactions. She needed a team of warm people who could see her soul even when she couldn't, forgive her if she screwed up, and be messy humans with her.

Most of us are so stuck in old family patterns that we don't know how to maintain conscious and loving relationships, because the ego-mind, which lives on fear (the opposite of love), determines everything. As we heal, loosen the ego, and begin living in the Heart, having a supportive community of the Heart is critical. Not a community where everybody's trying to one-up each other. Not a community where you're getting judged because you say something stupid. Not a community where how you look or present yourself is important. Not a community where your success determines how important you are. We are talking about a community where the soul is paramount, where the soul determines love, and where love is the basis of every interaction. This allows healing to rebuild every layer of the body with safety, worthiness, kindness, love, truth, and beauty.

I learned this through my own healing experience:

> On my personal path, my inner crisis occurred when I was 12 years old. After my parents' divorce, my father became an active alcoholic and drug addict, my mom checked out, and my family claimed bankruptcy. I became bulimic and severely depressed. My battle with bulimia lasted two years, and luckily, I hit a low point at 15 years old, where I ignited the inner will to heal. This was in 1991, when inpatient psychiatric treatment was available (versus outpatient short-term band-aids). I qualified for federal assistance for treatment, even though I wasn't suicidal, and I checked myself into Four Winds Hospital. It took 99 days of treatment for me to stop the addictive behavior of my eating disorder and establish a new normal.

My days at the inpatient psychiatric hospital were filled with people preparing healthy meals, caring mental health workers listening to me and holding groups to talk about feelings, and therapists challenging my belief systems and holding me accountable. It was my very first experience of consistently being held in a caring environment, having someone check in on me before bed and care for me if I was constipated. I grew close with the teachers, who helped me find joy in art and creativity. I felt love for the mental health caretakers who were in charge of watching over me, and essentially lived with us. They shared a personal connection with each of us. I felt close to the therapists who set boundaries. In fact, five years later, the administration allowed me to come back to intern there while in college.

This loving structure put me back together. I feel extremely blessed for the intensive care I received at such a young age, as it literally changed the trajectory of my life. It built the foundation of my work in the world.

Only after this inpatient setting could I receive the love that Jen provided at 16 years old, and Sally at 19 years old, and Matt at 22 years old. Had I not experienced this healing, I probably wouldn't have been stable enough to establish and maintain those relationships.

(Sadly, due to health insurance restrictions, this duration and level of care isn't available for those who can't afford $50,000–$150,000 for recovery treatment. Only the extremely wealthy can access this type of loving structure today.)

Tangible Examples of Love and Connection

Love is a vibration, a frequency, which is often distorted in our world. When we speak of love, we are talking about the purest, non-attached kind of love...Love that is the basis for every interaction. Unfortunately, many people don't know what this would even look like in practice. In fact, many healers and therapists aren't able to hold this for themselves, not to mention for their clients. Since many of the people who participate in my teachings and programs are therapists, yoga and meditation teachers, and healers, we share below what it looks like for a healing team to be capable of holding the container of love and establishing connection.

We must heal much of our own childhood trauma before helping others heal. We can't see their issues if we have the same blind spots. Unresolved issues will increase our vulnerability to merge with the client's fear beliefs. We will attract our family patterns with clients, and this will eventually drain our life force.

It's important to heal our own scarcity, powerlessness, entitlement, and control patterns. We must transform our habits of looking for safety, comfort, love, sex, power, or worthiness outside of self. Otherwise, we create a healing community that mirrors our own unmet issues and needs. Throughout history, we've seen many ashrams, churches, and personal growth movements create distorted organizations because of the leadership's confusion about value exchange, abuse of power, and hierarchy. To be a healer in community, this power needs to come from Source, and be implemented through love. The awareness body must be vigilant about trauma packet-induced distortions that could possibly lurk in the shadows of our personalities, and ultimately destroy sacred relationships.

We must have a regulated nervous system so we can help others regulate. If your nervous is dysregulated, you won't be able to hold the space for a client to regulate theirs.

We must hold the potential of others' souls even when they are projecting their ego's shadow. We can meet them in love (fifth-dimensional consciousness) when they are playing out their mother issues with us. If you can hold the vision of their soul essence in the presence of their shadow trying to provoke you, they will have the potential of shifting into their soul essence, through your courage and willingness to hold it. If you merge with their limitation, and get frustrated or hopeless as well, then you can't hold the infrastructure of their vision with them. This is the difference between empathy and compassion. In empathy, you merge with their low vibration of fear or suffering. In compassion, you hold your connection to your Heart and the vision of their soul, and see them grow into that vision. In compassion, you hold the vision's vibration to cheer them into this space of pure potential. Otherwise, through empathy, your personal suffering resonates with their suffering, and then you both struggle to keep your heads above water.

This empathy drain is one of the biggest barriers for those in the mental health field, many of whom we work with daily. The empathy is draining their pranic body, and their trauma packets are getting triggered with clients, so through empathy, they are swimming upstream each day. Many providers are self-medicating (e.g., overeating, marijuana) and limping through their work with clients. This empathic drain on the mental health field co-creates a system of the wounded helping the wounded, instead of the awakened holding the potential for others to awaken.

We must encourage clients with passionate motivation and inspiration without expectation, frustration, or judgment. As long as a healer's self-esteem and feeling of success are dependent on the client's healing, the relationship is bound in resistance. The healer must practice non-attachment to the results, trusting that if they show up in service while fully connected to their Heart, then the highest good will prevail.

It's so important to celebrate clients' soul qualities instead of reinforcing broken mentality by focusing solely on what's not working. We can balance their negative mind with observation of what's working. If someone comes in feeling broken, focusing solely on the broken aspects reinforces that as reality.

Build independence in the client rather than a dependency on our healing assistance. The longer they feel broken in our presence, the more we fortify their story. Bestow empowerment, rather than repeating the story of disempowerment, which will increase the client's confidence and sense of competency. Challenge clients through love and care, versus enabling the victimization patterns. Remember, the child self in the trauma packet was a victim, but the adult self has free will to change those victimization patterns in the present moment.

We can show up in unexpected ways that demonstrate authentic Heartfelt love. Unfortunately, the mental health front lines have established a sterile relationship full of boundaries to avoid clients' unhealthy attachments. However, love is anything but sterile. Those boundaries can remain in a warm and inclusive environment if built with care. Non-sterile, non-mechanical acts of love allow the person to re-learn what love feels like, how safety in a group feels. This is why our team works as a group with each client. The healing team creates the container, which isn't dependent on just one person loving and caring for the client. The client can experience different ways that love looks (fiery, earthy, or airy love,) and avoid clinging to one of us as *the* person to attach to.

While honoring self-boundaries, we can be responsive so they know we care. Since we work in a team, we always have someone available, night and day, weekdays and weekends. We help them work through challenging emotions or situations, and determine which rewiring practice to use. This level of responsiveness allows a quick shift from negativity into neutrality, so they can maintain the positive wiring they've worked so hard for. Our responsiveness teaches them that when they reach out for help, their needs are worthy of being met. Our response facilitates their empowerment to help themselves during real-time experiences, so they can anchor change into their daily lives with relevant situations. Once they have the capacity to show up for themselves, we remind them that they can do it and cheer them on.

We can reparent our clients so they can feel what it's like to receive the teaching, love, and growth they never received. As we model love with boundaries, boundaries no longer feel like the withholding of love. As you reparent them with love, empower them to learn to self-parent the same way.

Our own mistakes and failures can model that we too lose love and dip into fear. We can demonstrate how to be imperfect, acknowledge our own personal work, and apologize when we mess up. People will learn more from your processed failures than they will from your telling them how to do life. If they see your imperfection, they will get the signal that it's safe and reasonable to make mistakes in relationship.

We can teach them that healing is not about perfection, but recovery time. It's not how many times you fall, or avoiding falling into fear, because that's not realistic. It's about how much time we hang out in that fear—a year, a month, an hour, a minute. How quickly can you move out of fear and back into awareness, in the Heart? When the canoe tips, we can either spend a lot of time in the water, or we can find balance again quickly. This level of resilience and recovery is what allows us to avoid self-sabotage patterns of guilt, shame, self-punishment, or judgment—none of which are valuable if the goal is recovery time.

It's critical for the client to get their own lessons. To facilitate this, we can teach inductively, like a patient parent rooting for them to attain their own understanding themselves. When they do, the understanding is more meaningful and also serves as part of their new foundation of self. Allow them to put understanding together on their own, so they can have the *aha* they need for it to anchor in forever.

Modeling forgiveness is the most profound way to teach it. Show them how deeply you can forgive them, not because you spiritually bypass and ignore the situation, but because you know that there was a soul underneath the ego that made the error.

We can put into practice that only love is real. The rest is a play, a lesson, a game. It's not as serious as it looks. If it doesn't feel good, it's fear. If it feels like love, follow that. The rest is the wayward ego searching for temporary satisfaction through understanding.

Our own understanding of pain bodies and interference energy will allow us to teach our clients how to avoid getting caught up in energetic waves based in illusion. Help them understand that the interference energy is not who they are.

Uphold value. The value of your time. Their time. Money.

As healers, we can hold group sessions in love and safety. By redirecting a client who consistently dumps emotions, we let the group know that this is a no-dumping zone. By teaching them to process emotions before coming to group, we model emotional responsibility. Instead of fortifying co-dependent relationship patterns, we can teach others in the group to send Divine assistance to the rescue of others, not carry others' burdens themselves. We can do spiritual practices and visioning together, and hold space for each other with the Divine consciousness as the center (vs ego and personalities).

My hope is that all healers (e.g., yoga teachers, Reiki practitioners, mental health practitioners) can heal themselves so they can eventually model fifth-dimensional Divine love in every interaction. This is how we shift the consciousness of humanity one person at a time, one interaction at a time.

Chapter 14:
Inner Alignment Healing System

To explain how we facilitate the Inner Alignment process through a profoundly loving environment, allow me to explain the structure within which we deliver this profound work, so I can paint the picture of what the healing container looks and feels like.

Inner Alignment Soul Retrieval Program (Level 1)

There are seven aspects of our intensive Soul Retrieval for Healing Childhood Trauma (Level 1 Inner Alignment) program[5], which involves working with a team of about three healers and coaches over a two-month period. Helping people heal the effects of childhood trauma, and the root cause of anxiety and depression, requires an intensive approach because of the intricacies of rewiring the brain, nervous system, and

---

[5] All levels of Inner Alignment programs are offered virtually, across time zones in the US and internationally.

lower bodies. The neural pathways need to be developed in the brain, the hormones and neurotransmitters must be consistently established, and the neurotransmitter receptors in the cells must shift from fear-based emotion receptors to love-based emotion receptors. Science and our own experience have shown us that this deep rewiring process takes about 40 to 60 days from the point where soul retrieval has started planting these vibrations into the trauma packets. Once momentum has been created— i.e., soul retrieval keeps building deeper peaceful states, and the nervous system, emotions and thoughts can sustain them—a momentum occurs on each layer of the body, and by the end of about two months, enough wiring and momentum has been created for the participant to maintain this on their own.

The first and most important aspect of the work is the **Inner Alignment Soul Retrieval process**[6]. This takes about two hours a week for eight weeks. As discussed, this is where we work in the second dimension of consciousness, deep in the body where the trauma packets have stored the original experiences that tend to reverberate through daily life. We start with that week's current life triggers related to the client's healing goals, trace the trigger into the body, and work with the corresponding old situation that is still unreconciled. We do this work until every layer of the body has been shifted back to bliss body; thoughts are shifted to a place of safety, support, and empowerment; emotions are reconciled and connected to a sense of love, joy, peace, or happiness; energetics feel settled; physical body and nervous system are regulated in the trauma packet; and Divine Source becomes the source of love, warmth, and compassion. Also, within this dimension, the adult consciousness and what is known in mental body is bridged into the child's

---

[6] Inner Alignment Soul Retrieval process differs completely from traditional Shamanic soul retrieval work performed by other practitioners. Very often, people learn about this work and then search the internet for *soul retrieval* to find that other practitioners have a journeying process equivalent to a guided meditation, not an in-depth inner transformation process that works within the trauma packets across dimensions of consciousness.

consciousness, which releases the narrow perspective in the trauma packet. These vibrations settle into the body and vibration, and the original stimulus is rechecked to demonstrate neutrality. If upon recheck, the original vibrations are present, or a new negative sensation is there, we continue peeling the onion until love is restored in the trauma packet and safety is felt in the body.

The other six aspects of the work are focused on the rewiring process:

We have participants watch new **rewiring videos** each week, focused on topics that help to rewire the way they think and experience emotions, and the way they connect to self and Source.

With these weekly videos come new **daily rewiring practices** that they must do to create the habit of rewiring themselves. Each week focuses on different layers of the body, and the rewiring practices build on each other. Each day, clients spend about 20 minutes doing rewiring practices to build new neural circuitry that corresponds to their soul retrieval experience. This creates new auto-associations of positive thoughts, emotions, and vibrations.

Because showing up for self-care is usually difficult for those with anxiety or depression, we provide **daily and weekly Rewiring Coach support**. They meet with their Rewiring Coach every week, and check in with their coach every day to help stay accountable to the rewiring practices necessary for achieving their healing goals. This level of support is necessary to change the well-worn behavioral patterns and neural circuitry.

We hold **weekly Group Debrief Gatherings** to help mirror the participants' work. Typically, by Week 6 in the program, the person turns the corner on their issue and is feeling whole more consistently, so the reflection from the group serves as a profound experience, a benchmark for their work. Since most people have trauma around groups, this is an important step toward learning how to feel safe in a group setting. For them to feel safe, this container needs to be tightly held in upper dimensional space. The healing team is on the video conference, maintaining emotional responsibility and managing energetic pain body spillover that might leak into others' energy field. The key to this is the loving presence of the healing team holding the session.

One of the most important aspects of healing through this intensive format is to rewire the thoughts, emotions, and behaviors in real-time, while the participant is struggling with reactivity. This is the one thing missing from most modalities of healing, and can help turn the direction of the Titanic, when done well. To do this, we have our clients **texting the healing team 24/7.** We want to know how they are feeling, when they hit an issue, so that we can work with them when they are actively in a pain body. Doing so helps them learn how to reach out and ask for help (versus trauma patterns of hyper-independence), as well as how to transmute reactivity chains with awareness and rewiring practices. By the time they graduate, they can hear the whisper of our supportive responses to just about any situation.

The daily texting is where the rubber meets the road, where the auto-associated patterns can be noticed, diverted, and rewired with practice. Every day for two months, we lovingly help them see the vulnerabilities and triggers when their vibration is dipping into fear, and we work their vibrations back to their bliss body. We help them hold the vibrations from Inner Alignment Soul Retrieval sessions, so they can learn new ways of moving through their life. We help them build the new soul retrieval thoughts and actions into the different aspects of life very practically—with a spouse, a boss, or children—situation by situation. We hold the vision of them on the other side of an issue, send high vibrations, cheer them on, and provide real-time help so they can feel supported until they can provide themselves with that same care... this is love in action.

The last part of the program is an optional **couple's session** to ensure that long-term relationships are strengthened by the intensive inner work. Because of the rapid and profound shifts, we want to be sure the participant has the skills to up-level their primary relationship to be able to uphold this newly weaved version of themselves. We find that most of the time, when there is a deeply held love and commitment in the relationship (on both parts), the partner slowly up-levels with the primary participant. Once the participant gets back into their Heart, their partner finally gets the love they've been wanting (sometimes for decades) and the relationship begins to heal. Sometimes, the partner's trauma becomes exposed, which can be addressed in session. Other times, the couple needs to work specific trauma bonds that became ingrained over decades, or find new behaviors to engage with each other.

Instilling the Practice of Conscious Living

As you can see, the healing path can be intense. It must be to maximize the effect of healing trauma packets and quickly rewiring the brain, body, and behavior so that life can integrate the change that's happening. All layers of the body need to integrate at the same time, to create a new fabric of living, a new way of living in the Heart consciously. If done more slowly, over a longer period of time, it feels like ten steps forward and nine steps back because the inner healing occurs, but the person reverts back to the old neural wiring and behaviors. It could feel like chipping away at an iceberg.

In our work, there is a great deal of one-on-one interaction because trauma is so individualized, and group work usually doesn't feel safe enough to work in the deep, dark spaces of the death fear in the trauma packet. Often, group-based trauma work can be retraumatizing, or ineffective in getting people into the depth of pain living in the second dimension of their body consciousness.

Since healing requires deep one-on-one work, the healing team often becomes the model of what it is to live in bliss body. We become the model of awareness and bliss connection. (Otherwise, if we talk about it, but can't create the experience of it, it's just a concept.) Through nurturing ourselves and teaching the participant how to nurture themselves, the person learns what nurturing feels like. They see that it's not a chore or a burden, but something that feels good. They see us taking care of ourselves as we share examples of what practices we use, or how we choose to think about a tough situation. Through kindness and patience with the participant, the person learns that they deserve patience and kindness. They begin to model that toward themselves. They learn that they are worthy of that kindness, and how to set boundaries in their relationships if their values are not being upheld.

Through our authenticity, we model that the path is not perfect. When our ego-mind shows up, we model how we work with those thoughts. When our pain bodies show up, we use the examples from our week to model the path that we're teaching. We share our processed issues—meaning we share the experience once we've restored our vibration back to the Heart—so they can see this path in real-time, applied to real people. This keeps us off the pedestal so they don't believe that there are perfected beings who can live without real human emotions. (This level of sanitization has been a disservice to mental health clients because there is a sense that the healer or therapist is *fixed*. Since I've had the privilege to work with many of the people on the front lines, I can say that many are compartmentalizing their own traumas and getting retriggered in their work.)

When we make mistakes, we reconcile the situation with the other person. We model this as a team, by apologizing to each other and our participants. Admitting mistakes and failures without shame or self-punishment is a rare event in the world. In our work, we freely admit that we mess up all the time, and we demonstrate how OK that really is for everyone involved, if each person claims their responsibility and mends the situation.

Since we honor that the law of attraction and law of resonance is always in effect, we acknowledge that we attract every situation in our lives and help our participants see that responsibility without making it good or bad.

We model what living in neutrality, without good or bad or right or wrong, looks and feels like so it feels attainable.

Most importantly, with the healing team in deep alignment with our bliss body, we can hold the Divine potential for the healing of deep trauma wounds. We have the data that the system works, with repeatable processes in our toolbox, and our inner fire and concentration to hold the participant's vision. In holding this potential, and putting our will and desire behind it, there is a momentum that catapults forward, in a way that's not possible when doing this work solo. The unified vision of the team behind the participant, along with the unwavering trust that the healing will happen, carries the participant forward like they are kayaking down white-water rapids! When their boat flips, we straighten it back up and send it on back its way to the healing destination.

Sustained Healing

What does it mean to be *healed* from childhood trauma? What does long-term healing look like?

Once we've accessed and transformed vibrations within the loudest trauma packets, rewired the layers of the body to sustain the new vibrations, and created the foundation of love within and around someone to the point where they can sustain those vibrations on their own, they are ready for graduation. The foundation has been laid, and they know how their unique inner guidance system signals through emotions and thoughts. They can recognize their familiar reactivity chains and pain bodies. They know what to do in the presence of interference energy. When they get pulled into a low vibration, they can shift back to present moment and ratchet their vibration back up, with quick recovery time. They have new habits and new behaviors grounded in self-connection and self-care. They understand the signals of their layered body and have a desire, as well as the tools, to respond to the signals.

Physically, they notice when their nervous system gets dysregulated and can bring it back into balance. They know how to modify their breathing patterns to work with their heart rate variability to bring the involuntary, automatic systems of the body back into a parasympathetic state. They regularly and proactively move their bodies in ways that activate all layers of the body into Heart or bliss connection.

Energetically, they can clear their energy field, balance their imbalanced doshas, and work on their weakest chakras. They are able to see where the dosha and chakra imbalances are showing up on the layers of the body, and address those layers at the root cause.

Mentally, they can shift from limiting, fear-based thoughts into more balanced, neutral mind. They can transition from thoughts of the past to the present, and into Divine consciousness so the mental body can be a servant of the Heart, rather than the master. They see the ego-mind for what it is: somewhat helpful for caution and safety, but limited in its ability to create Heart expansion.

Emotionally, they can decode the messages from the inner guidance system and work with the lessons and wisdom. They can quickly recover from pain body patterns, and have awareness of the underlying trauma packets within, or interference energy that creates the chaos. They can work with emotional reactivity by developing awareness in every moment. They know how to steady their canoe and build neutrality.

Their awareness body is strong, awake, and regularly cultivated so that it consistently keeps the portal to the bliss body open and alive. It is the barometer for when vibration dips from love to fear, and has the wisdom to get back into the Heart.

Their bliss body is active and felt, and Divine messages and communication are clear. Manifestation from the Heart is fully engaged so that the Divine power within is activated.

They are not enlightened, or superhuman, so life has its storms and they will make mistakes. This keeps the humility in place and allows for continued surrender on the path of lessons that is this human experience.

However, they are no longer lost, stuck, or disconnected. They are no longer depressed or plagued with rage or anxiety. They have moments where emotions or negative thoughts are strong, but they have the wisdom and power within to be able to move through the storms, gaining lessons and evolving their souls.

They are surrounded by a loving community of real people, plugging away on their own paths, willing to lend a hand or provide support when needed. They feel equally privileged to do the same for others. There is no guru that holds more wisdom than their own Heart, only helpers who can ask questions to help them find their own answers.

This is what we call *healed*. Full self-understanding, self-acceptance, self-care, and self-love, and the ability to navigate and move through the circumstances that life presents without getting stuck in old patterns or limitations of fear. With this definition, it is possible for so many to build the inner connection to show up in a profound way for themselves, to release the broken mentality that keeps them stuck in trauma packet vibrations.

The "Will" to Heal

Inner Alignment Level 1 work has the most profound effect when a person has activated the will to heal. There is a certain type of hunger that develops within when someone has done absolutely *everything* they can think of to heal. Typically, our clients are far along their inner healing path and have exhausted the modalities available to them (e.g., 20 years of therapy, psychiatric medications, energy modalities, self-help books, daily yoga). They know they deserve to heal and are searching for the modality to catapult them forward. They see this system as the last stop on the train toward healing.

With this will activated, the Will Chakra has enough fire for the transformative process. Our team uses the client's Will Chakra energy to stoke the fire within, so that that inner power can be channeled toward transmuting the trauma in the trauma packets.

If this fire is not yet ignited, the Inner Alignment work is much less effective. We find this to be the case for people who are still deeply entrenched in addiction behaviors—getting that high from the outside world, through marijuana, alcohol, disordered eating, sex/porn, creating drama, or hoarding. These behaviors become a replacement for soul/Source connection. If the will to stop the addictive behavior has not yet been activated, they have some work to do in breaking the stimulus (trigger)/ response (addictive behavior) pattern. To stop the addictive pattern is an act of pure, fiery will and persistence—a significant achievement toward inner sovereignty, independence, and freedom.

A candidate for this work has tired of numbing, blaming, distracting, and changing the outside world for the temporary band-aid high. They have done their decades of talk therapy and exhausted their ability for self-healing. They are done controlling others, searching for love outside of themselves, and looking for worthiness through their results. They are ready to release that illusion, but don't know how because other modalities have failed to help them make the deep, transformative changes on every layer of the body.

What Other Modalities Lack

This Inner Alignment System stimulates healing because it intensively addresses every layer of the body, across all dimensions of consciousness; gets to the root cause of the issue; sustains the changes through neurosynaptic and behavioral rewiring; and provides a loving container of a healing team and ongoing online spiritual community. Other modalities touch parts of these criteria for healing but fall short of long-term, sustained healing of depression and anxiety.

My personal hope is to see other healers, and systems of personal growth, begin to leverage the wisdom of these three aspects of healing, so that clients can begin the deeper, more sustained healing they are meant to have.

Often people are piecemealing their healing together. They try a soul retrieval session, they go on a yoga retreat, they see a therapist. They get a massage or Reiki every once in a while. They are blindly trying different things that don't really lead them to a comprehensive approach to healing. Piecemealing healing can be a long and expensive road that creates a feeling of *I'll never be able to heal* when the negative vibrations persist.

In the Inner Alignment Soul Retrieval process, there is no need to piecemeal because the system is precise in addressing the specific trauma packets. It is a complete infrastructure that addresses every layer of trauma within. Working the trauma packets precisely allows for very quick healing that builds momentum and charts the course for inevitable future drops in emotional or mental vibration.

The comparison chart on the next page is an example of how other systems are missing major components for healing. It is not a comparison to suggest they don't work at all, or don't have a place in the healing of humanity. Most healing modalities are just incomplete, and incomplete systems can often leave people feeling broken and increasingly hopeless, thinking they will never find relief of their sustained low vibration.

Healing Modalities Comparison Chart

Criteria	Inner Alignment	Talk Therapy	EM DR	Plant Medicine	Yoga	Meditation	Reiki
Heals the **Root Causes** of trauma in trauma packets	✓						
Rewire all six body layers to sustain healing through	✓						
Physical Body: rewire and regulate brain/ nervous system	✓		✓	✓	✓		✓
Mental Body: transform thoughts/beliefs reactivity patterns	✓	✓	✓				
Emotional Body: process trauma packet emotion, pain bodies, or interference energy	✓	✓	✓				
Energetic Body: balances Chakras, doshas	✓				✓		✓
Awareness Body: develops present moment consciousness	✓	✓	✓	✓	✓	✓	
Bliss Body: Soul / Heart connection	✓			✓	✓	✓	✓
Loving Community: sustained authentic interpersonal connection	✓				✓		

Clinical Therapy—Mental Body Approach

The gift of clinical therapy is the consistent space to express thoughts and feelings with a non-judgmental compassionate human to receive it. This self-expression allows for the development of self-awareness depending on the skills (and blind spots) of the therapist, and hopefully an understanding of personal emotional responsibility in life.

Unfortunately, people spend decades in clinical therapy without much change in emotion, thoughts, beliefs, or behaviors. They develop an understanding of the patterns but struggle to overcome them. Yet, the mainstream world says, *If you have an emotional problem, get a therapist.* People continue therapy for 10 or 20 years, repeating the same stories and anchoring the old patterns. Eventually they feel defeated, and more hopeless.

Talk therapy typically accesses the stories of the past or present from the Thinking Brain, but trauma doesn't live in that part of the brain, nor does it heal from there, so all it can do is help people think differently about life. In this way, it helps to rewire the mental body, but the vibrations and emotions often don't clear up, because the pain body doesn't originate from the mind. The trauma packet pain body reactivity continues to replay when vulnerabilities and triggers arise, and the person doesn't feel like they can control the emotions or patterns.

While rewiring the mental body is important, without healing the root of the reactions, a disconnect is built between what is felt in the body versus what *should be* experienced from the rewired mind. The chasm between the present-moment feeling in the body and the rewired thinking creates further disconnection and frustration.

As discussed, therapy sessions are spaced out over weeks or months, so they don't work with the neuroscience of healing through repetition, with synaptic wiring that needs to be done to build new auto-associated experiences on all layers.

The therapist/patient relationship typically has its limitations. So much can get played out with a therapist, so they must create boundaries, but these boundaries usually create such a sanitized environment that the essence of love is lost. Without the inclusion of the therapist's path being modeled, the patient doesn't get the experience of learning through fellow journeys.

Further, while the awareness body and mental body are developed and rewired in therapy, the energetic, physical, and bliss bodies are usually left out of the process. You can't wire someone back to bliss body if you leave part of them out of the healing process. Since therapy operates in the fourth dimension of consciousness, healing doesn't occur in the second dimension, where the issue started, and typically doesn't open the upper dimensions for higher consciousness to bring bliss connection.

While Somatic Therapy allows deeper feeling in the physical body, bliss body and Source are usually left out. Often, little rewiring is done to create sustained change in day-to-day thoughts and emotional patterns. Typically, the client is simply feeling the smoke that is stirred by the fire of trauma in the basement.

Eye Movement Desensitization and Reprocessing (EMDR) therapy works with the physical body's neural synaptic pathways in the brain to process stored trauma that lives in the physical, mental, and emotional bodies. While this can provide some relief from PTSD, it tends to work the surface of the trauma in the mind, emotions, and body, without dissolving the loud trauma vibrations, beliefs, and thoughts that live deep within the body and create repetitive patterns, reverberating in the second-dimensional trauma packets. Unfortunately, this can close the portal down, making it difficult to heal the pain where it originated. We have seen many people come to us with less reactivity but not much joy or love built into their Hearts. Again, leaving out the spiritual connection, and Divine assistance, can leave a client disconnected from soul fragments.

Cognitive Behavioral Therapy will help develop awareness of reactivity, creating understanding in the mental body, which is important for rewiring but doesn't address the root cause.

Plant Medicine and Psychedelics—Physical and Bliss Body

If you've been on your path for a while, you may see the current trend toward going to South America for Shamanic Ayahuasca ceremonies. These journeys can be a euphoric experience (accessing bliss body) or difficult and devastating

239

experience (accessing trauma packets), depending on what shows up in a given experience.

This medicinal approach to treating depression or anxiety works with the physical and mental bodies to (hopefully) access the spiritual layers of the body. It does this by subduing the parts of the brain that are most responsible for the ego-mind, and activating the parts of the brain responsible for spiritual connection. This allows the person to have an experience beyond the physical and mental body, beyond the limitations of the brain and thinking patterns, so they are less encumbered by the ego. This can give temporary access to the bliss body or trauma packets.

These one-off journeys work very intensely and people have varying experiences. Positive effects can be awakenings, new awareness, spontaneous soul retrievals, meeting with Divine beings, epiphanies, out-of-body experiences, and perceptions of intense visualizations and color. Negative effects can be severe vomiting and diarrhea, frightening hallucinations, tremors, and increased blood pressure; as well as negative emotions such as fear, anxiety, grief, anger, or agitation. Some can feel disoriented or confused, lose control, or fear insanity or death. Others have violent or unpleasant imagery or sounds, or relive painful memories or traumas.

While this modality can jump-start the healing process, or remove a major blockage to healing, it lacks a number of critical factors for healing. It doesn't rewire your thoughts or emotions or change behavior, so after a big euphoric experience, people may revert back to old behaviors. It doesn't provide loving support or an ongoing community to integrate the *aha* moments and life upheavals that often follow. It doesn't balance your energetics, especially if the journey created imbalance from vomiting and diarrhea. It doesn't teach you how to maintain the new awareness and wire it into the six-layered body.

Yoga (Energetic & Physical Body) and Meditation (Bliss Body)

Most yoga is practiced in a mainstream approach. Instead of integrating the Eight-Limbed Path, which is more comprehensive, people practice yoga as a method to blow smoke out of the upper floors. They go to an asana (posture) class, and move their bodies in sacred forms, and they feel better afterward. The nervous system, breath, and heart are regulated and they feel that momentary bliss body connection. As they leave class and this feeling wears off, they often revert to the same thoughts, emotions, and patterns, and eventually get dysregulated again.

Even when yoga is paired more thoroughly with a regular meditation practice, which opens the upper chakras and the connection to bliss body, the trauma packets remain, and the mental and emotional bodies are not sufficiently healed or rewired.

With this, someone can be on their yogic path for decades, and while they've blown the smoke out of the upper floors, they haven't put out the fire in the basement. Trauma packets often remain and wreak havoc in their work and relationships, and within their karmic entanglements.

Energy Healing, Reiki, Astrology—Energetic Body

Reiki and other energetic healing modalities will often bring spiritual Light or frequencies into the energy channels of the body. Depending on the modality, frequency of work, and the skills of the practitioner, this can have effects on the physical or energetic bodies. Again, without addressing the issue at the root cause through the trauma packets, it is very difficult to translate this energetic shift into the emotional and mental bodies. Life patterns stay the same and the person will often feel stuck, getting temporary relief from the care and attention of the energy healer who may be in the resonance of love or bliss.

Modalities that utilize psychic readings, Astrology, or past life regression work with the mental body thoughts and beliefs. These modalities can give the mental body *answers* or understanding, but won't change the trauma packet body sensations, beliefs, or emotions to relieve the accumulation of karmic burden.

Psychiatric Medications—Physical Body

Many people, especially those who exhaust the benefits of talk therapy, will resort to psychiatric medications to address the brain chemistry imbalances inherent within the brain and body. This has an impact on the physical body but does not create new thought patterns, love-based emotions, balanced energetics, or a spiritual connection. This approach may work as a stabilizer, but will not address the other layers' root cause and will not build greater emotional and mental capacity for future transformation.

Helping Others Heal

I'm always amazed about the amount of pure life force that comes back into our clients once they have done the two months of Level 1 work. Before healing, the trauma packets burn so much prana, so much life force energy, stirring in the background of our lives like a computer application that is using up the battery and memory on your computer. As soon as you close the frozen program application, you get more function and quicker computer response, and the battery has more run-time available. The same is true when you heal underlying trauma packets. Your system doesn't need so much physical regulation, because the autonomic nervous system is resiliently staying in parasympathetic (rest and digest) mode. Your mind stops feeding you thoughts of scarcity, victimization, and unworthiness, so you get to think about more expansive things. Instead of your emotions being torrential waves thrashing you against the shore, there are just subtle ripples, so there's less emotional management happening. There's less leakage from your energy field, and less stickiness for interference to attach to you. You have a daily practice to tap you into the abundant flow of life, so there is an unlimited supply of Divine frequency moving through you.

Overall, people get their life back, and typically have more of themselves to share with the world—more patience, more care, more love. With the more abundant flow, there is often a desire to share the overflow with those around them. Some like to share their experience through personal stories or new insights on life. Others simply want to relieve the suffering around them now that they have new insight that people don't have to spend life suffering, that there's another way.

With the change in perspective, there is often a reevaluation of their life purpose. They start to ask themselves about the impact they want to make, what their role is in the awakening of others. This births the desire to serve others. Feeling whole, without the need to *fix* ourselves, allows us to lend a hand to others in need.

Many come out of Inner Alignment Level 1 wanting to provide emotional support, new mental perspective, or lessons on energetics and inner balance. They have the desire to share what they just went through because it was so powerful.

This desire from former clients called forth the Inner Alignment Coach (Level 2) and Healer (Level 3) Certification trainings that we now provide. Interestingly, training practitioners was not my original intent for this work, but after the requests started coming in, I realized that equipping former clients, who are therapists and spiritual seekers (those who have been on their path for decades and now have relief), with the tools to help others was the implementation of my highest vision of relieving the suffering of humanity.

Level 2 Coach Certification

Inner Alignment Level 2 Coach Certification is a training where we teach coaches how to hold sacred space and walk their own clients through the process of inner transformation. Holding a sacred container means that the Divine does the work while we keep our egos out of the way. We teach how to channel the Divine frequency into every session so that the session is held from the Heart while grounded in reality.

Coaches learn how to invoke the client's soul, rather than the coach advising or swaying the client's life direction based on their own bias. Giving advice or leading clients' choices will make the coach take on negative karma and feel drained by the sessions. We teach how to let the Divine work with the client's soul, so we are not the ones doing the work. We are not creating dependency on us as the coach. We are activating the client's wise soul to guide them. This is like teaching the client how to fish, rather than giving them the fish and making them dependent on us for their own nourishment.

We train coaches on navigating all dimensions with clients. We teach them how to protect their energy field. They learn how to avoid engaging with client ego resistance, by getting underneath the fourth-dimension consciousness and working in the trauma packets in the second dimension; and how to work with the upper dimensions of consciousness so the client can establish the upper chakras and channel their own wisdom.

Over the course of 10 to 12 weeks, coaches learn to:

- Teach clients about their energetic body, specifically doshas, chakras, and energy field;

- Establish a client's goal and vision through the law of attraction to manifest their desires through co-creation with Source energy;

- Unpack resistance, emotional turmoil, and fear-based thoughts that live within the body's trauma packets so that the client can feel the immediate healing of simply entering into the second dimension; and

- Rewire thoughts and beliefs systems that live in trauma packets, through second-dimension exploration.

Often, people who are called into coaching or healing roles don't have the business skills to establish their new work in the world. Therefore, we have developed a structure for this coaching work so that coaches have a business framework to offer assistance to others in need. We work with coaches to develop their program offers, websites, marketing communication, and business strategies in a way that aligns with Heart consciousness.

Level 3 Soul Retrieval Healer Certification

The deepest and most profound aspect of Inner Alignment work is the process of healing that is done through Inner Alignment Soul Retrieval process in the trauma packets. Before embarking into this healing work, someone must have a strong integration of Level 1 inner healing practices and Level 2 coach capabilities to hold sacred space.

Healer candidates need to have the ability to navigate their own trauma packets through their personal use of the Level 1 inner work and practices. They must develop their capacity to notice interference energy in their life, and transmute it before it wreaks havoc. They must have a solid recovery time from pain body reactivity—instead of weeks or months in an issue, they can move through it in minutes, hours, or a few days. As this capacity develops, they are better able to hold the space and lead the way as a Level 2 coach.

When Inner Alignment coaches have strong coaching skills, it means the coach can hold the container from their Heart. They don't get enmeshed in the client's issues. Their ego-personality and its desires stay out of the work. They are able to navigate freely from the client's mental body (middle dimensions) down into trauma packets (lower dimensions), and bridge into upper dimensional work.

With solid Level 1 and 2 skills, the coach can enter Phase 1 of the Level 3 Soul Retrieval Healer Certification to strengthen coaching skills. In Phase 1, we ensure that the coaches are providing a safe, solid, Heart-centered space for the client; are able to lead clients through Level 1 Rewiring Practices; and have a strong understanding of Level 1 and 2 curricula. No matter their background[7], everyone must go through the strengthening of these coaching skills before moving into learning the Soul Retrieval Healing process.

In Phase 2 of the Level 3 Soul Retrieval Healer certification, we teach the 10-step Soul Retrieval Healing Process, which includes accomplishing the following:

- Identifying trauma packets that correspond to healing goals;

- Precisely narrowing trigger portals;

- Following the tether through body sensations from trigger portal to trauma packets, journeying into the second dimension of consciousness to navigate the trauma packet;

- Working within the trauma packet to facilitate healing on all six layers of the body;

---

[7] Often, when clinical therapists join our work, they initially assume they already have Level 2 skills, but most are operating from the mental body (fourth-dimension consciousness). They are leading, advising, and talking significantly more than our coaches do. They are typically very active in the mind, rather than the Heart.

- Connecting the lower dimensions of consciousness to the higher dimensions to create a new frequency in the body vibration;

- Facilitating soul retrieval to restore soul embodiment;

- Helping recapitulation within the mental body; and

- Rechecking the vibration changes on the current life trigger.

Phase 3 of Level 3 Soul Retrieval Healer certification consists of submitting practice healing sessions for review and feedback. There is a standardized process for evaluating sessions with specific criteria. The healer apprentice evaluates their own sessions against the criteria, and the trainer also does this evaluation. Afterward, there is a discussion between the trainer and healer apprentice to provide additional training and feedback. This happens for a few iterations until the healer apprentice has achieved consistent soul retrievals and trauma packet healings. At this time, the healer is ready for graduation.

These phases of Level 3 Soul Retrieval Healer certification occur over 6 to 12 months due to the self-paced nature, and the fact that everyone learns at a different pace depending on their energetic constitution.

Life Path of Service

It is my sincere hope that those who have done their own inner healing move into service to others—Service that doesn't make people dependent on you for their healing, but in a way that allows people to feel empowered, and able to transform themselves. Helping others learn to fish, rather than being dependent on a healer to do the work for them. It is my belief that anyone who has walked this inner healing path can be of tremendous help to those suffering from the effects of childhood trauma. We don't need to be a therapist, enlightened, or perfected to guide others through Inner Alignment. We simply need to have done our own work and have the desire to be an instrument of Divine service.

Only when we move from a place of dependency to independence can we then shift into interdependence. Dependency is the state of depending on the outside world for our value, love, or truth. Moving to independence in Level 1 allows us the self-sufficiency to care for ourselves, so we're not dependent on others' help to feel safe or loved. We can do it on our own. Once independence is established, we can be of service to others, helping others become more emotionally independent. There's nothing more rewarding than empowering someone into their own self-sustained healing process. Once we are independent, and teach others that same self-sufficiency, we can move into a state of interdependence. Then we begin exchanging with each other from a place of: *I'm whole, you're whole. I have certain gifts that I can share* and *you have your gifts to share*. We exchange our soul gifts in the world from a place of inner alignment through unity consciousness.

Blessings!

Wishing you all profound healing on your path!

It is such an honor to share this wisdom with you.
Thank you for your openness to exploring
this mind-body-spirit approach to healing childhood trauma!

Join in the vision of relieving humanity's unnecessary
suffering from childhood trauma by joining our work.

Visit us at: **www.KimberlyBeekman.com**

Made in the USA
Las Vegas, NV
11 January 2024

84219548R00146